PUNISHING PERSISTENT OFFENDERS

CLARENDON STUDIES IN CRIMINOLOGY

Published under the auspices of the Institute of Criminology, University of Cambridge; the Mannheim Centre, London School of Economics; and the Centre for Criminological Research, University of Oxford.

Recent titles in this series:

Bar Wars
Philip M. Hadfield

Bouncers: Violence and Governance in the Night-time Economy
Hobbs, Hadfield, Lister, and Winlow

Courting Violence: Offences Against the Person
Fielding

Punishing Persistent Offenders

Exploring Community and Offender Perspectives

JULIAN V ROBERTS

Centre of Criminology, Faculty of Law
and Worcester College
University of Oxford

OXFORD
UNIVERSITY PRESS

OXFORD
UNIVERSITY PRESS

Great Clarendon Street, Oxford OX2 6DP

Oxford University Press is a department of the University of Oxford.
It furthers the University's objective of excellence in research, scholarship,
and education by publishing worldwide in

Oxford New York

Auckland Cape Town Dar es Salaam Hong Kong Karachi
Kuala Lumpur Madrid Melbourne Mexico City Nairobi
New Delhi Shanghai Taipei Toronto

With offices in

Argentina Austria Brazil Chile Czech Republic France Greece
Guatemala Hungary Italy Japan Poland Portugal Singapore
South Korea Switzerland Thailand Turkey Ukraine Vietnam

Oxford is a registered trade mark of Oxford University Press
in the UK and in certain other countries

Published in the United States
by Oxford University Press Inc., New York

First published 2008

British Library Cataloguing in Publication Data

Data available

Library of Congress Cataloging in Publication Data
Roberts, Julian V.
Punishing persistent offenders: exploring community and offender
perspectives / Julian V Roberts.
p. cm. — (Clarendon studies in criminology)
Includes bibliographical references and index.
ISBN-13: 978-0-19-928389-7 (hardback: alk. paper) 1. Recidivism—
Prevention. 2. Criminals—Rehabilitation. 3. Punishment—Public opinion.
4. Criminal justice, Administration of—Public opinion. I. Title.
HV6049.R59 2008
364.6—dc22 2007050085

Typeset by Newgen Imaging Systems (P) Ltd., Chennai, India
Printed in Great Britain
on acid-free paper by
Biddles Ltd., King's Lynn, Norfolk

ISBN 978-0-19-928389-7

10 9 8 7 6 5 4 3 2 1

General Editor's Introduction

Clarendon Studies in Criminology aims to provide a forum for outstanding empirical and theoretical work in all aspects of criminology, criminal justice, penology, and the wider field of deviant behaviour. The Editors welcome excellent PhD work, as well as submissions from established scholars. The *Series* was inaugurated in 1994, with Roger Hood as its first General Editor, following energetic discussions between Oxford University Press and three Criminology Centres. It is edited under the auspices of these three Criminological Centres: the Cambridge Institute of Criminology, the Mannheim Centre for Criminology at the London School of Economics, and the Oxford Centre for Criminology. Each supplies members of the Editorial Board.

Julian Roberts' carefully argued book, *Punishing Persistent Offenders: Exploring Community and Offender Perspectives*, contributes significantly to a longstanding tradition of key criminological analyses of punishment and sentencing. He investigates the important policy question of whether offenders should be punished more harshly when they have previous convictions—that is, for their 'criminal careers' or character, in addition to the punishment they receive for the offence that brings them to court. Many sentencers and criminal justice professionals see this as an intuitively appealing sentencing policy on the grounds that the offender is somehow more culpable, the offending 'more serious', and the perceived likelihood of re-offending higher. Others see it as an unjustifiable instance of double punishment for the same offence.

This clearly written and well researched book examines the 'recidivist sentencing premium' from a number of theoretical and empirical perspectives, addressing a common sentencing practice that has been insufficiently addressed by scholars to date. The volume demonstrates the near universal consensus that previous convictions should be considered at sentencing and then proposes a retributive justification for the practice. Particular attention is paid to the views of offenders and the general public. Offenders appear to support the principle of imposing harsher sentences on recidivists, but object to apparent inconsistencies in practice. The public endorse a recidivist sentencing premium but do not lose sight of the importance of proportional sentencing.

At a time when repeat offending is an issue of major concern to the public, and when imprisonment rates are rising steeply, this new look at the recidivist sentencing problem is both timely and valuable.

The editors welcome this important addition to the *Series*.

Alison Liebling
University of Cambridge,
September 2007

Commemoration

In winter's tedious nights sit by the fire
With good old folks and let them tell thee tales
Of woeful ages long ago betid;
And ere thou bid good night, to quit their griefs,
Tell thou then this most lamentable tale,
And send the hearers weeping to their beds:
For why, the senseless brands will sympathize
The heavy accent of thy moving tongue
And in compassion weep the fire out;
And some will mourn in ashes, some coal-black,
For the deposing of a rightful Queen.

Shakespeare, *Richard II*, v. i. 41–51.

Prologue

The sentencing of offenders attracts more public scrutiny and interest than any other stage of the criminal process. Sentencing decisions in high-profile cases receive intense media attention and often provoke heated debate among members of the public, politicians, and victims' advocates. Social reaction to such cases becomes far more negative if it transpires that the offender has a history of offending. Crime by repeat offenders generates criticism of the judiciary and of the legislature responsible for sentencing laws, and raises fundamental questions about the ability of the justice system to achieve one of its most basic functions: protecting the public. Over the years, legislators in all jurisdictions have devised sentencing laws to respond to recidivist offenders. Recently there has been an increased level of interest in the punishment of persistent offenders. Statutory reforms have promoted the use of previous convictions or introduced more punitive sentencing regimes for repeat offenders.

Two sentencing universals

Despite great variability in statutory sentencing frameworks, two elements emerge which are common to all jurisdictions. First, courts in all countries apply the principle of proportionality at sentencing. The proportionality principle is a simple one which has proven to have lasting appeal: the severity of the sentence should be proportional to the seriousness of the crime for which the sentence is imposed and to the offender's level of culpability.

The second universal feature of sentencing systems around the world is more controversial. All jurisdictions, whether developed, developing, or 'transitional' in nature consider an offender's *previous* convictions when determining the sentence to be imposed for his or her *current* conviction. This practice thus unites sentencers across the common and civil law worlds.

Analysis of sentencing statistics reveals a second kind of proportionality at work: between the severity of the assigned sentence and the seriousness of the offender's criminal history. The nature of the relationship may not be perfect, but as a general rule, increments in severity are imposed to reflect the number and nature of the offender's previous convictions.

In light of the importance of previous convictions, it is not surprising that a substantial scholarly literature has developed which focuses on a range of issues, including the extent to which previous convictions predict future offending. One issue on which much ink has been spilled is the justification for imposing harsher sentences of progressive severity to mark longer criminal histories. Sentencing theorists are divided: some assign an important role to previous convictions, while to others, such a policy is anathema. The debate has degenerated into a theoretical stand-off, with the advocates reaffirming their positions while calling into question the wisdom of opposing views.

This volume introduces two additional communities to this debate: the general public and convicted offenders. Why the public, and why offenders? The answer concerns the legitimacy of sentencing and therefore cuts to the heart of the criminal justice system. The sentencing process represents the expression of collective disapprobation for legally proscribed conduct. Sentences are imposed on behalf of the community against which the offence was committed. If a universal and abiding element of the sentencing process runs counter to community views, the legitimacy of the system is inevitably compromised. Legitimacy also derives from the reactions of the individuals on whom the practice falls. If convicted offenders oppose a fundamental principle of sentencing, they are unlikely to recognize the authority that imposes sentence. Absent the support of the public and the tacit acceptance of offenders, the legitimacy of the sentencing process and indeed the criminal justice system is open to question.

I explore the justifications for punishing persistent offenders more harshly and determine the degree of social consensus with respect to this controversial sentencing policy. I examine the reaction of the '*Intuitive Sentencer*' to the age-old question of whether previous convictions should count against a defendant at sentencing. During the course of the volume, I attempt to demonstrate that a sentencing policy which precludes consideration of the offender's prior criminal conduct is inconsistent with the views of community members, criminal justice professionals, crime victims, and even the group most affected by this policy: repeat offenders. All these constituencies incorporate an offender's past into their judgments of culpability and their preferences regarding the sentence that should be imposed. The intuitive sentencer appears to embrace a model in which the actor's characteristics have consequences for lay judgments of culpability and ascriptions of blameworthiness. These judgments then influence public sentencing decisions.

Flat-rate sentencing, in which previous convictions play no role at sentencing, would prove unacceptable to all but a handful of retributive sentencing theorists. The progressive loss of mitigation model—according to which first offenders receive a discount, but recidivists receive no harsher punishment once they have lost their first offender status—fares little better in terms of community support. The volume does not seek to promote a greater role for previous convictions at sentencing, but rather to recognize and better understand a universal feature of contemporary penality.

I take the approach that retributivism offers the most appropriate response to punishing repeat offenders. Crime control considerations should play only a modest role, except for exceptionally persistent offenders for whom proportionality-based considerations become progressively irrelevant. However, I argue that a retributive account which wholly, or almost completely, ignores previous convictions violates fundamental, consensual reactions to punishing offenders.

The conduct of the offender after the commission of the crime is relevant to sentencing. Thus courts should recognize and encourage actions by the offender to mitigate the harm of the offence. These actions in turn mitigate the legal punishment that will be imposed on the offender. However, no amount of reparative effort, or degree of remorse, may completely rectify the harm inflicted. For this reason courts should place limits on the power of this variable to mitigate sentence. Previous convictions also provide context in which to consider the offender's level of culpability for the current offence. While no amount of prior offending can alter the seriousness of the current offence, previous convictions do affect the degree to which the state should censure the offender. Thus limits should also be placed on the aggravating power of the previous convictions.

A sentencing scheme which follows this approach would:

(a) direct courts to consider previous convictions when imposing sentence;
(b) provide clear statutory direction to sentencers regarding the culpability-based rationale for considering previous

convictions at sentencing, including the limits upon the aggravating effect of this variable;

(c) identify the specific dimensions of criminal history that justify imposition of a harsher or more intrusive sanction when the offender has previous convictions;
(d) provide offenders with incentives to limit or efface previous convictions and clear direction regarding the steps they should take in this respect;
(e) encourage offenders to actively seek to regain their status as first offenders through the invocation of expungement provisions;
(f) identify in open court and in reasons for sentence the amount of punishment imposed on an offender as a consequence of any relevant previous convictions.

With respect to sentencing repeat offenders, the sentencing process stands at a crossroads. Current pressure to impose ever harsher punishments on recidivists may result in swingeingly severe sentencing for repeat offenders. One way of arresting the move towards a highly punitive, recidivist sentencing premium involves acknowledging the relevance but limiting the role of previous convictions at sentencing. My contention is that a sentencing process which followed these proposals would be more consistent with fundamental social reactions to the punishment of repeat offenders, the views of criminal justice practitioners, and would be more likely to be accepted as legitimate by the individuals on whom punishment is imposed.

Acknowledgements

The research reported here was supported by grants to the author from: the Nuffield Foundation; the Faculty of Law at the University of Oxford; and the Ducker Foundation, Oxford. I am grateful for this financial support without which the research could not have been completed. I am also grateful to Emily Gray for conducting interviews and recruiting interviewees, to the Probation Services in Oxfordshire for assisting in recruiting these participants and to Bob Gebotys for assistance with the statistical analysis.

The following individuals provided research assistance at various stages of the research: Karen Cooper; Bonnie Cheng; Robert Gebotys; Ester Herlin-Karnell; Nicole Myers; Tanya Skvortsova; Alex Sutherland; Cory Way. I am also grateful to the individuals who participated in the interviews for their time and patience in responding to questions about the role of previous convictions at sentencing.

I would like to gratefully acknowledge the feedback of the following people who read and provided comments on sections of the manuscript, or took the time to discuss these issues with me: Brandon Applegate; Andrew Ashworth; Estella Baker; Anthony Bottoms; John Braithwaite; Kathleen Daly; Jeremy Horder; Jan de Keijser; R.A. Duff; Jessica Jacobson; Stephen Nogera; Michael Tonry; Andrew von Hirsch. I thank in particular Allan Manson for discussing the issues with me at some length during his visit to Oxford in the spring of 2007 and Michelle Grossman for meticulous editing of the manuscript. I am grateful to Gwen Booth, Lindsey Davis, and Jodi Towler at Oxford University Press who were very supportive of the project throughout the gestation of this volume.

Finally, I am greatly indebted to Worcester College, Oxford, for providing me with the opportunity of spending time amidst its tranquil bowers and verdant gardens to reflect upon the issues discussed in this book.

Julian V Roberts
Worcester College, Oxford
July 2007

Contents

List of Tables

List of Figures

1

Paying for the Past: The Recidivist Sentencing Premium

Men's evil manners live in brass; their virtues we write in water.[1]

'They need to look more at what the person's achieved as well as what bad things he's done. The good things are never recognized in court.'[2]

Should previous criminal convictions count against offenders at sentencing? If they are relevant for the purposes of sentencing, how should they be considered? How much weight should they carry relative to the seriousness of the current offence? Does the use of previous convictions constitute double punishment for the same offence? These are among the oldest and most contentious questions in the field of criminal sentencing and have been addressed and contested by jurists, scholars, criminal practitioners, and legislators for centuries.

Previous convictions count against an individual with respect to decisions made throughout the criminal process from first contact with the police—where officers may exercise their discretion to charge rather than caution an offender with previous convictions—through to the determination of whether to release a prisoner on parole. The liberty interests of individuals passing through the criminal justice system are therefore affected by previous convictions in a myriad of ways, sometimes as a result of statutory provisions, sometimes as a consequence of the exercise of discretion by criminal justice professionals. In certain jurisdictions, accused persons are generally more likely to be denied bail if they have previous convictions.[3] Previous convictions may

[1] Shakespeare, *Henry VIII*, IV. ii. 45.

[2] Spontaneous comment of a repeat offender interviewed as part of the research for this volume (see Chapter 6).

[3] For example, in New South Wales, the Bail Amendment (Repeat Offenders) Act 2002 removed the presumption in favour of release on bail for persons accused of an indictable offence who have a previous conviction for an indictable offence.

disentitle an accused person to participation in a restorative justice program (rather than referral to the criminal justice system).

If sentenced to a term of custody, offenders with previous convictions are treated more severely than first offenders. Prisoners with substantial criminal records are classified at different security levels by correctional authorities (see Farrell and Swigert 1978; Horan, Myers, and Farnworth 1982; Bureau of Justice Statistics 1991). Inmates with lengthy criminal records are less likely to be granted early release on parole, or granted parole at a later point in the sentence.[4] In countries with home detention programmes, repeat offenders are less likely to be allowed to serve the last portion of their custodial sentence at home.[5] The consequences of previous convictions do not end with the expiry of the warrant of the court: possessing a criminal record has adverse effects upon the life opportunities of offenders as they attempt to regain their status in society (eg, Damaska 1968; Gardiner 1972; Reed and Nance 1972). As O'Neill, Maxfield, and Harer (2004) note, 'judgments about an individual's past behaviour take on a particular urgency in the criminal justice system' (p 245).

Previous convictions and sentencing

Determining sentence is arguably the most difficult task confronting a judicial officer. Judges must weigh a multitude of sentencing factors to determine those that are legally relevant to the objectives of sentencing. From the many factors considered by courts at sentencing, one in particular stands out: the offender's previous convictions. Empirical research in many jurisdictions has demonstrated that after the seriousness of the offence of conviction, criminal record is more important than any other aggravating or mitigating factor at sentencing (eg, Burke and Turk 1975; Sutton 1978; Albonetti 1991). All jurisdictions impose

[4] In Finland, first offenders can apply for parole after having served one-half of the custodial sentence while repeat offenders must serve two-thirds of the sentence before becoming parole eligible (see Tornudd 1997).

[5] Many jurisdictions employ home detention as an alternative to custody, or some portion of a custodial sanction, and repeat offenders are generally less likely to benefit from these programmes. For example, statistics from New Zealand demonstrate that approximately two-thirds of inmates serving their first prison sentence were approved for home detention release compared to less than one-third of prisoners with six or more previous convictions (see Spier 2001: Table 9.5).

harsher penalties on recidivists—a practice termed the '*Recidivist Sentencing Premium*'.

The recidivist sentencing premium

As the term implies, a recidivist sentencing premium mandates that as an offender accumulates more convictions, the sentence imposed at subsequent sentencing hearings becomes progressively more severe. Despite its intuitive appeal to many people,[6] the practice is fraught with normative dilemmas. Under a powerful recidivist premium, the sentence imposed on an offender with a substantial relevant record will reflect his previous convictions more than his current offence, unless the latest offending is very serious. When this occurs, the sentencing process moves from punishing the offender for the latest offence and towards punishing him for his criminal 'career'—whether long or short. Some people argue that when this happens, the sentencing process punishes defendants for their character—as evidenced in their past behaviour—rather than for their current criminal behaviour. Indeed in some jurisdictions the link is made explicit: courts are enjoined to consider an offender's character when imposing sentence, and given statutory authority to weigh previous convictions when evaluating the offender's character (see Chapter 5 of this volume).

Punishing people for their previous misconduct is not unique to the criminal justice system. Evidence of a more punitive response to repeated violations can also be found in the codes of professional conduct, the rules of professional sports, and all other domains in which social relations are regulated. The punishments mandated by various religions also increase in severity as the transgressions of the sinner multiply. Durham (1987b) provides examples from the Old Testament of punishments that become progressively more severe to match the repetitive disobedience of the sinner. Similarly, Oppenheimer (1913) notes the existence of graduated punishments under Mahometan law: 'for the first offence, the criminal is to lose his right hand; for the second, his left foot; for the third, his left hand; for the fourth, his right foot;

[6] Wasik noted over 20 years ago that 'few people would be likely to argue with the proposition that a defendant's criminal record is an important determinant of his sentence' (1987: 105).

and if he should continue to offend, he shall be scourged at the discretion of the judge' (p 110). Many people also punish their children more severely if the child has repeatedly behaved badly.

Historical origins

Although an offender's previous convictions have long played an important role in the determination of sentence in England and Wales, early criminal statutes contained no reference to repetition or indeed to offender culpability. The law of the talion is by definition blind to such considerations; the focus is exclusively on the harm caused by the crime. For example, the laws of Anglo-Saxon England under King Ethelbert, (written around 595) prescribe specific punishments for a lengthy list of offences (eg, 'if a freeman steal from the King, let him pay nine-fold bot'; Commissioners on the Public Records of the Kingdom 1831). The compensation due rises in relation to the harm of the conduct, but the statute carries no reference to the offender's previous conduct. Subsequent monarchs such as Alfred modified the enumerated punishments, but followed the same model of matching offences to penalties with no regard to the issue of repetition of offending.

Consideration of an offender's previous misconduct emerged as society moved away from a purely offence-based model of sentencing to one in which the offender's character became increasingly important. Although the evidence of sentencing practices is scanty during the sixteenth century it is clear that during this period offenders received harsher penalties if authorities were aware that they had previously been sentenced (see Ingram 2004). The historical record provides much and varied evidence of a concern for an individual's previous conduct, as the following examples reveal:

Alehouse Act, 1627[7]

(IV) And be it further enacted that if the said offender or offenders, being an unlicenced Alehouse-keeper, shall offend in any of the Premisses the second Time and be thereof lawfully convicted in Manner and form aforesaid, that then the said Mayor, Bailiff, Justice or Justice of Peace or other Head Officer, shall commit him, her or them unto the House of Correction...

[7] 1627 (3 Cha 1) c 4.

Frauds by Workmen Act, 1777[8]

Persons or Persons so buying, receiving, accepting, or taking, any such materials, should, for the first offence, forfeit the sum of twenty pounds...And in case of a further Conviction for or upon a second or any other subsequent Offence of the same Kind, the Person or Persons so again offending, being thereof convicted in Manner before prescribed by the Said Act, should for every second or subsequent Offence, forfeit the sum of Forty pounds.

Larceny of Cattle[9]

In the case of any further conviction for a second or other subsequent Offence of the same kind, the person or persons so again offending shall, upon every second or subsequent conviction, forfeit and pay for every such sheep or lamb the sum of five pounds of lawful money of Great Britain, and shall also suffer solitary imprisonment in the Common Gaol...

Evidence of a differential response to offenders with prior contact with the justice system can be found in legal statutes that exclude such offenders from consideration for leniency. In England and Wales the 'Benefit of Clergy' which permitted persons suspected of a clergyable offence to escape state punishment was available only to first offenders (Stephen 1883). After 1518, courts were required to maintain records of individuals to whom the benefit of clergy had been extended—perhaps the earliest version of a criminal records register (Baker 2003). By the seventeenth century the effect of an offender's previous convictions was discernible in sentencing practices. Shoemaker analysed sentencing decisions in London courts and concluded that 'the age, social status, attitude and previous criminal history of the accused played a crucial role in shaping sentencing decisions' (Shoemaker 1991: 190; see also Beattie 1986).

The number and severity of recidivist sentencing provisions accelerated in the eighteenth century and by the Victorian era, a clear transformation in sentencing had occurred. Concern with the punishment of repeat offenders became a near obsession for many Victorian jurists and legislators. Perhaps the leading exponent of the use of previous convictions was the penal reformer Barwick Baker, who argued for the total abandonment of the principle of proportionality between crime seriousness and sentence severity in favour of a rigid recidivist structure. He argued that sentence

[8] 1777 (17 Geo 3) c 56.

[9] Larceny of Cattle, 1819, S III.

severity 'should depend, not on the estimated amount of guilt of the crime, but upon the simple fact of whether the criminal had or had not been previously convicted' (1889: 40). Under his scheme, the severity of the sentence imposed would double with each conviction, regardless of the seriousness of the offence, the relationship between past and current offending or the individual circumstances of the offender.

Why did interest in an offender's previous convictions intensify at this time? Until this point, an ex-offender could move from the town in which he had been convicted to another part of the realm with little fear that his previous conviction would come to light. As the Report of the Advisory Council on the Penal System noted 'before a man could be treated as a persistent criminal he must be recognized as such' (1978: 45). Determining whether an offender had previous convictions was never easy. The Advisory Council's report suggests that the procedure of branding offenders served as an early way of marking recidivists apart from first offenders.[10] At the beginning of the nineteenth century, an early form of record keeping for offenders was instituted for this very purpose. Towards the end of the nineteenth century, the recording of criminal convictions was placed on a statutory footing. Thus Section 6(1) of the Prevention of Crime Act 1871 stated that:

> Registers of all persons convicted of crime in the United Kingdom shall be kept in such form and containing such particulars as may from time to time be prescribed, in Great Britain by one of Her Majesty's Principal Secretaries of State, and in Ireland by the Lord Lieutenant.

From this point forth, the institutionalization of criminal records ensured that offenders with previous convictions would repeatedly suffer the consequences of their former transgressions (see also discussion in Hebenton and Thomas 1993).

Is this practice of punishing offenders for previous offending a fair and effective element of the sentencing process? Is it defensible from an ethical or utilitarian perspective? Opponents of the use of previous convictions at sentencing argue that it constitutes double punishment for the same offence. The phrase 'double punishment' recurs throughout the literature; however, under a cumulative sentencing model, multiple recidivists will incur additional

[10] The practice of branding offenders was abolished in England and Wales in 1799.

punishment for the original offence every time that they reoffend. In this sense the additional punishment visited on repeat offenders snowballs with repetition: each additional sentence imposed on the repeat offender includes a component reflecting the first conviction. 'Multiple punishment' may be a more appropriate term for cases involving repeat offenders.

Reflexive punitiveness?

Populist justifications for the recidivist premium abound; some people may wish to punish recidivists more harshly out of a sense of mere punitiveness: bad people deserve bad outcomes; worse people deserve worse outcomes. For others, the justification lies in a sense of frustration bred of unrealistic expectations concerning desistance. How many times does an individual need to be punished before he desists from offending? Why has he not learned his lesson? For many people, the search for a justification is needless; it seems to be a case of justifying the obvious. As Rudenstine, cited in Singer (1979) noted, people justify the recidivist premium by 'simply throwing up their arms in frustration and saying "I don't know what the rationale is, but it strikes me as ludicrous not to pay attention to the fact that this person did the same act once or twice before" '.

One of the goals of this work is to try to understand the origin and consequences of this common reaction to the sentencing of recidivist offenders. Is there any defensible justification for the practice? The challenge is to understand whether punishing recidivists more harshly is an example of mere punitiveness or whether it reflects a more fundamental, principled, and desirable sentencing policy.

Justifying the recidivist sentencing premium

The practice needs a clear justification, if only to explain to offenders who may believe that they are being punished twice for the same offence. Why then do so many jurisdictions punish repeat offenders more harshly? Two general accounts may be offered. They are derived from the principal (and competing) sentencing perspectives. One of these perspectives aims to reduce crime in the future, the other is primarily concerned with imposing a sentence that reflects the seriousness of the offence, without consideration of the offender's future conduct. Advocates of utilitarian sentencing seek to prevent crime through a number of ways, including specific deterrence and incapacitation. According to the logic of deterrence, an offender's previous convictions are a reliable predictor of future offending—and offer putative evidence that previous sentencing decisions were insufficiently severe. Harsher sentences for repeat offenders are therefore justified in order to prevent further offending.

An alternative perspective is that recidivists are more culpable than first offenders and therefore deserve more punishment, and that the quantum of additional punishment should rise in direct proportion to the seriousness of their previous offending. This justification is offered independent of any crime prevention benefits that may arise from the use of a recidivist sentencing premium. The proposition that repeat offenders are more culpable or more blameworthy is usually asserted rather than demonstrated. For example, the US federal guidelines manual simply states that: 'A defendant with a record of prior criminal behaviour is more culpable than a first offender and thus deserving of greater punishment' (US Sentencing Commission 2006: 354).

Conflicting approaches to the use of previous convictions at sentencing

Different sentencing perspectives prescribe different approaches to previous convictions at sentencing. Three clear models can be distinguished. One is derived from a consequentialist perspective that seeks to prevent crime, the other two from a retributive approach in which the primary focus is upon the seriousness of the crime of current conviction.

(i) Cumulative sentencing

According to the '*cumulative sentencing*' model, previous convictions should always be used by a court at sentencing—unless they are too old, or for some reason they are considered to have little predictive utility for the sentencing of the individual now appearing before the court. The cumulative sentencing model is most often justified by reference to preventing crime through individual deterrence or incapacitation. The penal logic underlying this model assumes that reoffending constitutes evidence that the sanction imposed at the previous sentencing was insufficiently harsh to deter the offender. The consequence is that the severity of sentences will increase constantly as the offender's criminal record grows ever longer. This view distinguishes between repeat offenders with different numbers of previous convictions.

(ii) 'Flat-Rate' sentencing

One opposing view—called '*flat-rate*' sentencing—is based on a purely retributive sentencing model.[11] According to this perspective, previous convictions should never count against a defendant at sentencing on the grounds that the criminal law should punish people for their current actions, and not because they have developed bad characters—as revealed by their criminal antecedents. The consequence of this view is that offenders convicted of the same crime will receive the same penalty, regardless of whether one is a first offender and the other a multiple recidivist with many previous convictions. In short, this model makes no distinction between offenders on the basis of their past offending: all offenders are, and always remain, first offenders for the purposes of sentencing.

(iii) The progressive loss of mitigation

In between these two extreme views lies a *via media* reflected in the doctrine of the '*progressive loss of mitigation*'. According to this model, an offender's previous convictions play a very limited role at sentencing: first offenders should receive a discounted or mitigated sentence, but once they have lost their first offender status they lose this discount. The important distinction between the progressive loss of mitigation approach and cumulative sentencing model is that under the former, convictions acquired after the first offender discount has been exhausted do not result in a harsher penalty. The progressive loss of mitigation model therefore distinguishes between first offenders and all recidivists, but does not prescribe differential sentences to reflect different levels of recidivism. This model affords some limited leniency to first offenders, but this concession does not justify a recidivist premium. The

[11] Newman (1983: 54) referred to advocates of this approach to sentencing as the 'old retributivists' yet there a number of more recent retributivists who hold this view (eg, Bagaric 2001).

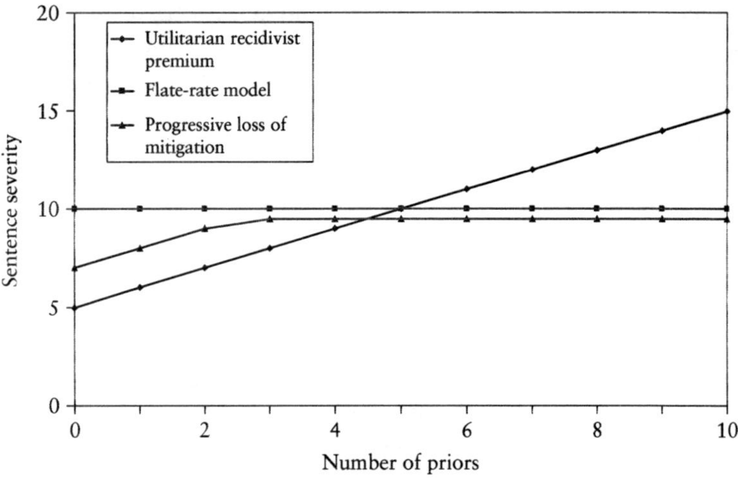

Figure 1.1 Sentence severity as a function of criminal history: theoretical curves

three theoretical positions regarding the relationship between sentence severity and criminal history are represented graphically in Figure 1.1.

Two universal features of sentencing

Proportionality

This general principle of proportion between crime and punishment...is hardly less familiar or less important than the principle that only the guilty ought to be punished (Gross 1979: 436).

Few sentencing theorists—and even fewer members of the public, or criminal justice professionals—would contest the assertion that the severity of penalties should escalate to correspond to increases in the seriousness of the crimes for which they are imposed. As Tonry (1996) observes, 'no one argues that desert has no relevance to justice in sentencing' (p 187).[12]

[12] Some advocates of restorative justice may object to the principle of proportionality at sentencing. While a number of scholars argue that proportionality has a role to play in restorative justice, others suggest that proportionality considerations may impede or undermine efforts to achieve restoration between the victim and the offender. Scholars such as Van Ness and Strong (2002) advocate a form

Articulated as a sentencing principle, proportionality thus carries great popular appeal, in part because it reflects an even broader principle pertaining to human behaviour, namely that outcomes—positive or negative—should reflect equity considerations. For example, the demoralization which ensues among employees when salaries or promotions are allocated on the basis of fortuity or pulchritude rather than industry or merit reflects an enduring and universal human desire for fairness. In the domain of legal punishment, this emerges as the principle of proportionality, according to which the severity of sentences reflects the seriousness of the crimes for which these sentences are imposed.

The cross-jurisdictional importance of proportionality can be demonstrated by noting the constitutional protections against violations of the principle. For example, article 49(3) of the Charter of Fundamental Rights in the European Union states that the severity of penalties 'must not be disproportionate to the criminal offence'. The universal appeal of proportional sentencing is also clear from the large number of domestic sentencing statutes that place this principle on a statutory footing. The principle may be discerned in sentencing statistics and statutory frameworks around the world. Public reaction is negative when sentences are disproportionately lenient, or disproportionately harsh—relative to the perceived gravity of the crime.[13]

The recidivist sentencing premium

The widespread public support for proportional sentencing—demonstrated in all countries in which researchers have explored the issue—demonstrates that the principle of proportionality attracts a great deal of community support (see Roberts and Hough 2005). This appears true across a wide range of countries and cultures. However, little is known about public reaction to the second most important sentencing factor: an offender's

of 'restorative proportionality' between the severity of harm and the degree of restorative effort on behalf of the offender that is needed to respond to the harm (see discussion in Van Ness and Strong 2002:176–9; and in Daly 2003).

[13] News media coverage of sentencing creates a clear asymmetry in this regard: the disproportionate sentences which disturb the public are inevitably examples of apparent leniency. This explains the ubiquitous public dissatisfaction with sentencing and the low levels of public confidence in judges (see Roberts and Hough 2005, for a review of research).

criminal record. As will be seen, prior convictions constitute an important sentencing factor around the world. In some jurisdictions the two universals of proportionality and criminal history are fused into a single purpose. For example, according to the sentencing guidelines in the US state of Washington, when sentencing offenders, courts should 'ensure that the punishment for a criminal offense is proportionate to the seriousness of the offense and the offender's criminal history' (Washington State Sentencing Guidelines Commission 2006: II-23). Similarly, the statement of the purpose and principles of sentencing in the state of Oregon notes that 'the appropriate punishment for a felony conviction should depend on the seriousness of the crime of conviction when compared to all other crimes and the offender's criminal history' (Oregon Criminal Justice Commission 2007: 2).

If sentencing theorists remain divided with respect to the use of previous convictions at sentencing, where does the public stand? This question is addressed in depth in subsequent chapters of this volume. Proportionality in sentencing is a most intuitive concept. Ignoring an offender's previous convictions and sentencing him only for the current crime is highly counter-intuitive.[14] In everyday life when expressing censure of others, we generally consider much more than the act giving rise to the censure. The context of the conduct is very important, and central to that context are inferences drawn about the offender's attitude to his 'offending'. It does not follow from this that the criminal law must assume an intuitive 'layperson's' approach to sentencing. The reality however is that retributive theories are confronted with a problem regarding community values: the spine of retributivism—proportionality—resonates with lay perceptions of legal punishment but the retributive perspective regarding previous misconduct can only perplex and possibly antagonize the 'intuitive sentencer'.

Conceptualizing the recidivist premium

Considerable variation exists regarding the ways that previous convictions should count against the defendant at sentencing.

[14] Imagine the reaction of the average layperson to the following statement which is representative of the 'flat-rate' retributive perspective: 'people who commit like offenses should (it would seem) be treated alike, whether the offense is the first or the ninety-first' (Adler 1991: 167).

Statutory provisions across the United States incorporate criminal history in a variety of ways. Some statutes require a misdemeanor to be reclassified as a felony if it is the offender's second or subsequent conviction; others require or permit the imposition of enhanced sentences in the case of recidivist offenders, while the most severe recidivist sentencing laws require offenders with extensive previous convictions to be sentenced as career or habitual offenders. Elsewhere, the criminal codes of many countries define the specific circumstances that should give rise to the imposition of a harsher penalty. In some jurisdictions, courts are simply directed to consider previous convictions as an aggravating factor at sentencing. Most criminal justice systems consider an offender's previous convictions in light of their relationship to the current offence of conviction. Thus related priors generally count more heavily than previous convictions of a different offence category.

Another common feature is the practice of discounting priors to reflect the passage of time without the accumulation of any more convictions. In most countries, older previous convictions[15] carry less weight at sentencing, and ultimately are discounted entirely. Once this happens the ex-offender is considered as a first offender and punished accordingly at any subsequent sentencing hearing. By allowing an offender's previous convictions to 'decay' and eventually be completely expunged, the criminal justice system offers offenders an incentive to desist from crime. In this way, ex-offenders ultimately regain their original status as citizens with no criminal past. Unfortunately, the legal provisions by which this transformation is achieved are generally not well known; the justice system is scrupulous in ensuring that previous convictions are recorded and considered at sentencing, but less effective in helping ex-offenders shed their past. As Beccaria noted over 200 years ago: 'A man accused of a crime, who has been imprisoned...ought not to be branded with infamy' (1764; 1963).[16]

[15] Homicide is an exception to this generalization. In most jurisdictions a conviction for murder or some form of homicide will remain 'alive'—to be considered at any subsequent sentencing hearing.

[16] It is rather surprising, however, that in his classic volume *On Crimes and Punishments* Beccaria was silent with respect to the question of punishing persistence and in fact offers no commentary on the issue of offender culpability.

Evaluating the impact of previous convictions: the invisible premium

How powerful is the recidivist sentencing premium? The answer will vary from jurisdiction to jurisdiction, but a clear deficiency of sentencing statistics published by most statistical agencies is that the magnitude of the recidivist sentencing premium is hidden from view. Sentencing statistics are generally broken down by the specific offence or offence category. Thus if we read that the incarceration rate for assault is 30%, or that five years imprisonment is the average sentence imposed for a conviction for rape, these aggregate statistics usually include all offenders, first and recidivists alike. Recidivist statutes such as the 'three strikes' laws make plain the nature of the enhanced penalty that will be imposed on recidivist offenders who meet the triggering criterion. But for the vast majority of repeat offenders, the recidivist premium is hidden within a sentence which reflects many sentencing factors.

Sentencing statistics

When the impact of an offender's previous convictions is masked in this way, it has consequences for the interpretation of sentencing statistics. Sentence lengths for crimes which are committed more often by recidivists will reflect this fact and it will appear as if courts treat these offences with more severity than is in fact the case. The point can be readily illustrated by examining sentencing statistics from any jurisdiction. For example, in Western Australia, almost one-third of theft and burglary offences resulted in imprisonment for a period of at least one year while only 18% of crimes against the person attracted this length of sentence (Ferrante, Loh, Maller, Valuri and Fernandez 2005). Similarly, in England and Wales, 28% of offenders sentenced for a violent crime were imprisoned compared to half of those sentenced for theft or burglary (Home Office 2007: Table 6.3). The explanation for these trends is not that crimes of violence are perceived by the court to be less serious but rather that offenders convicted of theft typically have much longer criminal histories.

Recent research published by the British Home Office demonstrates the variability in reoffending rates between categories of offending. Thus Shepherd and Whiting (2006) report the reoffending rates for a cohort of offenders sentenced in 2003. The 'window' of reoffending used in the study was two years. Within two years, approximately 80% of offenders convicted of theft from vehicles, theft in general, or burglary had been reconvicted. Rates of reoffending were significantly lower for offenders convicted of personal injury offences. Thus approximately 20% of offenders convicted of a sexual offence and less than half the offenders convicted of a violent offence were reconvicted within two years. The lowest two-year reoffending rates were associated with drink-driving offences and sexual offences—two categories of offending of great concern to the public (see Shepherd and Whiting 2006). Similarly, recidivism statistics reported by the Washington State Sentencing Guidelines Commission (2005) demonstrate that the more violent crimes resulted in the lowest recidivism rates. For example, approximately one-quarter of manslaughter offenders were subsequently reconvicted compared to over two-thirds of property offenders (Washington State Sentencing Guidelines Commission 2005: Figure 3).

Evolution of penal policy regarding repeat offenders

Although the recidivist sentencing premium has been around for centuries, some recent developments are noteworthy. Historically, the premium has been justified by reference to prevention. The highly punitive recidivist statutes of the nineteenth century in England were founded upon a desire to incapacitate a wide range of offenders and thereby prevent further offending.[17] Little consideration was given to retributive concerns—either to justify or limit the scope of the premium. Today, the use of previous convictions at sentencing rests upon a dual justification. Recidivists are judged by many to be more deserving of punishment. Yet at the same time, concern about proportionality in sentencing has limited the severity of all but the most punitive recidivist laws. For example, the recidivist premium for a third domestic burglary committed in England and Wales is three years imprisonment—a far cry from the severity of Victorian recidivist statutes.

[17] Referring to the schemes of cumulative sentencing in the mid-nineteenth century, Radzinowicz and Hood observe that 'they were aimed at incapacitating a whole class rather than a selected few' (1990: 227).

Public input into sentencing policy and practice

The second development consists of an increased sensitivity to the views of the public with respect to sentencing (see discussion in Roberts 2008; Parker 1998; Freiberg 2006). Forty years ago, public opinion was a subject that attracted little interest from sentencers or scholars in the field of criminal justice. That has all changed. Today the importance of community views can be seen in a number of ways, as illustrated by the following examples:

- *Sentencing guidelines councils and commissions*: In England and Wales, the Sentencing Advisory Panel provides advice to the Sentencing Guidelines Council which subsequently issues guidelines to judges in England and Wales (see Ashworth 2006; <http://www.sentencing-guidelines.gov.uk> for further information). The Panel has commissioned three systematic investigations into public attitudes to specific offences, with a view to informing its recommendations regarding sentencing guidelines.[18] Sentencing Commissions in the US and in Canada have conducted analogous surveys of public attitudes to sentencing (see Rossi and Berk 1997; Canadian Sentencing Commission 1987). In the United States, a number of sentencing guidelines commissions formally acknowledge the link between public views and the structure of guidelines. For example, the Washington Sentencing Guidelines are designed to 'make the criminal justice system accountable to the public'.[19]
- *Sentencing advisory councils*: Many sentencing advisory bodies such as the Sentencing Advisory Council in the Australian state of Victoria have members drawn from the general public in addition to criminal justice professionals such as judges and prosecutors.[20] The statutory functions of the Sentencing Advisory Council in Victoria include the following: 'to gauge public opinion on sentencing matters' and 'to consult, on

[18] The three research projects explored public attitudes to the sentencing of burglary (Russell and Morgan 2001), rape (Clarke, Moran-Ellis, and Sleney 2002) and driving offences resulting in death (Hough, Roberts, Jacobson, Bredee, and Moon 2007).

[19] RCW 9.94A.010; see Washington State Sentencing Guidelines Commission (2005).

[20] The Sentencing Advisory Council has published a review of research on public attitudes to sentencing (see Gelb 2006) and held an international conference on the role of public opinion in the sentencing process (see Freiberg and Gelb 2008).

sentencing matters with... the general public'.[21] By appointing community members in this way, these councils hope to ensure that the sentencing process is in some way reflective of community views. The Sentencing Council in New South Wales also attempts to incorporate public views into the development of sentencing recommendations (see discussion in Hutton 2008).

- *Sentencing policy*:[22] The Home Office Sentencing Review in England and Wales conducted extensive polling into the views of the public prior to publishing its report in 2001. The report noted that 'achieving a satisfactory level of public confidence is therefore an important goal of sentencing, and the framework for sentencing needs to support that goal' (2001: 1). Moreover, the report clearly acknowledges the influence of public views in a passage that states: 'The [sentencing] Review's assessment of public views on how sentencing should operate has informed its recommendations for a new framework, especially for persistent offenders' (p ii). These recommendations were influential in determining the direction of sentencing reform and ultimately resulted in the Criminal Justice Act 2003. This Act assigns a more central role to previous convictions at sentencing, and represents a clear departure from previous sentencing policy (see discussion in Chapter 5).
- *Legislative interest*: A number of legislatures have conducted inquiries into the state of public opinion regarding the sentencing process. In Scotland, for example, the Justice 1 Committee commissioned a deliberative poll upon the issue of sentencing (see Hutton 2005).

Most western governments have identified promoting public confidence as an important policy goal, and sentencing is front and centre in attempts to increase public confidence (see Hough and Roberts 2004). Britain is not alone in viewing public opinion as an important consideration at sentencing; many other governments repeatedly conduct public opinion research to determine

[21] Sentencing (Amendment) Act 2003, section 108C (1) (d) and (e).

[22] Courts have also become increasingly sensitive to the views of the public with respect to sentencing decisions. Shute (1998) reviewed this issue and concluded that 'all the judgments... indicate that sentencing judges are at the very least duty-bound to consider the relevance of public opinion... and possibly even required to factor that consideration into any sentence they pass' (p 475).

the tenor of public opinion regarding sentencing and sentencing reform proposals. Finally, all this activity has not escaped the attention of scholars; the views of the public and their relationship to sentencing policy and practice have emerged as an important topic in the field of criminology (see Freiberg and Gelb 2008; Hutton 2005; Roberts 2008; Parmentier et al 2004; Kommer 2004).[23]

If public opinion is now playing a greater role in determining sentencing policy, it is not surprising that an issue of great concern to the public—repeat offending—has risen to greater prominence. In light of this development, this is a propitious time to examine public reaction to the role of previous convictions at sentencing. In addition to the increased attention to the views of the public, a number of other explanations may be offered to account for the renewed interest in persistent offenders.

Explaining contemporary interest in the recidivist sentencing premium

(i) Rise of penal populism

Lenity reigns in moderate governments (Montesquieu 1784: 80).

A great deal has been written about the increasingly political nature of criminal policy development. Throughout the 1990s a number of western nations experienced the paradox of declining crime rates accompanied by a rise in punitive sentencing policies, including and especially mandatory sentences of imprisonment. These sentencing policies are in part a response to continued public pressure for harsher sentencing laws, as can be seen in answers to polls that ask about sentencing trends. Public opinion surveys around the world converge on a common finding: most people subscribe to the view that sentences are too lenient. Table 1.1 summarizes trends from eight countries during the decade

[23] In the 1960s, almost nothing was published on the topic except for a brief commentary in the Criminal Law Review (see Silvey 1961) which provoked no further publications. Nigel Walker conducted a number of unique experiments relating to public opinion on sentencing (see Walker and Argyle 1964). In addition, a seam of scholarship developed in the 1970s under the general heading of 'Knowledge and Opinion about Law' (eg, Podgorecki, Kaupen, Van Houtte, Vinke and Kutchinsky 1973).

Table 1.1 Perceptions of judicial leniency, eight jurisdictions

Jurisdiction	Date of survey	Percentage of respondents expressing the view that courts are too lenient
England and Wales	1996	79%
United States	1998	74%
South Africa	1999	83%
Northern Ireland	2000	76%
Scotland	2001	70%
Barbados	2003	76%
Netherlands	2004	84%
Canada	2005	74%

Sources: Hough and Roberts (1998); Sourcebook of Criminal Justice Statistics (2005); Institute for Social Studies (1999); Amelin et al (2000); Justice 1 Committee (2002); Nuttall et al (2003); de Keijser et al (2006); Roberts, Crutcher, and Verbrugge (2007).

1996–2005.[24] A later chapter of this volume will demonstrate that the public over-estimate recidivism rates. The two perceptions may well be linked: people may infer that sentences are too lenient because so many offenders reoffend.

Clear evidence of the public scepticism regarding the ability of the system to reduce reoffending can be found in responses to a survey of the British public conducted in 2003. Respondents were asked to express the degree of confidence they had that the criminal justice system was achieving a number of important objectives, including dealing with crime promptly, creating a safe society, and responding effectively to drug-related crime. It is significant that people expressed the least amount of confidence that the system was effective in 'stopping offenders from committing more crime'. Fully three-quarters of the public responded that they were not very or not at all confident that the system was achieving this objective (Roberts and Hough 2005: Table 2.2).

[24] Research in other jurisdictions using a somewhat different methodology generates the same pattern of findings. For example, in Belgium, respondents were asked whether sentences for a series of offences were punished too severely, with sufficient severity, or not severely enough. Very high percentages of respondents chose 'not severely enough'; see Parmentier, Vervaeke, Doutrelepont, and Kellens (2004).

Increasing the general punitiveness of the sentencing process comes with a price: rising prison populations result in higher correctional costs. Most governments have eschewed this approach in favour of a more selective response that targets repeat or persistent offenders. The goal of promoting cumulative sentencing in England and Wales was made crystal clear by the then British Home Secretary, David Blunkett, in a speech to the National Probation Service in which he focused explicitly on the issue of previous convictions: 'Sentencing should send a clear message that the more you offend, the greater the punishment you can expect.'[25] As will be seen in a subsequent chapter, repeat offenders are now receiving harsher punishments and this objective has been achieved by increasing the importance of prior convictions at sentencing.

A consistent pattern across jurisdictions has emerged: politicians have identified repeat offenders as the offender category justifying a mandatory sentence. In recent years, most western nations have introduced punitive sentencing legislation aimed at repeat offenders. The focus on punishing persistent offenders encompasses both common law and civil law jurisdictions. This interest is partly populist in nature; politicians in many countries have sought to mobilize penal resources against the profile of offender for whom the public has least sympathy: recidivists. In 2007, the Scottish Conservative leader proposed to crack down on 'a cancer of repeat offenders' by imposing a recidivist sentencing premium on any offender sentenced to custody for the third time.[26]

In addition to creating mandatory sentences for repeat offenders convicted of the most serious forms of offending, politicians have also focused on the general concept of repeat offending. This is particularly the case in Britain where the pendulum swung away from a desert-based sentencing model at the beginning of the 1990s to one which focused on punishing persistence (see Tonry 2004, for discussion). These reforms often involve mandatory sentences of imprisonment triggered when the offender accumulates a number of convictions for serious offences. The most visible of these laws are the 'three strikes' statutes in the United

[25] Speech to the National Probation Service conference, 5 July 2001.

[26] The length of the additional period would be determined by the average of the offender's previous custodial term. Thus an offender sentenced to first two years, then three, then four years in prison would receive an additional three year term on top of the final four year sentence (BBC News, July 16, 2007).

States which prescribe life imprisonment or a long period of custody for offenders convicted of a third serious felony. But most common law jurisdictions have also created recidivist sentencing provisions for a wide range of lesser offences. One justification for these laws invokes community support, although the research record on which this invocation rests is slight (see Roberts 2003c, for a review). Members of the public may find the recidivist premium an obvious, intuitive consideration at sentencing. Repeat offenders probably represent a greater threat to society. Recidivists may even be regarded as increasingly reprehensible as their previous convictions accumulate, but the practice of inflicting progressively harsher penalties upon persistent offenders requires careful scrutiny if it is to be theoretically defensible.

(ii) Evolution of risk-based sentencing and the movement away from desert-based sentencing

Much has been written in recent years of the rise of what Beck (1992) called the 'risk society'—one seeking to measure and control all manner of threats to state or individual security. This transformation has had predictable effects upon the sentencing process. Repeat offenders represent an easily identifiable risk to the community, one that should be subject to the most advanced risk management strategies. This movement is also consistent with an earlier paradigm shift in the field of legal punishment. Sentencing in the 1970s and 1980s emerged from an era in which judges exercised relatively untrammeled discretion, and engaged in what has been described as the 'intuitive synthesis' of relevant sentencing factors, from which a specific disposition ultimately emerged.

This discretion has been progressively curtailed in many countries, but particularly the United States where sentencing guidelines have been adopted. A good example can be found in the state of Utah, where risk is privileged above other considerations at sentencing. Specifically, the Utah Sentencing Commission adheres to the following policy position:

> The first and foremost objective in the sentencing of offenders is to protect the public.
>
> (a) Risk to the public should be of paramount consideration at sentencing and in probation/parole deliberations.
>
> (b) All other positions taken herein are considered secondary. (Utah Sentencing Commission 2006: 1).

The promulgation of guidelines will naturally promote a search for the specific variables that should be incorporated into the guidelines. Judicial intuition has been replaced by the application of actuarial measures of the probability of recidivism. This movement is consistent with a desire to make the sentencing process more scientific, and less subjective. Clinical judgments have been replaced by aggregate risk scores based upon scales such as the Violence Risk Assessment Study.[27]

Many jurisdictions employ risk-based sentencing scales that have become increasingly sophisticated, although their application remains normatively controversial. Previous convictions constitute a relatively reliable predictor of future offending (eg, Gendreau, Goggin, and Little 1996). For this reason an offender's criminal record is a central component of the most common risk-based scales such as the Statistical Information on Recidivism (SIR) scale or the Level of Service Inventory–Revised (LSI-R) used in Canada or the salient Factor Scale used in the United States (see Andrews and Bonta, 2003). The increasingly actuarial approach to sentencing, in which the severity of sentence reflects the risk level ascribed to the offender, pays great attention to the offender's previous convictions.[28] The number, nature, and recency of any prior convictions are primary determinants in many risk-based prediction schemes. Beyond the political and popular levels, criminologists too have evinced growing interest in the role of previous convictions at sentencing. Criminal history has emerged as the sentencing factor on which the greatest amount of research has been conducted.

This increased concern with reducing risk to the community has the obvious consequence of diminishing interest in the retributive character of sentencing: sentencers become more interested in reducing the likelihood of future offending than recognizing the seriousness of past offending. It is easy to understand sentencers' attraction to record-based risk scales as well as their reluctance to

[27] The number of previous adult arrests is one of the predictors in this scale; see Dolan and Doyle (2000) for a summary of risk predictors used in various risk prediction scales.

[28] Harcourt (2007) argues that 'today the criminal sentence is related primarily to prior criminal history' (p 188). This is an overstatement; analyses of sentencing statistics demonstrate the primacy of crime seriousness over criminal record as a predictor of sentence severity. Nevertheless, there is no denying the growing influence of actuarial devices to which Harcourt rightfully calls our attention.

ignore risk predictions when placed before the court. A judge confronted with a categorical risk level has a finding on which to rely when imposing sentence. In addition, if the court discounts or ignores a prediction of reoffending and the offender subsequently reoffends, blame will accrue to the original sentencer. Judicial 'error' in the other direction (imposing a term of custody when the risk of reoffending is lower) will have no consequences for the judge and this makes sentencers impervious to criticism for what may be termed 'false positive' sentencing decisions in which a sentence is imposed to prevent a crime that in fact would not have been committed.

Criminal justice policymaking in a number of countries has moved towards a crime prevention agenda, one that stresses the reduction of reoffending. For example, the British government has identified reducing reoffending rates as a primary criminal justice objective. The Home Office Sentencing Review of 2001 took the position that sentencing arrangements in England and Wales reflected a 'muddled approach to persistent offenders' (2001: 2). It produced a set of proposals in which the new sentencing framework would 'in particular do more to target persistent offenders' (p 11). In addition, as noted in a recent publication, the government has set a target to reduce overall crime rates by 15% by 2008 (Home Office 2006). In 2007 the newly-formed Ministry of Justice issued a penal policy paper in which it declared that 'sentencing is central to...protect the public and reduce reoffending' (Ministry of Justice 2007: 8). This reorientation of sentencing is likely to come at the expense of policies that stress the retributive sentencing perspective. Reducing recidivism is an ancillary goal of retributive sentencing, but it lies at the heart of utilitarian schemes.

(iii) Legislative intervention in sentencing

Legislatures around the world have become increasingly interventionist with respect to sentencing policy. Many areas of the criminal law have become increasingly subject to statutory regulation, and sentencing is no exception. Thus, sentencing objectives and factors have been placed on a statutory footing in a number of countries,[29] and the ambit of specific sanctions has been

[29] In Canada in 1996, New Zealand in 2002, and England and Wales in 2003 (see Roberts and Baker 2007).

determined or curtailed by parliamentary intervention. It is hardly surprising therefore that the second most important consideration at sentencing should be the target of reform legislation. This has had a number of effects, including a rise in attention to the goal of preventing reoffending. Many jurisdictions have introduced legislation mandating harsher penalties for specific categories of repeat offenders or promoting the use of previous convictions for sentencing repeat offenders in general. France is the most recent country to introduce tough mandatory sentences for repeat offenders. Legislation introduced in June 2007 creates mandatory sentences of imprisonment for offenders with previous convictions.[30]

Focus of volume

With the resurgence of interest in the use of previous convictions at sentencing, the time has come for a more detailed examination of the practice and a more thorough exegesis of its justifications. The current volume examines the recidivist sentencing premium from a number of perspectives, both theoretical and empirical. The volume thus explores a universal sentencing practice that has been insufficiently addressed by sentencing scholars to date (for earlier publications, see Durham 1987b; Roberts 1997a). Particular attention is paid to the experiences and perceptions of ex-offenders and the reactions of the general public. Sentencing policy must attract the tacit support of both of these groups if the sentencing process is to enjoy some degree of legitimacy. Moreover, these two constituencies have been overlooked in the literature on the subject of the recidivist premium which has tended to explore normative questions or research issues pertaining to predicting reoffending. The focus is on the general punishment of offenders with previous convictions, and not upon the more radical habitual offender laws that apply only to offenders with very long criminal histories.[31] The reason for this is that

[30] The press release describing the new sentences makes it clear that repeat offenders are viewed in a very different light: 'Recidivism, particularly when it involves violence, constitutes an unacceptable harm to the security of the public and must be addressed in the most effective manner possible, whether the offender is an adult or a juvenile' (Communication de Madame Le Garde des Sceaux, 13 June, 2007, translation by author).

[31] Davis (1992) makes a distinction between external and internal approaches to justifying recidivist sentencing laws. By external he means a justification which

considerable consensus exists with respect to two propositions. The first is that first offenders should be treated with more leniency than recidivists. The second is that offenders who have accumulated a very large number of convictions—particularly serious offences—should receive harsher punishments.[32] As will be seen later in this volume, however, first offenders and highly-persistent offenders account for a minority of offenders appearing for sentencing. Consensus does not exist, however, with respect to the sentencing of the majority of offenders, namely those who are neither first nor highly-persistent offenders.

Plan of the volume

Chapter 2 documents the different ways that the principal utilitarian sentencing perspectives incorporate criminal history information. There is considerable consensus among advocates of utilitarian sentencing with respect to this issue. As will be seen, whether for the purposes of deterrence, incapacitation, rehabilitation, or restoration, an offender's previous offending is relevant for the purposes of sentencing.

Chapter 3 explores some non-consequentialist or retributive justifications for considering an offender's past at sentencing. The most popular justification for a very limited use of previous convictions is based on the idea that anyone may 'lapse' and commit a crime. It has also been argued that harsher sentencing is justified because crime by recidivists is inherently more serious.

Chapter 4 proposes a retributive justification for the recidivist premium. Over 25 years ago George Fletcher concluded that previous convictions had no role to play according to a retributive

is unrelated to criminal law principles—by dealing with exceptional offenders, recidivist statutes occupy a zone beyond important considerations such as proportionality. The internal approach to which he refers is the one taken in this volume which seeks to justify harsher treatments on the grounds that they deserve additional punishment.

[32] Utilitarian sentencers would endorse a rigorous recidivist premium for such cases on the basis of risk, with the specific mechanism to prevent reoffending being incapacitation. Retributive theorists would probably accept that at some point, the most extremely persistent offenders should be assigned to a 'proportionality-free' sentencing zone, and detained on the basis of public protection. Even von Hirsch, who is sceptical of claims to impose extra punishment on offenders who display 'incorrigibility', concedes that 'the issue may be worth debating' (1991: 56).

account of sentencing. However, he challenged the field to 'come forth with additional and stronger arguments' (1982: 59) to justify the consideration of prior offending. A considerable amount of scholarship has accumulated since then, although Ryberg (2004) recently concluded: 'the principles that underlie [the dimension of criminal record] are—if not defective—theoretically underdetermined'. This chapter proposes that prior convictions enhance the repeat offender's level of culpability in much the same way that evidence of premeditation enhances blameworthiness. Both circumstances reflect a higher level of moral turpitude at the time of commission of the offence. A number of scholars have evinced renewed interest in justifications based on enhanced culpability (eg, MacPherson 2002), and this is therefore a propitious time to revisit the relationship between previous convictions and offender culpability.

Chapter 5 documents the range and diversity of recidivist sentencing laws in a number of representative countries. The chapter makes two important points: first, that the recidivist sentencing premium appears across a wide range of countries, and second, that criminal history information is conceived and implemented in a diversity of ways across jurisdictions, although some common elements clearly emerge. The chapter also summarizes sentencing statistics that reveal the strength of the recidivist premium, and provides a limited exploration of the concordance between theoretical justifications and sentencing trends at the trial court level.

Chapters 6 and 7 examine the opinions of the most overlooked constituency in the debate about sentencing reform: sentenced offenders. The views of this group are sometimes dismissed by populist politicians (and cynical members of the public, perhaps) as being predictable and self-interested; yet if offenders reject the recidivist sentencing premium, the practice of imposing progressively harsher penalties may backfire. Perceptions of injustice on the part of offenders may undermine any deterrent effects associated with a recidivist premium. A considerable volume of research has demonstrated the importance of perceptions of legitimacy in securing compliance. Legitimacy is conferred upon a practice when the individuals most affected (offenders) regard it as appropriate. Offenders sentenced capriciously, or as a result of the application of extra-legal factors, will never accept the legitimacy of the sentencing process. Offenders who perceive that they have been unjustly treated may return to crime out of a sense of injustice, regardless of the enhanced deterrent threat of the criminal law arising from a recidivist sentencing premium.

Chapters 8 and 9 explore community reaction to various ways of using an offender's previous convictions at sentencing. As noted, proportional sentencing derives much of its strength from an appeal to community values: few people take issue with a sentencing philosophy that assigns progressively harsher sentences to progressively more serious crimes. But can the same be said for the recidivist sentencing premium? At some point, cumulative sentencing will violate proportionality requirements, and how do the public react when this occurs? One of the most robust findings in the field of public opinion is that members of the public are very critical of sentencers and the sentences that they impose. The fact that most people underestimate the severity of sentencing patterns helps to explain this public criticism of the courts.[33] But if courts adhere to a sentencing model that is clearly at odds with the views of the public, this discrepancy may explain some of the antagonism expressed towards judges. Further to this, which of the competing theoretical perspectives attracts the greatest degree of support from the public? This chapter also reports findings from a recent survey using a representative sample of the British public. Chapter 9 attempts to explain these views by drawing upon research exploring the social psychology of attributions of criminal behaviour.

Chapter 10 summarizes the principal findings and draws some conclusions about the future of the recidivist sentencing premium. I argue that consensual conceptions of culpability incorporate considerations of the offender's criminal antecedents and that flat-rate sentencing will never likely prove acceptable to the community. An account of sentencing practices which failed to incorporate an offender's previous convictions would fail to be perceived as legitimate by members of the public, crime victims, and even offenders themselves. At the same time, allowing previous convictions to enhance the severity of sentence without limit would result in disproportionate punishments which themselves would generate opposition from the community.

[33] The most recent survey of the British public found that 76% of the sample expressed the view that sentences are too lenient (ICM Research 2006b).

2

Reductivist Sentencing Perspectives and the Role of Previous Convictions

Ask the man in the street why a thief is sent to prison, and in all probability you will receive one of two answers: he will say, 'because he has stolen', or 'because it would not be safe to allow him to remain at large'. These two homely replies illustrate the two fundamental principles which have competed, since Grotius's time, for supremacy in the theory and practice of punishment. (Oppenheimer 1913: 179)

Desert or dangerousness? Punishment or prevention? Recognizing past harm or preventing future crime? These antimonies encapsulate the two perspectives that continue to compete for support in the discourse of sentencing reform and the practice of the courts. Like the ancient Roman deity Janus, the sentencing process gazes simultaneously in two directions: backwards to consider the offence of conviction, and forwards to evaluate the likelihood that the offender will reoffend. The nature and quantum of punishment is therefore based on a combination of the seriousness of the crime, the offender's level of culpability, and the probability of reoffending. How do the competing theoretical perspectives react to, and incorporate an offender's previous convictions? As noted in Chapter 1, there is a divergence of approaches, even within the same theoretical perspective. The following three chapters all share a two-fold goal: they seek to determine whether previous convictions are relevant to a range of sentencing objectives, and if so, whether these objectives can justify progressively increasing sentence severity to reflect the number and nature of an offender's previous convictions—the recidivist sentencing premium.

Overview

This chapter explores the relevance of previous convictions for a number of sentencing objectives and perspectives, including individual and general deterrence, incapacitation, and restorative justice. The focus is on sentencing purposes that attempt to reduce crime directly, by means of threats or detention, or indirectly through some other purpose such as restoration. At first glance, utilitarian theories—and in particular incapacitation—offer the most persuasive rationale for a recidivist sentencing premium. To the extent that an offender's criminal history is a good predictor of future offending, there will be some crime prevention benefit associated with imposing harsher sentences on recidivists. Upon closer examination, however, it is clear that individual deterrence rests on the dubious assumption that progressive increments of severity will deter offenders more effectively than a 'flat rate' approach, while incapacitation is a sentencing model applicable principally to the most serious offenders. However, as will be seen, all sentencing perspectives take an interest in the nature of the offender's criminal record.

Consequentialist approaches to sentencing: deterrence and incapacitation

Not even the offender himself can be certain that he or she will or will not reoffend (Floud and Young 1981: 39).

The justification for incorporating an offender's previous convictions appears straightforward from the perspective of utilitarian sentencers. Utilitarians are concerned with preventing crime by means of one or more of a number of specific objectives, including incapacitation, general and specific deterrence, and rehabilitation. All these sentencing purposes share a concern with the future conduct of the offender; they all seek to prevent reoffending, albeit by different means. A vast literature has by now accumulated on predicting reoffending. This research confirms what the intuitive sentencer over the centuries would have concluded, namely that previous crimes predict future crimes. Reoffending rates increase rapidly as the number of previous convictions (and sentencing decisions) increases (Cunliffe and Shepherd 2007; Gabor 1986; Ruddy 2007).

The monotonic relationship between number of previous convictions and probability of reoffending can be seen in recidivism statistics from many jurisdictions. Table 2.1 provides reoffending rates for the cohort of offenders convicted in England and Wales and Northern Ireland in 2003. As can be seen, the recidivism rate for offenders with one or two priors is more than double the

Table 2.1 Reoffending rates and criminal history category of offenders convicted in 2003, England and Wales; Northern Ireland

Percentage of sample reconvicted within two years

Criminal history category	England and Wales	Northern Ireland
No priors	13%	25%
1–2 priors	30%	37%
3–6 priors	45%	40%
7–10 priors	56%	50%
>10 priors	76%	57%

Source: adapted from Shepherd and Whiting (2006); Ruddy (2007)

rate for first offenders. The reoffending rate for offenders in the most serious criminal history category (more than 10 priors) is approximately five times the rate for the first offenders (76% compared to 13%—see Table 2.1). These are aggregate custody rates for the total cohort, but offence-specific studies find the same clear correlation between offending in the past and the future (eg, Rose 2000). This not a new phenomenon: statistics from over a century earlier reveal the same pattern. Grunhut (1948) reviewed statistics collected in Germany in 1902 and concluded that 'the probability of recidivism increases with the number of previous sentences' (p 389).

There is also a robust relationship between number of previous convictions and the severity of sentencing practices. Konecni and Ebbesen (1982) reported a linear relationship between the number of previous felony convictions and the probability of committal to state prison. Thus only 7% of first offenders compared to 29% of multiple recidivists were sentenced to prison (see Konecni and Ebbesen 1982: Table 11.5; see also Spohn 2002: Exhibit 3.2). (Sentencing trends as a function of criminal history are explored in more detail in Chapter 5.) The relationship between prior and future offending also transcends the nature of state intervention and is not limited to the criminal justice system. Repeat offenders participating in a restorative programme rather than the criminal justice system were significantly more likely to reoffend. Hayes and Daly (2004) report that approximately three-quarters of the offenders with previous convictions participating in restorative conferences reoffended within five years. In contrast, only approximately one-third of the first offenders committed additional offences.

The consequentialist justification for a recidivist premium may be uncontroversial but the utilitarian perspective is nevertheless problematic. While there is considerable evidence that an offender with four prior convictions for robbery represents a higher risk to reoffend than an offender with a single conviction, there is no guarantee that either offender will in fact reoffend. Indeed, research suggests that the relationship between the number and nature of previous convictions and the likelihood of reoffending is complex and attenuates more rapidly than is commonly believed. This raises the much-discussed problem of false positives. A significant number of offenders predicted to reoffend will in fact desist. The utilitarian sentencer is therefore punishing offenders on the basis of an ascribed risk based upon research findings involving categories of offenders: for example, fourth-time offenders are more likely to reoffend than second-time offenders. Utilitarians thus have to overcome the moral objection raised by retributivists: offenders are being punished in large measure for what they (or other potential offenders) might do, rather than what they have actually done. Ultimately, the utilitarian justifications for a recidivist sentencing premium are founded upon the empirical observation that repeat offenders represent a greater risk to reoffend.

Advocates of general deterrence would take a similar line. The crime control benefit from a general deterrence perspective arises from the inhibition of offending as a result of potential offenders refraining from offending through fear of harsher punishment. Recidivist sentencing laws relating to drink-driving are often justified on the grounds that potential offenders with a previous conviction for impaired driving will be deterred by knowing that reconviction will result in a significantly harsher sentence. In order to be effective however, recidivist statutes of this kind must be well-known to potential offenders. The research record is not encouraging; surveys of the general public generally reveal low rates of awareness of sentencing provisions, even for common or well-publicized offences such as drink-driving (Roberts and Hough 2005).

The objectives of individual and general deterrence as well as incapacitation rest upon the assumption that harsher penalties for recidivists are justified because repeat offenders are more likely to reoffend than novice offenders. There are two empirically-testable elements to the argument. First, it is necessary to establish that there is a significant association between the extent of past offending and the likelihood of future offending. This relationship is easily demonstrable (see Table 2.1). But it is also necessary to demonstrate that the imposition of progressively harsher penalties—the recidivist sentencing premium—will result in lower recidivism rates. This is the 'verifiable good' to which Bagaric (2001) refers. The evidence for this proposition is far from convincing.

Most of the empirical research on individual and general deterrence has addressed the crime preventive power of sentencing: to what extent do variations in the certainty, severity, and celerity of punishments affect the aggregate crime rate? The most important variable in the present context is severity of the sentence, and a number of reviews have concluded that changes in the overall severity of punishments have little impact on aggregate crime rates (see for example, von Hirsch, Bottoms, Burney, and Wikstrom 1999; Doob and Webster 2003). But this literature sheds little light on the crime-preventive effectiveness of a specific deterrent policy, namely the imposition of progressively harsher sentences to reflect an increasing number of previous convictions.

Consider sentencing under one of the two-dimensional guideline grids used across the United States. The US federal sentencing guidelines contain six criminal history categories. The median sentence of imprisonment imposed rises from 24 months for category I to 27 months for category II, 30 months for category III, 37 months for category IV, 50 months for category V, and 60 months for category VI (US Sentencing Commission 2006). Thus each additional conviction results in an additional period of custody. From an incapacitation perspective, there will be a modest crime preventive effect arising from the fact that offenders in the repeat offender categories are more likely to reoffend. But what evidence is there that the more severe sentencing ranges provide any additional individual deterrent value?

Ideally, one needs to compare recidivism rates in comparable jurisdictions, some which adhere to one of the retributive accounts of sentencing and ignore criminal record, and some which pursue a rigid cumulative model of sentencing. If the recidivist sentencing premium is effective, recidivism rates should be systematically lower in the cumulative model countries. However, the ubiquity of the practice of employing a recidivist sentencing premium precludes a comparative analysis of this kind at present.

Assumptions of deterrence theory

A deterrence-based justification for the recidivist sentencing premium makes a number of dubious assumptions about the impact of such a premium on offenders' behaviour. It assumes that offenders are rational calculators, who consider the 'expected gain' and 'expected penalty' of future offending. Of course, this assumption applies to deterrent policies in general, but a recidivist premium further assumes that offenders consider the additional punishment that will be visited upon them, and that the increased punishment provides a sufficient deterrent.[1] The imposition of additional punishment each time the offender reappears for sentencing is unlikely to have any significant impact on aggregate crime rates or individual reoffending rates. Andrews and Bonta (2003) review a number of studies upon the impact of shorter versus longer prison sentences on reoffending. They conclude that recidivism rates were actually slightly higher for offenders released from longer rather than shorter prison terms. Sentencing outcomes—particularly with respect to the issue of severity—have little impact upon the causes of reoffending. This suggests that a rationale for the imposition of harsher penalties on repeat offenders must be found elsewhere.

Advocates of selective incapacitation would argue that the imposition of a harsher penalty will incapacitate the offender, thereby preventing further offending during the additional period in which the offender is imprisoned. However, the propriety of adopting such a rationale for the general offender population is highly questionable. Selective incapacitation is most effective when applied to a relatively small group of highly repetitive offenders (Champion 1994). The increments in number of months of custody for offenders with a relatively small number of convictions will generate only a modest incapacitative benefit.

Finally, it is worth recalling that under most US sentencing guidelines, criminal history points are assigned to reflect issues such as the recency of the previous convictions and whether the offender was on parole at the time of the commission of the current offence. The imposition of metronomically regular increments of

[1] A subsequent chapter in this volume will discuss interviews with individuals who have been sentenced on many occasions, and that offer no support for the deterrence-based assumption that severity increments reduce the probability of further offending.

punishment to reflect the number of previous convictions cannot be predominantly risk-driven. A truly risk-based sentencing premium would be sensitive to variables such as the offender's age, any substance abuse problems, and other variables that relate to offending. This suggests that in practice the recidivist premium in the US reflects an alternate model. Indeed, many guidelines manuals argue that harsher punishments are justified both because repeat offenders represent a higher risk and because they are more culpable. The question of whether repeat offenders can be considered more culpable for their current offending is addressed in Chapter 3.

To summarize, although the individual deterrence model carries considerable popular appeal as a justification for the recidivist sentencing premium, at the end of the day, whether it is effective is an empirical question, one which has yet to be answered affirmatively. The imposition of a recidivist sentencing premium requires a more principled justification. Incapacitation seems even harder to justify as a general sentencing policy. The vast majority of offenders are convicted of crimes the seriousness of which cannot justify such a severe sentencing policy.

Rehabilitation

Rehabilitation is one of the oldest sentencing objectives, although support for this purpose has waxed and waned over the years. Consistent with individual deterrence, rehabilitation aims to reduce reoffending, although by changing the offender—not simply through threat of further punishment. How does the rehabilitation-oriented sentencer respond to the issue of the offender's previous convictions? One of the abiding criticisms of the rehabilitation movement in sentencing is that it is hard to identify a single strategy or specific criminal sanction which will rehabilitate a wide range of offenders. What 'works' with one offender may well fail to have any impact upon another individual. By definition, rehabilitation focuses on the individual before the court, and in particular, his specific needs. The nature and seriousness of the offence diminish in significance as the focus turns upon the person.

This said, some general conclusions may be drawn. Rehabilitationists make a clear distinction between first and repeat offenders. A policy of penal restraint may offer the greatest rehabilitative potential with respect to first offenders; the experience of having been called to account, the process of conviction itself may suffice—hence the near universal use of suspended or conditional sentences for first offenders convicted of less serious crimes. However, a more interventionist strategy may be necessary for repeat offenders. Another critical distinction involves the question of previous custodial experience. Offenders who have not served a term of imprisonment should be spared the experience for as long as possible, in recognition of the generally accepted view that rehabilitation is harder to achieve when the offender is in prison rather than the community (Wright 2005).

Like deterrence, the effectiveness of rehabilitation can be empirically established. Recidivism bespeaks failure and although reoffending may (in fact, usually does) reflect factors other than the nature or severity of the sanction imposed, the offender's re-appearance for sentencing will provoke questions about the effectiveness of the previously-imposed sentence. The response to these questions may well be a change in sanction strategy, and this may involve the imposition of a more punitive disposition. The rehabilitationist may seek to make a non-custodial sentence more intrusive, with a view to disrupting the offender's criminogenic lifestyle. A term of probation might now include more onerous conditions, or more intensive treatment of some kind.

To ignore the offender's record—to treat, for the purposes of rehabilitation, all offenders as first offenders—makes little sense and will undermine the rehabilitative effectiveness of the sentencing process. However, it is clear that rehabilitation cannot justify a recidivist premium which consists of imposing a harsher or more intrusive sentence each time the offender is reconvicted. Finally, to be effective, rehabilitation strategies need to be well-resourced. This means concentrating time and attention on the individual offenders who have the greatest needs and who represent the highest risk to reoffend. A lengthy criminal history is evidence of such persons and as such, previous convictions are a useful guide to allocating correctional resources. Ignoring an offender's previous convictions would therefore violate a sound principle of effective rehabilitation. At this point I turn to sentencing perspectives that do not explicitly aim to reduce offending.

Punishing defiance of the law

Can defiance of the law justify the recidivist premium? Here the idea is that the accumulation of additional convictions constitutes wilful defiance of the law and thereby justifies harsher treatment. Progressively harsher sentences are imposed until the defiant offender desists. The concept of defiance is often heard in popular discourse about punishing repeat offenders.[2] According to this logic, the previous sentence carried an implicit appeal to the offender to desist, and this appeal has had no effect—as evidenced by his reappearance for sentencing.

Over a century ago Cox (1877) argued that 'he who has had so emphatic a warning as a trial, a conviction, and punishment can plead none of the excuses which may be properly urged in behalf of first offenders' (pp 146–7). This quote suggests that the repeat offender, having been warned through the imposition of punishment, is disentitled to mitigation, but it does not imply sentencing to reflect different levels of defiance. How might the defiance justification be conceptualized to justify a recidivist premium? Offenders will be seen to fall at some point along a continuum or axis of compliance-defiance. With each episode of offending they assume a more defiant posture, and this justifies the escalating severity of imposed penalties.

Ensuring compliance with court orders is essential to a functioning judicial system. Indeed as MacPherson (2002) notes, defiance 'could cripple the operation of the criminal justice system' (p 208). Offenders are sometimes punished for defiance in the context of failing to comply with a judicial order such as a probation order. Failure to comply with a condition of probation (such as reporting to a probation officer) is a criminal offence in most jurisdictions and may result in the offender being committed to custody. However, there is an important difference between the two contexts. Desistance from offending is not a condition of the

[2] A desire to punish defiant individuals underlies many institutional recidivist rules. Oxford students are required to report for their exams in sub-fusc, an antiquated form of academic attire. Students who appear improperly attired for an examination for the second time are reported to the university disciplinary authorities. Rules of this nature clearly reflect the assumption that repetition constitutes defiance of authority, and that this should be punished. Failure to comply with authority is regarded as being more serious than the nature of the actual predicate conduct.

previously imposed sentence but simply an expectation on the part of the sentencing authority.

Defiance in practice: punishing the recalcitrant offender

In practice it is likely that some judges respond to recidivists more punitively out of an all-too-human reaction to an affront to their judicial authority. This seems clear from comments sometimes heard in court where judges may note that the offender had appeared for sentencing mere months before—as though this rapid reappearance justified the imposition of additional punishment. Similarly, the veiled judicial threats to offenders at sentencing 'let this be a warning to you, that if you come before me again…' echo the same sentiment. Any offender brazen enough to reappear for sentencing following additional offending can expect a harsher sentence. Public reactions to sentencing repeat offenders often echo this notion that having been served notice by the previous sentence, the offender's reappearance can reflect only moral turpitude. Barwick Baker, the Victorian advocate of cumulative sentencing captured this sentiment when he noted that if an offender was sentenced for the third time he was effectively sentencing himself (see Radzinowicz and Hood 1980: 1324).

Most sentencing guideline systems in the United States consider the offender's custody status at the time of the offence to be relevant to sentencing. An offender who committed his latest offence while on probation or parole is assigned an additional criminal history point and this subsequently results in harsher punishment. It may be argued that custody status is confounded with recency: the current and previous offences may be relatively contiguous in time. A more plausible explanation invokes defiance: the offender has elected to reoffend even before warrant of the previously imposed sentence has elapsed. The fresh offending may be interpreted as wanton disregard of the authority of the court.

The language used to justify the recidivist premium in some recent policy documents relating to sentencing often carries the same tone. The Home Office Sentencing Review of 2001 in England proposed a series of reforms which would increase the role of previous convictions at sentencing (discussed in a subsequent chapter of this volume). The Review's report asserted that there were two justifications for a recidivist sentencing premium: 'The justification for [the imposition of harsher sentences on recidivists] is two-fold. A continuing course of criminal conduct in the face of repeated attempts by the State to correct it, calls for increasing denunciation and retribution' (2001: 13).[3] This language suggests that the offender's recidivism constitutes a culpable rejection of the State's legitimate attempts to elicit desistance. The sentiment expressed by courts and the language of the report may be understandable but does it constitute safe ground on which to justify incrementally severe punishments?

Finally, appellate courts in a number of jurisdictions have acknowledged the relevance of defiance or disobedience to the sentencing process. For example, in *Veen v The Queen*, the Court of Criminal Appeal in New South Wales stated that an offender's previous convictions are relevant 'to show whether the instant offence is an uncharacteristic aberration or whether the offender has manifested in his commission of the instant offence a continuing attitude of disobedience of the law' (p 477).

Retributivist objections to punishing defiance

Unsurprisingly, retributive theorists object to the defiance argument. Von Hirsch (2002) takes the view that the justification assumes wilful defiance on the part of the offender, who may have reoffended with no such wilfulness in mind. Defiance is inferred on the basis of the offender's reappearance for sentencing, not demonstrated. Offenders reoffend for a variety of reasons, and it would be naïve (and, ultimately unfair) to impute one particular motive to all repeat offenders and punish them all accordingly. Moreover, even if the intention to defy the law lay behind the offence, this does not make the crime more seriousness or the offender more culpable for the crime. Von Hirsch writes that: 'theft of a CD player from a shop, with the animus shown by a deliberate flouting of the rule against theft, is still just stealing an article of modest value' (2002: 202).

The defiance justification is thus rejected by George Fletcher (1978), von Hirsch and other retributivist theorists who argue that disobedience is a transgression with important collective consequences in some societies—such as the military where refusal to

[3] The report goes on to add that persistent criminality 'justifies the more intensive efforts to reform and rehabilitate which become possible within a more intrusive and punitive sentence' (2001: 13).

comply with a legitimate order 'is grounds for disciplinary action irrespective of any risks or injurious consequences of the conduct itself' (von Hirsch 2002: 202). But this does not apply to civil society. An analogy may be made to discipline in the home. When Jack hits his sister Jill for the second time, having been disciplined by his parents for the same conduct five minutes earlier, his punishment is now likely to be more severe. But here the harsher treatment is imposed as much (or more) to reflect his flagrant flouting of parental authority as his much as his gesture against his sister. Compliance with parental instructions is a prerequisite of a functioning family, without which the structure of the familial unit is threatened. The relationship that exists between the citizen and the state is of a quite different nature. Moreover, the causes of non-compliance with respect to criminal conduct are much more complex. A criminal court cannot match the expectation of compliance and desistance that a parent makes of a child.

If there is evidence that the offender is in fact wilfully defying the authority of the court, defiance of the law may be a justified ground for imposing an additional or a more severe penalty. However, defiance alone does not constitute a sufficient normative basis on which to base a sentencing policy that has consequences for a high proportion of sentencing decisions.

The pedagogy of legal punishment

An important pedagogical function of the criminal law aims to educate members of the community about the boundaries of acceptable conduct and the relative seriousness of different offences. Statutory maximum penalties should contribute to this pedagogical effect, and a number of writers have drawn attention to the pedagogical function of specific sentencing decisions (see discussion in Walker 1985).

This perspective is often associated with the writings of AC Ewing (1929) who regarded the sentencing process as a means to educate the offender as well as society about the moral wrongfulness of criminal conduct. Intuitive or lay accounts of sentencing often invoke the concept of teaching offenders to comply with the law. This perspective is reflected in comments such as 'he obviously hasn't learned his lesson'—to describe a repeat offender who appears for sentencing, particularly when the interval between court appearances is relatively short. (As will be seen in Chapters

7 and 8 of this volume, offenders as well as members of the public appear to subscribe to this justification of a recidivist sentencing premium.) Sentencing scholars, too, have identified learning as an appropriate goal for sentencing. Walker (1985) for example notes that 'the repetition of an offence for which the offender has already been sentenced strongly suggests that the sentence was ineffective in changing his conduct in which case it is reasonable to resort to a different kind or greater severity' (p 44). The perspective carries the assumption that the imposition of punishment should result in desistance. Having been called to account for his offending (through the imposition of a penal sanction) the offender should thereafter desist.

Insufficient punishment or lack of responsiveness to a specific sanction

Lessons may be learned in various ways and the pedagogical perspective is susceptible of multiple interpretations. One perspective is based on mere punitiveness: the logic here is that the aversiveness of the response should inhibit subsequent manifestations of the stimulus (the offending behaviour). This version would prescribe a more punitive punishment when the behaviour is repeated. It reflects a punitive and rather simplistic approach to regulating human behaviour. On the other hand, the *nature* of the punishment may change with a view to educating the offender and encouraging desistance. An individual on whom a community penalty was previously imposed may now be committed to custody not simply to escalate the punitive bite of the sanction but to convey a message that the offending is more serious than the offender appears to believe.

The pedagogical perspective fits well with the cumulative sentencing model although the magnitude of the premium may not follow a true linear equation. Instead, the severity of penalties may rise more sharply. A sentencer may reason that an offender who received a six month term and then a twelve month term on the second occasion may 'require' a more rigorous premium—the extra six months having failed to have the desired effect. The escalation in sentence severity may also reflect a practical desire on the part of the court to detach the offender from a criminogenic lifestyle, or to ensure treatment in a way that is impossible if the offender remains in the community. Finally, using the sentencing process to 'teach the offender a lesson' may ultimately be self-defeating. Such a policy invites the following logic: the offender is punished and then reoffends. He is punished again, this time with more severity. The additional record-based punishment may provoke further defiance rather than elicit compliance.

Awareness of illegal nature of specific conduct

A related justification concerns the offender's state of awareness of legal rules. People convicted for the first time could argue that they were unaware (or insufficiently aware) of the truly criminal nature of their conduct. One justification for the first offender discount is that we accord some degree of mitigation to people who may have failed to fully appreciate the criminal consequences of their behaviour, even if they were well aware that the conduct was illegal. But relying on this justification requires the sentencing system to offer a blanket 'diminished awareness' discount—or to hear evidence in court with respect to the offender's actual level of awareness. Neither solution appears satisfactory.

In addition, once the offender has been punished once or twice, no plausible appeal may be made on the grounds of lack of awareness. As with most other justifications for the use of previous convictions, the 'lack of awareness' argument justifies a mitigated response to first offenders. However, it fails to offer a plausible rationale to distinguish between repeat offenders with different criminal histories, all of whom are presumably aware of the illegal nature of their conduct.

Preventing public demoralization

One last perspective on sentencing requires commentary in this chapter. It is sometimes argued that a primary purpose of the criminal sanction is to prevent the demoralization of the public which may arise if offenders are seen to commit crime with impunity. The Canadian Sentencing Commission noted that this objective 'rests on the premise that the majority of the population need to be spared more from the outrage and demoralizing effect of witnessing impunity for criminal acts than to be deterred from indulging in them' (1987: 151). The perspective assumes that demoralization will ultimately result in a number of adverse consequences, such as low levels of public confidence, and possibly, direct action against offenders. If offenders escape any punishment for offending it seems likely that at some point demoralization and retaliation will ensue. In theory at least, crime that results in derisory punishment may well have the same effect, although no empirical research has explored the hypothesis. Similarly, awareness that the imposition of punishment is routinely followed by reoffending is likely to diminish public confidence in the sentencing process.

The concept is related to the notion of denunciation. A denunciatory sentence aims to convey a message to the wider community about the gravity of offending. The degree of expressed denunciation reflects the gravity of the crime—proportionality is once more a relevant consideration. But community values are also germane; the criminal conduct that constitutes the greatest affront to society requires the most denunciation. The literature on denunciation generally focuses on the offence. However, offender characteristics are also relevant. Repetitive criminal behaviour, particularly of a serious nature, calls for greater denunciation. In this respect previous convictions play a role in determining the nature of the sanction imposed from the perspective of denunciation.

Restorative justice and the role of the crime victim

Unlike the reductivist models of sentencing that have been discussed, or the retributive perspective which will be explored later, restorative justice comes in many forms and encompasses a wide variety of practices (Braithwaite 1999). Dignan (2005) identifies the following five categories of restorative approaches to offending: court-based reparative programmes, victim-offender mediation programmes, conferences, community reparation boards, and healing or sentencing circles. It is harder, therefore, to encapsulate this approach to offending within a brief description. This explains why classifying any particular practice or programme as restorative 'remains a matter of controversy' (Dignan 2005: 107).

Nevertheless, some common elements emerge across a variety of restorative programmes. Restorative justice initiatives are (or should be) inclusive, community-based, and involve consensual decision-making. Some initiatives may seek to achieve reconciliation between the victim and offender and restoration of the offender to the community against which he or she has offended. What role might an offender's previous convictions play within a restorative justice approach? The answer may depend upon whether the question pertains to the admission of recidivists to a restorative justice programme or whether it involves the continued participation of repeat offenders who have already participated in such programmes.

There would appear to be no principled, a priori reason why recidivists would be disentitled to participate in a restorative resolution. Restorative programmes do sometimes involve offenders with previous convictions. For example, Maxwell et al (2005) report findings from an analysis of data concerning adolescents referred to a family group conference in New Zealand. One-third of the juvenile offenders referred to a conference had previously appeared in Youth Court. However, it seems likely that previous convictions would constitute a less important impediment to referral to a restorative programme at the juvenile level: Hayes and Daly (2004) report that slightly more than half the offenders participating in their conferences had prior convictions.

Although members of the public appear to oppose the inclusion of recidivists in restorative programmes (see Roberts and Stalans 2004, for a review), their opposition probably reflects a sense of proportionality or a tendency to regard restorative justice as a less onerous (and therefore in this case, less appropriate) response to offending. This public opposition may explain why in many jurisdictions, restorative programmes are restricted to less serious forms of offending such as crime by juveniles or adults convicted of crimes against property. But there is nothing in the theory of restorative justice that defines this approach to justice as being of exclusive or primary relevance to first offenders or offenders convicted of the less serious offences. Indeed, some reviews of the empirical research on restorative justice conclude that the potential for a restorative justice solution is even greater in the cases involving serious harm. Sherman and Strang (2007) for example, assert that 'restorative justice may reduce crime more effectively with more serious crimes' (p 70). This said, there are practical reasons why repeat offenders may be less appropriate candidates for a restorative justice programme.

First, there is the straightforward issue of resources. As Daly (2003) and others have noted, restorative interventions such as conferences usually consume far more time and resources than a conventional criminal justice response to offending. Sentencing circles or victim-offender reconciliation sessions take longer to arrange and conduct than a conventional sentencing hearing.

Indeed, this enhanced attention to the cause of the offending is one of the putative advantages of the restorative justice approach. A system which needs to conserve its resources will focus on the cases most likely to result in a positive restorative outcome. On a practical level then, previous convictions may therefore serve as a filter, with a lengthy criminal record disentitling the offender to consideration of a restorative rather than criminal justice response. Von Hirsch, Ashworth, and Shearing (2003) propose an alternate restorative justice model which they refer to as a 'making amends' model. This involves a response negotiated between the victim and the offender consisting of an acceptance of responsibility and an agreement to undertake a reparative task. Here too, the offender's reoffending has consequences; further offences undermine the offender's 'regretful stance for criminal behaviour' that is necessary for the model to succeed.

The second consideration concerns the reactions of repeat offenders, and the response of crime victims to the participation of recidivists. There is evidence from some restorative justice programmes that offenders with previous offences may well be less willing partners in a restorative conference.[4] For example, Rugge and Cormier (2005) note that offenders with criminal histories typically do not volunteer for the Collaborative Justice Project, a victim-offender programme in Canada. Many, but by no means all, restorative justice programmes require the consent of the victim. For example, the restorative justice programme for Aboriginal offenders in Toronto requires the approval of the victim before a referral is made to the programme (Roche 2003) as does the Community Accountability Programme in the North Island of New Zealand (Morris and Maxwell 2003) and the sentencing circles conducted in western Canada (Roberts and Roach 2003).

Victims appear to see mediation and reparation-based initiatives as inappropriate for repeat offenders. Thus Warner (1992) found that victims were opposed to the referral of persistent offenders to victim-offender mediation. Similarly, Maxwell and Morris (1996)

[4] One counter argument to this generalization is that a multiple recidivist with a lengthy history of involvement in the criminal justice system may be seen as an appropriate candidate for a restorative programme on the grounds that restorative justice may succeed where the criminal justice system has so patently failed. In fact, this logic was responsible for the first sentencing circle in Canada (see *R v Moses* (1992) 71 CCC (3d) 449 (Supreme Court of Canada).

found that victims participating in family group conferences in New Zealand were least satisfied when the offenders participating had extensive records of offending.[5] Vanfraechem (2005) reports that the juveniles participating in conferences for 'serious juvenile offenders' in Belgium were unknown to prosecutors, suggesting that repeat offenders 'did not get a chance to participate' (p 290). Seriousness was defined in terms of having been charged with a serious offence rather than possessing a history of previous convictions.

Thus in practice, multiple recidivists are less likely to enter a restorative justice environment—whether as a result of formal diversion by criminal justice professionals or through reluctance on the part of victims to engage with such a profile of offender. What happens when an offender has commenced, or completed a restorative programme, and then reoffends? The exclusionary approach to the use of previous convictions is unlikely to attract much support from restorative justice advocates.

Consider the following sequence of events. An offender convicted for the first time is offered and accepts the opportunity to participate in a restorative justice programme. Having completed the programme's requirements he is later reconvicted and is offered another entry into the programme. If he reoffends again—now his third conviction—his desire to participate once more is unlikely to meet with the endorsement of the crime victim. Offenders who repeatedly reoffend and repeatedly engage in a restorative justice programme are likely to undermine confidence in the restorative justice movement in the same way that recidivism undermines confidence in the conventional criminal sentencing process. The offender's pattern of repeat offending provides the background against which judgments are made about his or her suitability for a restorative referral.

The acknowledgement of responsibility and the expression of an apology are central to the restorative justice experience. These gestures carry an implicit acceptance on the part of the offender that desistance will ensue. As Roche notes, 'the vengeful victim

[5] Some may argue that the offender's history of offending should not be revealed to the victim contemplating participation in a restorative encounter. This seems unethical; crime victims should have an accurate and comprehensive picture of the other party in order to make an informed decision regarding participation in a victim-offender meeting.

becomes forgiving while the hardened offender becomes remorseful, promising to make amends and never reoffend' (2003: 11–12; emphasis added). If the victim has repeatedly been victimized by the same offender, further participation in the restorative programme is unlikely, unless there is a relationship between the victim and the offender sufficiently robust to accommodate such behaviour. Repeat victims in the criminal justice system are likely to lose faith in the sentencing process, but this loss of faith will be particularly striking in the restorative context since, in many cases, the victim must make a personal commitment to engage in dialogue with the offender.

A restorative justice system which ignored reoffending would inevitably lose credibility with its most critical constituency: crime victims. Of all participants in the criminal process, crime victims are especially likely to seek some assurance that the offender will desist. Indeed, a victim who learns of (or worse, witnesses) reoffending by an offender who has been through a restorative programme is likely to feel particularly punitive and may experience exactly the kind of hostile emotions towards the offender that restorative justice seeks to purge. Victims may also become cynical and believe that the repeat offender is manipulating the restorative system by affirming his commitment to a restorative option simply in order to avoid a more aversive criminal justice outcome. Such victims may also conclude that the reoffending could have been prevented had the offender been referred to court rather than a restorative programme, thereby undermining support for restorative, compared to criminal, justice.

Thus restorative justice models would consider previous misconduct to be relevant to whether the offender is invited to engage in a restorative process. The offender with many previous convictions has repeatedly rejected overtures of a restorative nature—the distinction between the offender and the law-abiding community to which he belonged becomes increasingly clearer with each criminal conviction. In the event that a victim has been victimized repeatedly by the same offender, it is unlikely that this individual will see much benefit in participating in a restorative process. This suggests that the offender's previous offending will play a role in determining whether a restorative resolution is possible or desirable.

This analysis is consistent with Braithwaite's pyramid-shaped conceptualization of responses to offending in which the majority of offenders are offered a restorative opportunity; a deterrent-based response is appropriate for a smaller group of recidivists, while a very few cases (the apex of the pyramid) are subject to an incapacitative sentence (see Ahmed, Harris, Braithwaite, and Braithwaite 2001: Figure 2.1). Thus first offenders are engaged at the first, broadest level of the pyramid. As they reoffend they are more likely to be subject to the non-restorative interventions that occupy the higher levels of the conceptual pyramid. Hudson notes: 'ultimately a repeat offender or a non-complying offender could be diverted back to conventional court processes' (2003: 87). From a restorative justice perspective then, it is hard to overlook an offender's previous offending in the way advocated by the 'flat-rate' or progressive loss of mitigation schools identified in the previous chapter. Before leaving the restorative framework, it is worth making a comment about the interests of the crime victim.

The special case of the crime victim

Research reported by Wake, Homes, and Wright (2006) involved focus groups with crime victims. The offender's previous offending emerged as an important focus of discussions. The authors of the report concluded that 'there was general agreement that previous offences and convictions should be taken into account when deciding on the appropriate punishment' (Wake et al 2006: 22). This is consistent with the responses of crime victims to criminal mediation. Warner (1992) for example, found that victims held the view that mediation and reparation were appropriate when the offence was 'out of character'—when committed by a first offender. In Canada, interviews with victims of serious personal injury offences revealed that victims were more critical of the leniency of the sentencing process when they learned that the offender had previous convictions (see Roberts and Roach 2005).

Knowing that the offender has previously been convicted of the same crime may be particularly demoralizing for crime victims. An offender who offends repeatedly will be perceived by victims as treating the sentencing process as a penal tax, simply one of the costs of offending. Although it is seldom discussed in the literature, a censure-based model of sentencing carries a clear appeal to crime victims. Von Hirsch notes that: 'Censure addresses the victim. He or she has not only been injured, but wronged through someone's culpable act...Censure, by directing disapprobation at the person responsible, acknowledges that the victim's hurt occurred through another's fault' (1993: 10). There is evidence that victims appreciate judicial recognition that they have been wronged (Roberts and Roach 2005). However, crime victims are likely to see little appeal in a retributive approach to sentencing once it becomes clear that the offender's previous convictions have little or no role to play. Victims of recidivist crime are unlikely to share either the exclusionary or progressive loss of mitigation model. In short, although the research record is rather scanty, it seems clear that an offender's previous criminal conduct is important from the perspective of the crime victim.

Summary and conclusion

Several conclusions may be drawn from this brief review of some competing sentencing perspectives. First, while criminal history information is used in different ways by competing theories, an offender's previous convictions are relevant for all perspectives, including restorative justice and crime control approaches. Some objectives invoke a severity premium for each additional conviction, on the basis of risk or retribution.[6] Other perspectives change the nature of the penal response, or possibly disentitle the repeat offender to particular response options. The next two chapters examine in more detail other arguments to justify the use of an offender's previous convictions at sentencing.

[6] As noted earlier, a number of sentencing guidelines manuals in the US affirm that a severity premium is justified both because the offender represents a higher risk to reoffend and should be considered more culpable. The enhanced culpability argument falls within a retributive framework and will be discussed at greater length in Chapter 4.

3

Retributive Approaches to Previous Convictions

For retributivists the problem is to explain how a single act of wrongdoing can deserve more punishment than another if the two differ only in that the doer of one is a recidivist while the doer of the other is not (Davis 1992: 36).

This chapter and the next move the focus from consequentialist to retributive and related approaches to sentencing. As noted in Chapter 1, retributive sentencing theorists fall into one of two camps: advocating a flat-rate approach in which prior convictions play no role, or espousing the very limited use of priors in a way consistent with the principle of the progressive loss of mitigation. The so-called 'flat-rate' approach to the use of prior convictions in which they play no role at all is inescapable if one accepts the proposition that previous convictions can have no impact upon the seriousness of the crime or the offender's level of culpability. For this reason, the debate about the use of prior convictions engages only those theorists who see a limited role for criminal history along the lines of the 'progressive loss of mitigation'.

Overview

I begin by exploring the most widely-held justification for the limited use of previous convictions—the so-called 'lapse' theory. Thereafter I address an alternate communicative theory of sentencing proposed by RA Duff as well as some other common justifications that have been advanced to support the use of previous convictions at sentencing. These fall into a retributive framework in that they are allegedly related to the seriousness of the offence or the offender's level of culpability. For example, it is sometimes argued that crime by repeat offenders is more serious and therefore should be punished more severely. These alternate justifications are reviewed and found wanting as adequate justifications for considering previous convictions.

Although many retributive theorists oppose even the limited use of previous convictions, earlier writers used retribution to justify harsher treatment for repeat offenders. An early English sentencing text (Cross 1971) contains the following, rather Delphic, statement: 'a man must not be punished twice for his past offences but his record may justify a severer sentence for the current offence' (p 148). Cross continues his analysis by asking 'how can past offences affect the gravity of the current crime? Resort may be had to the retributive theory for an answer. Repeated floutings of the law call for higher punishment on each occasion on which they occur... repetition also negates such possible extenuations as the fact that the offender did not know or fully appreciate that he was breaking the law, or that the incident was a mere isolated lapse' (p 149).

Cross appears to be making two claims here: first, that repetitive criminal conduct justifies the imposition of a harsher sentence by virtue of mere repetition, and second, that the existence of a criminal history disentitles an offender to the mitigation that would be accorded first offenders. Both of these claims will be examined over the course of this chapter.

It is easy to see the retributivist objection to the use of previous convictions at sentencing. According to a retributive perspective, legal punishment conveys blame and expresses societal disapprobation—but only for a specific criminal act. Sentence is imposed for a particular offence without which no legal censure is justified. If this were not the case, we would live in a society in which, from time to time, people were held accountable for their lives to that point. Under a 'flat-rate' retributive account, the sanction should reflect the seriousness of the crime and the offender's level of culpability for the offence for which he is called to account. Previous convictions should play no role—any more than other extra-legal considerations that nevertheless may have some intuitive appeal as a sentencing factor.

For example, many people may wish to mitigate punishment for offenders who have made a significant contribution to the community, although there is little room for such considerations within a principled retributive sentencing framework, since they are unrelated to crime seriousness or offender culpability. As

Bagaric (2000b) observes: 'people should be punished only for what they do; not according to the type of people we think they are...In a community governed by the rule of law...people are judged by their actions not their values or beliefs' (p 15; see also Gross 1979; Galligan 1981; Bean 1981; Fox 1994).

Other communicative theorists such as Duff (2001) are equally clear with respect to the role of previous convictions: 'the mere fact that an offender who is now convicted of a crime has a prior criminal record can make no justified difference to his sentence' and 'the fact that this is the offender's twentieth burglary does not justify a harsher punishment than was imposed for the tenth burglary' (p 167; 169). Davis (1992), too, regards the issue as unproblematic: 'The principle of just deserts does not allow a criminal to be punished more severely than he deserves for what he did' (p 132). These statements are consistent with the exclusionary model identified in Chapter 1. How then do retributivists justify even the limited use of previous convictions at sentencing?

Pessimism and optimism about offenders

Gross (1979) offers one justification for incorporating previous convictions to a limited degree in a way consistent with the progressive loss of mitigation. His account emphasizes societal expectations of the offender. Gross argues that sentencing reflects 'an implicit optimism about future conduct, for there is good reason for punishing less severely than culpability would warrant those persons who are first offenders and others who have not yet shown themselves to be dedicated to crime. It is a matter of giving them the benefit of the doubt so long as there is a reasonable doubt about their intentions' (p 456).

With repetition by the offender, however, optimism is dispelled with respect to the individual's future behaviour, and according to this view the full force of the law should thereafter descend upon the recidivist. The pessimism/optimism account fails to distinguish between repeat offenders with variable criminal histories (unless the optimistic view of offenders slowly evaporates). In this sense, this account offers no justification for incrementally increasing the severity of sentences in response to additional criminal convictions. This justification for the use of prior convictions has not been embraced by the field, and will not be discussed further here.

The progressive loss of mitigation: the lapse theory

Progressive loss of moral credit

Proponents of the alternative retributive perspective argue that previous convictions should play a limited role at sentencing—encapsulated in the progressive loss of mitigation. There are in fact two versions of the principle. In its earliest incarnation the principle of offering some mitigation towards first offenders or people with relatively short records was justified in terms of their character. In the first edition of his sentencing text, Thomas (1970) describes the 'progressive loss of credit' approach to offenders with no or few prior convictions (p 197). By this term he refers to the credit accumulated by the offender as a result of his crime-free life to that point. The credit is progressively lost with each accumulating conviction. Thomas notes the following: 'The fact that a man with previous convictions receives a longer sentence than a first offender and that a man with five previous convictions receives a longer sentence than a man with two previous convictions, is the result not of progressive aggravation of the basic penalty but a progressive loss of credit for good character until the offender's record is so bad that nothing could be used in his favour in that regard.' (1970: 174). This version[1] of the leniency principle has been largely supplanted in the literature by the lapse theory, which justifies the mitigation for first offenders in a quite different way.

Progressive loss of mitigation

In the seminal publication *Doing Justice*, von Hirsch (1976) took the position that previous convictions increased the offender's level of culpability and therefore had a role to play within a desert-based sentencing framework. I shall return to the culpability argument in the next chapter. For the present however, it is simply worth noting that with the publication of *Past or Future Crimes* (in 1985) von Hirsch refined his approach to the use of previous convictions at sentencing. In the later volume he abandoned the recidivist premium based on enhanced culpability in favour of a far more limited model which came to be characterized as

[1] It is unclear why the early interpretation proposed by Thomas failed to become widespread. One explanation is that the emphasis on the character of the offender was inconsistent with retributive theorizing following the publication of *Doing Justice* in 1976.

the progressive loss of mitigation. In the 1985 volume, and subsequent writings (1991; 1993) von Hirsch has elaborated upon the justification for this limited use of previous convictions although it is fair to say that the field awaits a thorough exegesis of the issue (see Ryberg 2004).

Wasik and von Hirsch (1994) offer the following succinct explanation of the justification in terms of tolerance for a lapse in behaviour:

> Our everyday moral judgments include the notion of a *lapse*. A transgression (even a fairly serious one) is judged somewhat less strictly when it occurs against a background of prior compliance. The idea is that even an ordinarily well-behaved person can have his or her inhibitions fail in a moment of willfulness or weakness. Such a temporary breakdown of self-control is the kind of frailty for which some understanding should be shown. In sentencing, the relevant lapse is an infringement of criminal law, rather than a more commonplace moral failure, but the logic of the first offender discount remains the same—that of dealing with a lapse more tolerantly. A reason for so treating a lapse is respect for the process by which people attend to, and respond to, censure for their conduct. A first offender, after being confronted with censure or blame, is capable—as a reasoning human being presumed capable of ethical judgments—of reflecting on the morality of what he has done and of making an extra effort to show greater restraint. What we do, in granting the discount, is to show respect for this capacity—and thereby give the offender a so-called 'second chance'. With repetitions, however, the discount should diminish, and eventually disappear (p 410).

Critiques of the progressive loss of mitigation doctrine

By drawing upon everyday moral judgments as a justification, the 'lapse' theory invites these views to influence the treatment of the recidivist. This is part of the popular appeal of retributivism in general, which, as Matravers notes, 'seeks to capture an intuition that wrongdoers deserve punishment' (2000: 95). Later chapters of this volume (8 and 9) will explore laypersons' reactions to the use of previous convictions at sentencing. But an appeal to everyday or intuitive conceptions of punishment might require the theory to consult this same constituency with respect to other elements of sentencing—a position generally rejected by retributive sentencing theorists (eg, Singer 1979; Bagaric and Edney 2004, and discussion of the issue in Chapter 10). However, this approach to the use of previous convictions involves more than simply a populist addition to a proportional sentencing model.

Although there is a link to intuitive reactions to wrongdoing, the 'lapse theory' approach to previous convictions is more complex. It incorporates notions of tolerance for imperfection in human behaviour, and a desire to extend leniency on more than a single occasion. This indulgence towards offenders arises in part out of recognition that offending reflects a multiplicity of influences and that many members of society are subject to forces that make compliance with the law more demanding.[2]

Ambit of application

The doctrine or policy of the progressive loss of mitigation has been criticized by other desert theorists (eg, Bagaric 2000a, 2001; Ryberg 2004). Bagaric (2000a) for example argues that this constitutes an unwelcome discretionary intervention into the principles of sentencing (p 14). In addition, a number of writers have pointed out the inconsistency with which the principle is applied. Although there is a policy of offering mitigation to first offenders that carries considerable intuitive appeal, it seems inappropriate to extend this leniency to certain kinds of crimes. A first offender convicted of assault will receive a significant discount to reflect his previously law-abiding life. He or she may advance the plausible argument that circumstances explain a temporary lapse: 'I don't know what came over me—that's not me at all'. But the discount is less plausible when proffered by an offender convicted of an offence that requires a considerable amount of premeditation and planning, or a spontaneous but very serious crime such as aggravated assault or rape.

Marijuana growing operations or 'grow-ops' are big business in some parts of North America. These 'farmers' cultivate large swathes of land in the countryside, or grow rows of plants in specially prepared basements illuminated by arc lamps drawing upon illegally diverted electricity. It is hard to justify a first offender discount on the grounds that individuals convicted of this form

[2] One of the unexplored issues in the literature concerns the role of social adversity. It may be argued that offenders who have suffered considerable social adversity may be entitled to additional consideration—for these individuals the state may need to extend mitigation beyond the second or third conviction out of recognition that they have been subject to extraordinary pressures to offend. The state may also have to accept some responsibility for the adversity and one way of so doing is to extend more mitigation at the time of sentencing.

of offending were suddenly overcome by greed to which we all might occasionally succumb. After all, they have been confronted by the machinery necessary to commit the crime on a daily basis. Similarly, offering an offender a mitigated punishment because he had not, until this point, ever raped anyone could only bring the sentencing process into disrepute. For this reason, as Ashworth (2005) observes, the progressive loss of mitigation does not apply across a wide range of offending, but is restricted to certain offences and certain offenders.[3] This is clearly the case in practice where the first offender discount carries little weight for the most serious crimes.

On a theoretical level, however, the interaction of crime seriousness and applicability of the discount seems puzzling. It is unclear why the nature or the seriousness of the offence should override this particular argument in favour of mitigation. People may 'lapse' into committing a serious offence just as easily as a minor transgression. Crimes of violence often occur when the offender is intoxicated, under the influence of drugs, or subject to a transitory but intense emotion; these circumstances may result in the 'lapse' that results in an appeal for mitigation at sentencing. Seen in this light it seems less like a theoretically indispensable sentencing principle, and more like a limited concession to human frailty. For reasons that remain to be elucidated in the literature, this concession is denied to offenders convicted of the most serious crimes.

Why is the mitigation progressively withdrawn?

If the ambit of application is unclear it is also not apparent why the mitigation accorded first offenders is *progressively* withdrawn rather than offered on only a single occasion. An employee convicted for the first time of defrauding her employer may reasonably ask a sentencing court for a 'second chance' on the intuitive grounds that the offence was out of character and reflected a temporary slip, an aberration in a normally law-abiding life. It would be a severe judge indeed who would deny some mitigation in response to such an appeal. But if the offence occurs a second and then a third time, the claim for mitigation seems far less plausible.

[3] In an earlier publication von Hirsch raises but does not resolve the question of whether the most serious forms of criminal behaviour fall outside the 'human fallibility' justification for the first offender discount (see von Hirsch 1991).

Why then does the progressive loss of mitigation extend some mitigation, albeit less, on the second, third and possibly subsequent occasions? There is some recognition in the literature of the problematic nature of repeated mitigations. For example, Adler (1991: 171) argues that a moral theory that allows for one lapse or offence is 'more plausible than the theory that allows for many'.

The progressive nature of the loss of mitigation is inconsistent with the oft-encountered description of the principle as 'a second chance' (Wasik and von Hirsch 1994: 410). Desert theorists offer no precise number of convictions after which the severity of sentence should asymptote. The nature and seriousness of the offending and the severity of the first sentence may influence the number of convictions that may accumulate before mitigation is lost. A person convicted of robbery and sentenced to custody may be denied further mitigation because he cannot claim the indulgence of the state having been censured to such a degree. However, an offender convicted of a minor fraud, and who receives a suspended sentence may more plausibly argue that he had transgressed mildly and the sentence imposed was insufficiently severe to call him fully to account and to make him appreciate the wrongfulness of his conduct. Von Hirsch (1981) suggested that there was no specific number of repetitions that could be acquired before the mitigation was exhausted, although the description in one publication suggests a relatively protracted period of withdrawal.[4]

Wasik (1987) proposed five as the magic number: 'the crucial point is that after those five convictions, reconviction would not attract greater severity' (p 118; see also Wasik and Taylor 1991: 28). But only a very credulous judge would accept an argument that the current conviction was out of character when the offender had four previous convictions. In the terms of a 'tolerance for a lapse', it would be a very tolerant court that can still extend some mitigation to an offender with such a number of prior offences. Most recently, Ashworth adopts a more conservative (and credible) position that 'the third offence may be censured fully' (2005: 188), suggesting the discount is exhausted after two convictions.

If the justification is based upon recognition that anyone may lapse into offending, then the mitigation should surely apply to all

[4] 'With repetitions, however, the discount should begin to diminish, and eventually disappear' (Wasik and von Hirsch 1994: 410).

forms of offending and be withdrawn after the first conviction. Desert theorists are at pains to avoid punishing bad character and therefore should be equally scrupulous to avoid rewarding good character. The phrase used by Thomas (1970) namely a 'progressive loss of credit' seems a better fit for a mitigation that is progressively withdrawn. The first offender has accumulated credit as a result of his law-abiding lifestyle to that point. A criminal conviction now deprives him of some of this credit, particularly if it is a less serious crime. She may have some residual credit on which to draw to obtain some mitigation for the second and third minor thefts, but eventually it is all dissipated. The language of a lapse suggests a more dichotomous discount, based upon a quite different justification.

Progressive loss of mitigation and principles of retributive sentencing

It is hard to see how extending and then progressively withdrawing mitigation to novice offenders promotes desert principles such as parity or proportionality. A proportional sanction is one the severity of which is commensurate with the seriousness of the crime and the offender's level of culpability. Crimes by first offenders are no less serious, and as noted, von Hirsch and other retributive theorists have rejected the position that first offenders are less culpable, or that repeat offenders are more culpable. Far from promoting proportionality, offering a discount to first offenders may weaken the principle—however appealing it may be as a concession to human frailty.

The practice of reducing the severity of sentence for first offenders is therefore not an essential requirement of retributive sentencing. Indeed, the link between the principle of progressive loss of mitigation and censure based accounts is also rather obscure. Sentencers and sentencing theorists of all stripes (as well as most members of the public) can probably agree that first offenders should be treated with more leniency than recidivists—retributive accounts are not unique in this respect. Advocates of individual deterrence would also accept the principle. First offenders may well be deterred by the experience of trial, conviction and sentencing—no further punishment may be necessary to prevent further offending. Proponents of restorative justice would take the position that reconciliation and restoration is more easily accomplished in cases in which the offender has transgressed on only a single occasion. This may explain why public support for restorative justice is strongest when the offender has been convicted for the first time and declines as convictions accumulate (see Roberts and Stalans 2004). Finally, rehabilitationists would also respond very differently to first offenders, for whom minimal intrusion is necessary to return them to a law-abiding lifestyle. Thus there is no unique or inherent link between the first offender discount and retributive sentencing rationales.

The progressive loss of mitigation principle serves two functions in a retributive sentencing framework. First, it introduces an intuitive element into the determination of sentence. The intuition—shared by members of the public and many sentencing theorists—is that everyone may make a mistake. Second, by permanently withdrawing this concession, the principle allows the sentencing process to thereafter ignore an offender's previous convictions, regardless of how many he has accumulated. This second feature preserves a certain kind of ordinal proportionality: one based on the seriousness of the offence. Thus an offender with 20 convictions for shoplifting cannot be punished more harshly than say, an offender convicted of a more serious crime such as assault, simply because of his criminal record. The principle assumes that the determination of the offender's level of culpability is unaffected by the number of previous convictions. I shall contest and explore this assumption in the next chapter.

Penitential theory of sentencing

RA Duff (2001) proposes an intriguing 'penitential' theory of legal punishment that conceives of sentencing as a communicative enterprise. The purpose is to communicate to the offender a message of censure which ultimately should result in a form of secular penitence. This in turn will lead offenders to reform themselves and achieve reconciliation with the individuals whom they have wronged. Although proportionality has an important role to play in Duff's theory of sentencing, he rejects the affirmative or 'positive' version of proportionality propounded by von Hirsch in favour of a negative form not unlike that advocated by Morris and Tonry (1990). Negative proportionality does not require a careful scaling of offences and punishments, although it does set a constraint on the severity of imposed sentences which must not be disproportionate to the crime (see Duff 2001: 143–4).

With respect to the recidivist sentencing premium, Duff rejects any model that prescribes increasingly severe penalties to reflect increments in the offender's criminal record, but does allow a modest degree of mitigation for the first offender or the offender with only one or two priors. In this respect at least his theory is consistent with the principle of the progressive loss of mitigation. Duff's reasoning is that the mitigation accorded first offenders is appropriate because it 'makes sense of the intuitively plausible thought that, in the criminal law as in other contexts, the fact that this is the offender's first offence should be a modestly mitigating factor' (p 169). Although he does not discuss the issue in detail, it seems that Duff's approach to the use of previous convictions would assign a more modest degree of mitigation to first offenders. In addition this mitigation would exhaust more rapidly than the retributive model proposed by, among others, von Hirsch (1993) which emphasizes the *progressive* loss of mitigation

But if sentencing consists of an attempt to communicate censure to an individual, that person's reactions to previous communications are relevant. In everyday life, when we attempt to communicate with a person who has ignored our previous message,[5] we often adopt an alternate form of communication. For some people this may mean shouting—the same message is conveyed again, but now at a different volume. This is the equivalent of a progressive recidivist premium; six months now rises to a year of custody in response to reoffending. Other people try different forms of communication: the original appeal to the individual's conscience may now be replaced by a threat of reprisal or reference to an incentive for compliance.

Courts may also vary the nature of message by moving from one kind of sanction to another—following a form of 'penal escalation'. Having imposed a non-custodial sanction on two or three occasions, only for the offender to return before the court, a sentencer may now resort to custody. This kind of penal escalation may be construed as simply getting tougher and in these terms it is often condemned. Some sentencing statutes mandate an escalation from community to custody for this purpose; other statutes prevent or discourage courts from imposing custody simply because a community penalty has been repeatedly imposed on

[5] I am assuming that the message communicated to the offender includes an appeal to desist from further offending.

previous occasions. The Youth Criminal Justice Act in Canada for example has a provision (s 39(4)) which states that 'the previous imposition of a particular non-custodial sentence... does not preclude a youth court from imposing the same or any other non-custodial sentence for another offence'.

But it may equally reflect a sentencer's intention to select a penalty more likely to change the offender's lifestyle; moreover, it could follow a decremental trajectory: the court may reason that since repeated incarcerations have had no impact upon the offender, and may even have impeded attempts at desistance, a community penalty may now be more appropriate. The general point, however, is that the offender's repeat appearances for sentencing change the court's response, and in this respect previous convictions enter the equation, albeit not necessarily in a way consistent with the cumulative sentencing model.

A communicative account of sentencing should therefore consider the reaction of the person with whom communication is attempted. Unlike the first offender who has never before been sentenced, an offender with many prior convictions assumes a response to the communication expressed by the court. There may be many reasons for this response, including defiance, weak will, force of circumstances, or even physiological causes (the offender may have an addiction that is responsible for his offending) but at the end of the day the response involves rejection of the previous penal communications. The offender who repeatedly reoffends is communicating a message that the sentencing process represents a penal tax, one with a rate set at a tolerable level. If this is an accurate interpretation of the offender's response, the message is likely to prove unpalatable to the community at large. It is not unlike a wealthy offender who repeatedly parks his car illegally, happy to pay the fine imposed on each occasion.

If the offender has adopted an attitude of defiance, any communication designed to elicit repentance is likely to fail. The search for a sanction that will elicit penitence and lead to reformation and reconciliation cannot proceed in the same direction on every occasion. The consequence is that the sentence imposed on the offender with ten priors may justifiably be different than the one imposed on the offender with three priors, although both have long exhausted any mitigation they might have claimed as first offenders.

The mercy model

If the first-time offender 'discount' is a concession to human frailty can it be conceived within a framework of mercy? Is the limited mitigation offered first offenders justified as an example of merciful criminal justice? When we protect first offenders from the full reprobative power of the criminal law it might be said that we are acting out of a sense of mercy. We grant a limited degree of clemency not because first offenders *deserve* less punishment but because the full severity of the law seems inappropriate or unnecessary when considered in light of their law-abiding lives to that point.

There are sound reasons to reject mercy as the justification for considering an offender's past at sentencing. When X is merciful towards Y it is in full recognition that the mercy is unjustified by any utilitarian or retributive consideration. It is not extended in order to achieve any obvious benefit to the merciful individual or the wider community. It more closely resembles a partial amnesty for wrongful conduct. But human mercy has its limits; the mitigation is offered once, and not repeatedly. Mercy may seem consistent with a very limited consideration of previous convictions since according to a mercy model there is no justification for mitigating punishments beyond a first conviction. Repetition of the conduct giving rise to punishment undermines the justification for a merciful response. It makes little sense for the sentencing system to be 'progressively merciful'.

There are several reasons why the expression of mercy can justify only a 'one-off' concession. First, the quality of mercy is unique; if the state exercised mercy repeatedly the exceptional nature of the gesture would be lost. Fox (1999) provides a list of principles to guide the use of mercy. One of these is that mercy 'should only be exercised sparingly and in exceptional circumstances' (p 25). Since there is nothing exceptional about first offenders this suggests that mercy is an unsound basis on which to justify a 'first offender' sentencing discount. Second, as Smart (1969) points out, being merciful towards an offender who repeatedly commits assaults is inappropriate since the extension of mercy in such case comes at the cost of others' interests. Thus mercy might justify a significant difference in severity of sentence between first and repeat offenders but should not be offered and then slowly withdrawn. It cannot therefore sustain a policy of distinguishing between repeat offenders with different criminal histories, but can only represent a potential justification for treating first offenders with more leniency.

However, there is an important reason for rejecting mercy as the doctrinal basis for treating even first-time offenders with leniency. Mercy carries a clear element of charity. Walker (1999) distinguishes mercy from mitigation in large measure because the former is motivated by compassion for the offender, while mitigation reflects considerations relating to the offence or the offender's level of culpability. Tasioulas (2003) defines the concept as 'a form of charity towards wrongdoers that justifies punishing them less severely than they deserve according to justice' (p 101). Similarly, Murphy and Hampton (1988) describe mercy as 'a free gift' (p 166). Mercy reflects more the magnanimity of the agent extending a merciful response than the qualities of the individual on whom mercy is bestowed. To the extent that this is true, it conveys an inappropriate message to offenders. It states that were it not for their unblemished past, they would have been treated more harshly. The system seems to be saying: 'you deserve more, but on this occasion I shall punish you less than you deserve. Others may not be so magnanimous.' Murphy and Hampton (1988) observe that mercy is found where 'a judge, out of compassion for the plight of a particular offender, imposes a hardship less than his just deserts' (p 166). But the point is surely that the first-time offender deserves less punishment; the mitigation associated with the first offender 'discount' is his due.

Mercy thus conveys the wrong message to the offender, the crime victim, and the community. The sentencing process should acknowledge the reduced culpability of first offenders, not simply give them a break for their first offence. A clear parallel exists between mercy and amnesties. Many jurisdictions such as South Africa and France periodically release a proportion of the prisoner population to mark an auspicious state occasion or simply to relieve prison overcrowding. But this 'mitigation' is unearned; prisoners are not released early because they deserve a shorter period of detention.[6] First offenders however, are in a different category; their sentences are more lenient out of recognition of their law-abiding lives to date—for which they are responsible.

[6] The unearned nature of the amnesty may explain why amnesties are criticized by public and professionals alike.

Finally, if mercy is invoked as a justification for considering the offender's previous conduct, it can only justify a reduction for first offenders. In order to justify distinguishing among recidivist offenders we need to look elsewhere.[7]

Enhanced seriousness of crime by recidivists

Can the recidivist premium be justified by reference to the impact of the offender's criminal record on the seriousness of the current crime? Durham (1987b) refers to this as the 'elevated harm' justification. At first glance it would seem an unconvincing argument: in what way is the seriousness of the offence affected by a characteristic of the perpetrator of the crime?[8] Fletcher for example states that 'it is hard to see how a string of burglary convictions could increase the wrongdoing of the current burglary charged in the indictment' (1978: p 462). The answer may depend upon the way in which crime seriousness is defined. To a large degree, determining the seriousness of a criminal offence is a matter of considering objective elements of the crime. How much harm was inflicted on the victim? How many days of remunerated work were lost as a result of injuries sustained by the victim? What was the value of property stolen or damaged? Answers to these questions are readily ascertainable. Sentencers typically steer clear of subjective accounts such as the victim who reports being traumatized for months as a result of a crime that might not trouble the vast majority of people.

There may be a more plausible justification for the enhanced seriousness argument if crime seriousness is defined by the views of the crime victim. If crime victims perceive particular criminal acts as being more serious when the offender is a recidivist, this

[7] A thorough discussion of when mercy is appropriate is beyond the scope of this volume. However, in my view mercy should be bestowed to reflect circumstances unrelated to the seriousness of the offence or the offender's level of culpability. A good example of merciful sentencing would be the case of an offender who, as a result of criminal dangerous driving, causes the death of a close friend or family member. Although he may deserve to serve a term of custody, the offender's loss elicits a merciful response from the court with the result that he is spared imprisonment. The state acts mercifully out of recognition of the offender's immanent punishment arising from the offence.

[8] As will be seen in Chapter 5, a number of statutes, including the Criminal Justice Act 2003 in England and Wales, identify the offender's previous convictions as a factor determining the seriousness of the offence for the purposes of sentencing.

may be taken as a justification for a harsher sentence. There is little relevant research on the question, although anecdotal evidence suggests that when victims learn that the offender had prior, related offences, their reaction to the offence and ultimately their views regarding the appropriate sentence may change (see Roberts and Roach 2005). But should this affect the court's determination of the seriousness of the crime?

Are the views of the general public relevant to the determination of the seriousness of the offence? Communities may be more alarmed by crime committed by repeat offenders. In my view, using this heightened concern argument to enhance the seriousness of the offence is unreasonable, from a number of perspectives. First, the offender has no advance notice of the magnitude of the sentencing premium that will be imposed simply because he happens to have committed an offence currently giving rise to considerable public alarm. Second, courts would need to hear evidence—presumably from public opinion surveys, in order to have systematic information about community reaction rather than simply assuming this fact. Third, community concern about particular crimes waxes and wanes, often in response to media coverage of specific incidents rather than the actual incidence of offending. The sentencing process should not attempt to keep step with such fluctuating opinions.

Conclusion

To conclude, none of the justifications reviewed here offer a convincing argument for the use of a recidivist sentencing premium. They either support a very limited or crude distinction between first offenders and recidivists (mercy, the progressive loss of mitigation), or distinguish between offenders on grounds that seem inappropriate (mercy, or victim/community perceptions of crime seriousness). The next chapter is devoted to exploring a culpability model which asserts that the degree to which the offender is considered blameworthy is affected by his or her state of mind at the time of the commission of the offence. The thesis advanced here is that repeat offenders are more culpable by virtue of their mental state at the time of the crime, in much the same way that offenders who plan their offending may be seen as being more blameworthy. The degree of aggravation created by previous convictions is however constrained by proportionality considerations.

4

The Enhanced Culpability Model

In previous chapters I argued that a policy of distinguishing between offenders with different criminal histories cannot be adequately justified on the basis of mercy, enhanced crime seriousness, defiance of the law, or by reference to the need to 'educate' offenders or the community. Can recidivists be considered more culpable than first-time offenders? Should the seriousness of offenders' *previous* convictions be taken as evidence of their enhanced culpability for the *current* offence? If previous convictions are irrelevant to the determination of crime seriousness, do they have a bearing on the second branch of proportionality, namely the offender's level of culpability? Of all justifications for distinguishing among offenders on the basis of their previous convictions, this one is both the most prevalent and the most convincing.

Overview

This chapter begins by noting the ubiquity of a culpability-based approach to previous convictions. Statutory provisions and sentencing guidelines in a wide range of jurisdictions affirm that repeat offenders are more culpable as a result of their previous convictions. The analysis then explores the retributivist objection to a culpability argument before unfolding arguments why the existence of prior convictions should enhance the offender's level of culpability. Previous convictions speak to the offender's state of mind prior to the commission of the offence in the same way that premeditation reflects an individual more worthy of censure, and the expression of remorse lowers an offender's blameworthiness. The position advanced is that previous convictions are relevant to an offender's level of culpability and therefore have a role to play within a retributive sentencing framework. However, any aggravating factor (such as previous convictions) that arises from the consideration of the offender should be subordinated to offence-related factors. This means that previous convictions should aggravate the severity of the sentence imposed, but only within limits.

Enhanced culpability in practice

The legal discourse surrounding the punishment of repeat offenders is suffused with references to culpability. In addition, many statutory sentencing provisions and sentencing reform proposals take the position that previous convictions affect the offender's level of culpability. One of the clearest examples can be found in a proposal from the Law Commission of Ireland. The Commission proposed the following statutory framework for the consideration of previous convictions at sentencing:

(a) The sentencer, in determining the severity of the sentence to be imposed on an offender, may have regard to any offences of which the offender has been found guilty in the past which may be considered to increase the culpability of the offender.
(b) In considering whether such prior offences aggravate the culpability of the offender for the offence for which he is being sentenced the sentencer should have regard to:
    (i) the time which has elapsed between the prior offence or offences and the offence for which the offender is being sentenced;
    (ii) the age of the offender at the time of commission of the prior offence;
    (iii) whether the prior offence or offences is or are similar in nature to the offence for which the offender is being sentenced;
    (iv) whether the prior offence or offences are similar in seriousness to the offence for which the offender is being sentenced.

(Law Reform Commission of Ireland 1993: 378).

The sentencing manual used in the Australian state of Victoria also links prior offending to culpability: 'Prior criminality is also relevant to the weight to be given to different sentencing purposes and to the assessment of the offender's moral culpability' (Victoria Department of Justice 2006). Many American sentencing guidelines manuals describe recidivists as being more culpable, and therefore deserving of harsher punishments. Chapter four of the guidelines manual of the US Sentencing Commission asserts that: 'a defendant with a record of prior criminal behaviour is more culpable than a first offender and thus deserving of greater punishment' (US Sentencing Commission 2006). Similarly, according to the sentencing guidelines in Utah, 'guidelines should reflect the culpability of the offender based on the nature of the current offence and...overall likelihood to recidivate as inferred by the offender's "Criminal History Assessment" '.[1]

A number of other sentencing guidelines manuals in the US make it clear that an offender's previous convictions have a role to play that is independent of any light they may shed on the seriousness of the crime or the offender's likelihood of reoffending. For example, a recent document published by the Ohio Criminal Sentencing Commission states the following: 'In determining the sentence, the court would consider the nature and circumstances of the offense or offenses, the offender's criminal history and character, and whether the offender is likely to commit further crimes' (2005: 14). This passage implies that if previous convictions are to be considered independently of the seriousness of the crime and the likelihood of reoffending, they must be relevant to the offender's level of culpability.

In England and Wales, guidance to sentencers is provided by the Sentencing Guidelines Council. In 2004 this body issued guidance to judges with respect to the critical issue of determining the seriousness of an offence. The Council's guideline with respect to seriousness cites a number of factors that indicate a higher level of culpability on the part of the offender. Some of these factors relate to the nature of the offence, or the manner in which the offence was committed (for example, committing the offence while under the influence of drugs or alcohol). However, the list of culpability-related factors also includes: 'previous conviction(s), particularly where a pattern of repeat offending is disclosed' (Sentencing Guidelines Council 2004: 6). Finally, a number of appellate judgments have linked previous convictions to the question of culpability. For example, in *R v O'Brien and Gloster*, a judgment from the Victoria Court of Appeal, it was stated by Charles JA that 'an adverse criminal record may impact on the sentencing

[1] The Utah Guidelines manual describes this as a 'basic concept of justice' (Utah Sentencing Commission 2007: 2).

process in a number of ways; for example, as an indicator of the offender's moral culpability'.

Retributivist critiques of the enhanced culpability argument

As with other elements of the debate, sentencing scholars have strong opinions on the subject. Bagaric flatly asserts that: 'there is no place for previous convictions in the culpability variable' (2000a: 245). Much of the debate among desert-oriented sentencing theorists with respect to this issue emerged as a result of the publication of *Doing Justice* by Andrew von Hirsch (1976). That work included a chapter on previous convictions which contains the clear articulation of the position that previous convictions should influence the severity of punishments under a desert-based scheme: 'the reason for treating the first offense as less serious is...that repetition alters the degree of culpability that may be ascribed to the offender' (p 85) and: 'a repetition of the offense following conviction may be regarded as more culpable, since he persisted in the behaviour after having been forcefully censured for it through his prior punishment' (p 85). As noted, von Hirsch subsequently moved away from this position in his later writings in favour of the more limited use of prior convictions incarnated in the progressive loss of mitigation.

These statements from *Doing Justice* may suggest that this early formulation of desert-based reasoning conforms exactly to the cumulative model of recidivist sentencing: sentence severity should increase to reflect the number and seriousness of the offender's previous convictions. There are two critical differences between the two perspectives, however. First, cumulative sentencing rests upon an empirical foundation: if research demonstrated that fifth-time offenders were less likely to reoffend than third-time offenders—suggesting an 'inverted U' or curvilinear relationship between criminal history and the probability of reoffending—utilitarian sentencers would have to abandon the cumulative, linear model in favour of a curvilinear alternative. Second, as von Hirsch has noted (1976: 87–8), preventive, risk-based models that incorporated previous convictions would also have to include many other predictors of reoffending—employment status for example—that are unrelated to the offender's level of blameworthiness.

Conceptualizing culpability

Should recidivist offenders be considered more culpable, as originally asserted by von Hirsch? Since the publication of *Doing Justice* other retributivist theorists have rejected the view. According to George Fletcher (1978), culpability does not conform to a continuum, with culpability levels or scores increasing indefinitely to reflect an offender's previous convictions. Rather, a score of unity should be assigned to the offender who is found beyond a reasonable doubt to be responsible for the crime without any mitigating circumstances that might reduce his culpability level (such as social deprivation or provocation). Culpability 'scores' will then range downwards to reflect the impact of these factors; offenders convicted of crimes under conditions of reduced culpability will attract diminished culpability scores, all fractions of 1.00. Thus, according to Fletcher's analysis there is no such thing as 'hyper culpability'. He writes that: 'Perhaps the offender's persisting in crime demonstrates his greater resolve to flout society's values. But how can the offender's resolve be greater than that represented by the voluntary commission of the offence? Is there a degree of resolve that renders the conduct "super-voluntary"?' (1978: 59). Numerically, 'culpability scores' cannot rise above 1.00. Culpability is not measured in the way that seriousness ranges from very low to very high values. Crime seriousness is not 'capped' in this way.[2]

When culpability is conceptualized in these terms it can be distinguished from crime seriousness, which does conform to a continuum with no cap. According to Fletcher, no amount of previous offending can increase an offender's level of culpability for the current offence (Fletcher 1978). Culpability thus reaches an asymptote. In this way culpability may be likened to a salary scale with a fixed 'cap': incomes may vary widely but no employee can earn more than, say, £50,000. The analogy illuminates a weakness of Fletcher's analysis: it constrains the ability to distinguish between different individuals. Pursuing the analogy, under a £50,000 salary cap, a significant number of senior employees would earn the same salary as soon as their salaries hit the ceiling. With respect

[2] There is no sense in which crime seriousness scores scale downwards from unity; they range upwards continuously to reflect the degree of harm inflicted or threatened.

to criminal culpability, a large number of offenders would be considered equally culpable—presumably when they have acquired a third conviction.

This conceptualization of culpability appears to import the logic of criminal responsibility into the analysis. Assuming that two offenders have conceived and executed a burglary with exactly the same degree of involvement in the crime, they would be considered equally responsible for the offence. Each individual has contributed equally to the planning and execution of the offence; the two offenders are equally responsible for the ensuing harm. If they really are equal partners in the enterprise, it makes little sense to assert that one is more responsible than the other for the crime. Such an assertion confuses culpability or blameworthiness with responsibility. The language of legal discourse on the subject sustains this interpretation. For example, the very phrase 'diminished responsibility' suggests a concept in which responsibility is present in its entirety or at some reduced level.

However, the fact that both offenders are equally responsible for the crime does not mean that they must be regarded as equally culpable individuals. If offender A is 40 years of age, and has five prior convictions for burglary, while offender B is a 20-year old with no previous convictions, it is reasonable to regard the former as more blameworthy than the latter. Absent any other grounds for mitigation an offender with nine prior convictions is regarded by the flat-rate school as being no more culpable than the one with no prior convictions. Is this a plausible account of culpability?

On a popular level,[3] culpability is best represented as a continuum, like an uncapped salary scale or indeed like crime seriousness with no apparent maximum limit. Understanding why this is so requires some consideration of the concept of culpability. For the intuitive sentencer, repetition of offending enhances ascriptions of blame or culpability. At first glance this position may seem no different than punishing defiance. Why is the repeat offender more culpable, more blameworthy? Because he repeatedly flouts the law? We appear to be back to defiance of legal authority as a justification for harsher sentencing. But there are

[3] Empirical research on public attitudes suggests that ascriptions of blameworthiness rise with each successive reconviction; this issue is explored in detail in Chapters 8 and 9.

alternate grounds for considering repeat offenders to be more culpable.

Culpability and responsibility

One argument rests on the premise that criminal responsibility and culpability are independent concepts with very different conceptual topographies.[4] Establishing that the offender is responsible for the offence is a legal requirement for a conviction. Culpability on the other hand reflects the degree to which blame may reasonably be ascribed to the offender. Many factors will affect the degree of blame imputed to an offender, and the level of culpability ascribed to him. Consider two offenders convicted of assault. Offender A's crime was committed with considerable planning and forethought, while Offender B struck out spontaneously. The harm inflicted is comparable and both offenders would be considered equally responsible for that harm. But would we regard the two individuals as equally culpable? (The issue of premeditation will be explored later in this chapter).

The conduct of the offender before and after commission of the crime

It is worth reflecting on the relationship between the offender's actions before and after the commission of the current crime and the sentencing outcome. Under a strict retributive rationale, there is little or no room for the sentencing process to recognize compensatory gestures or expressions of remorse made by the offender after the offence, or following conviction. This is a short-sighted approach to punishment that is inconsistent with some fundamental social values which the sentencing process should promote. Despite the problematic nature of this variable from the perspective of retributive theories, the sentencing process has long taken the offender's conduct after the offence into account. Thomas (1970) noted that 'the behaviour of the offender since the commission of the offence may be a highly significant mitigating

[4] The two terms are often used interchangeably. For example, according to s 718.1 of the Criminal Code of Canada, a sentence must be 'proportionate to the seriousness of the offence and the offender's degree of responsibility'. I would argue that the statute means culpability in this context.

factor' (p 195). Vidmar and Miller (1980) note that an unrepentant offender attracts greater hostility and incurs more severe punishment, while a contrite individual can expect less severe punishment.

The remorseful offender

Consider the case of an offender who has committed a relatively serious assault and who almost immediately afterwards appreciates the wrongfulness of his conduct. This realization leads him to assist the victim while the latter is hospitalized, to plead guilty at the first court appearance, and to issue a written and oral statement. Let us further imagine that in this document he accepts responsibility for the offence, expresses remorse for his unlawful actions, offers to compensate the victim, condemns his own behaviour (the assault), and undertakes not to act in such a fashion in the future. These actions are of benefit to the victim, the criminal justice system, the community at large, and indeed the offender as well; in this sense they serve an important instrumental purpose.

The benefit to the offender may be easily or often overlooked but there is much to be said for encouraging people to distinguish commendable from reprehensible behaviour, and to encourage them to forsake the latter for the former. These values are fundamental to the concept of law. For example, Raz (1979) includes preventing undesirable behaviour and securing desirable conduct among the primary functions ascribed to the law. Remedial actions may carry some benefit in terms of crime prevention. Taking these steps helps the offender to redefine him or herself as a member of law-abiding society by creating distance from the offence. The offender would feel a state of psychological dissonance if he or she performed these actions and simultaneously remained committed to offending.[5]

There is also an argument to be made that conferring upon the offender the ability to mitigate the harm caused and thereby the severity of any consequent penalty provides him with a partial 'second chance'. The challenge to the sentencing process arises from the question of whether such mitigation should be

[5] Encouraging offenders to feel remorseful for their offending thus carries a potential utilitarian benefit; it may make desistance from offending more likely.

institutionalized—in the form of a guideline for sentencers—or even codified as a sentencing principle. If this happens it runs the danger of being differentially beneficial to certain offenders: offenders with more resources, legal or financial, may be more able to engage in the kind of behaviours necessary to elicit some mitigation from the court, but this is an insufficient reason for ignoring it entirely.

The sentencing process should encourage such actions on the part of convicted offenders and one way of doing this is to recognize them when determining sentence.[6] These actions may be taken as evidence of 'good character' by some judges who may then impose a mitigated punishment to reflect this evaluation. This conceptualization is inappropriate; the consequence would be that the taciturn offender with little or nothing to say at sentencing is penalized more severely as a result of inappropriate inferences about his character based upon his reticence.[7] But the actions of the offender after the commission of the offence can be seen within a more circumscribed framework; they speak to the actor's relation to the act for which he is being punished. The remorseful offender is concerned with achieving some (partial) rectification of his wrongdoing—he is taking a step away from his offending.

Public reaction to the expression of remorse

An examination of public reaction to offenders who are remorseful exposes the gap between a retributive model and sentencing and community sentiment. Remorse is a sentencing factor that may be considered extra-legal from a retributive perspective. Since the expression of remorse cannot alter the seriousness of the offence or the offender's responsibility for the offence, retributive theorists reject the consideration of this factor at sentencing (eg, Bagaric 2001; Bagaric and Amarasekara 2001). However,

[6] In a recent publication von Hirsch and Ashworth (2005) acknowledge the relevance of such behaviour under the heading 'voluntary reparation'. They note that one of the values underlying desert theory is giving the defendant 'the opportunity of providing recognition of how he has wrongfully injured the victim' (p 177 at footnote h).

[7] Interviews conducted for this volume sustained a finding emerging from the previous literature: offenders often find the experience of attending court intimidating and this may inhibit them from speaking.

empirical research has repeatedly demonstrated that the expression of remorse has an important influence over public attitudes to sentencing as well as actual sentencing decisions.[8]

Members of the public attribute less blame when offenders apologize—a concrete manifestation of remorse. Experimental studies have found that the expression of remorse decreases the severity of recommended sentences (Robinson, Smith-Lovin, and Tsoudis 1994; Robinson and Darley 1995; Scher and Darley 1997). The mitigating effect of remorse can be seen even with regard to the punishment of the most serious crimes such as rape (see Kleinke, Wallis, and Stalder 1992). This public sympathy towards defendants who express remorse is not restricted to experimental studies involving volunteer subjects or college students. Research with actual jurors conducted by the National Capital Jury Project finds that the expression of remorse is an important determinant of penalty phase decision-making by capital juries (see Sundby 1998). The consequence is that remorseful offenders are less likely to be sentenced to death. It seems unlikely that the public are less punitive towards remorseful offenders simply because they are seen to be less likely to reoffend. Sentencers and the general public respond to remorseful offenders with leniency because they make a more global assessment of the seriousness of the case, and this approach incorporates factors considered extraneous by retributive or utilitarian sentencing theories.

Remorse entails the expression of regret for harm caused. Apologies require the offender to go a step further, and involve the victim: the apologetic individual both regrets his wrongful actions (a self-reflective response) and extends apologies to the wronged party, the crime victim. Most traditional sentencing perspectives have trouble incorporating the existence of an apology into the sentencing decision. Unless apologetic individuals are less likely to reoffend, utilitarian sentencers will not be interested in moderating the sentence imposed in such cases. From a desert perspective the result is the same as it is for mere remorse: an apology does nothing to mitigate the seriousness of the crime, or reduce the offender's level of culpability. However, the intuitive

[8] The expression of remorse has long been recognized by the Court of Appeal. Over 40 years ago, in *R v Harper*, the Court noted that: 'It is... of course proper to give a man a lesser sentence if he has shown genuine remorse'. [1967] 3 All ER 617; 52 Cr App R 21.

sentencer and many judges will reduce the severity of the sentence if the offender makes a convincingly sincere[9] apology to the crime victim.[10]

The remorseful defendant is not simply saying 'go easy on me your Honour, I'm not such a bad sort after all'. She is taking a stand in a public forum *against her own offending*. The expression of remorse is an offence-related communication. It speaks to the relational nature of sentencing from the perspective of the intuitive sentencer. The offender has effectively signalled her intention to rejoin the community against which she offended, and this is recognized by members of the public who subsequently impose less severe punishments.[11] In this way the expression of remorse may be distinguished from less plausible pleas for mitigation that are also character-based—such as having a good war record, or a history of volunteering for the community.

The rebarbative offender

Now consider an offender convicted of the same offence but one who displays a very different attitude to the crime. This second individual is not just negligent of the harm he caused or indifferent to the legal censure and any legal consequences that may ensue from conviction—he actively maintains his conduct towards the victim. By words and gestures he expresses an attitude of contempt towards the crime victim and disregard for the consequences of his criminal actions. Such an individual protracts and exacerbates the victim's suffering. This person is different from the offender who is simply defiant of authority, or the offender who is abusive towards the court or its officers. As a result of his behaviour after

[9] A common objection to recognizing remorse as a sentencing factor involves the difficulty of knowing whether the offender is truly remorseful. If remorse is allowed to mitigate sentence some offenders feigning remorse will benefit from this mitigation along with the truly repentant individuals. But eliminating remorse on the grounds that we can never be sure of the genuineness of the offender's statements is a classic case of throwing the baby out with the bathwater.

[10] A number of empirical studies of actual sentencing decisions have demonstrated that offenders who express remorse are sentenced more leniently (eg, Harrel 1981).

[11] Vidmar (2002) makes a similar point when he suggests that remorse 'appears to serve the function of reaffirming moral values held by members of the community' (p 305).

the offence was committed, most people would regard this second offender as being more blameworthy than the first. Should the sentencing process not recognize, albeit within limits,[12] the reprehensible nature of such conduct? Again, the argument is not a general one based on character; the individual is not being punished for being a bad person, but rather for his conduct in relation to the offence of conviction. The actions of the remorseful, repentant offender diminish her level of culpability. This reduces the degree of blame which the community expresses.

If the offender's conduct after the commission of the offence is relevant to the offender's level of blameworthiness it opens the door to a consideration of the offender's actions prior to the offence, namely his previous convictions. An offender convicted of assault for the fifth time is more blameworthy not because he is a bad person, but because his conduct prior to the commission of the crime creates a relational context for judgments of the act giving rise to sentence.

This analysis of blameworthiness is thus retrospective and prospective in nature. The offender's conduct before and after the offence provides a context in which to judge not the seriousness of the crime (which cannot be affected by antecedent offences or the offender's post-conviction conduct) but the extent to which the offender should be considered blameworthy. Since this judgment takes place within a retributive framework in which proportionality is the primordial guiding principle, and since blameworthiness or culpability considerations are secondary, neither the previous misconduct nor the post-offence conduct can fully eclipse the seriousness of the crime as a determinant of sentence severity. But neither should these considerations be ignored.

Previous convictions and other sources of aggravation

> According to the retributivist, the moral seriousness of an offence is a function of two factors—the harm done by the offence and the culpability of the offender as indicated by his mental state at the time of committing the offence (Ten 1987: 155).

> As a matter of principle the greater the planning or premeditation that proceeds the commission of the offence the greater the culpability of the offender (Victorian Sentencing Committee Report 1988: 253).

[12] The limits are placed in order to protect the principle of proportionality.

Consider now some of the grounds for enhanced culpability or blameworthiness. Evidence of planning and premeditation is a powerful aggravating circumstance (see Ashworth 2005).[13] The link between motive and premeditation is made explicit by Pillsbury (1998) who asserts that aggravated forms of murder should be defined in terms of motive rather than premeditation. When premeditation constitutes an element of the offence it results in a much higher penalty than that which is imposed on people convicted of the crime without such planning.[14] Premeditation also has an important impact when cited as an aggravating circumstance at sentencing. But exactly why are offenders held to be more culpable or blameworthy simply because they planned the offence? Like previous convictions, this factor is external to the crime and does not affect the seriousness of the offence: the harm of an assault or a burglary does not change because the offender planned the act rather than having committed it spontaneously. An assault victim is unlikely to be comforted by knowing that his assailant assaulted him on the spur of the moment rather than as a result of having planned the act. Indeed, the victim may be, and may always remain, totally oblivious to the offender's level of preparation for the offence. How then does premeditation aggravate the sentence? Premeditation reflects the mental state of the offender, his state of mind prior to committing the offence.

In fact, the offender's state of mind is a factor that may aggravate or mitigate punishment. Evidence of premeditation will usually (but not always—see below) result in a harsher sentence, while the impulsive, spontaneous act can mitigate the punishment

[13] There are many other aggravating factors relating to the offender's mental state to which the arguments made here also apply. For example, motive is very relevant to judgments of blameworthiness and sentencing (eg, Bean 1981). An offender who steals out of necessity will be considered less blameworthy than one whose crime is motivated solely by cupidity. Similarly, racially-motivated offences provoke a harsher sentence in part because offenders convicted of this form of offending are considered more blameworthy (Roberts and Hastings 2001).

[14] For example, in Canada, murder is first degree when it is 'planned and deliberate' and carries a mandatory penalty of life imprisonment with no prospect of parole until the offender has served at least 25 years in prison. Second degree murder also carries a mandatory life sentence but with a non-parole custodial term of between 10 and 25 years in prison (although in practice almost all convictions for second degree murder result in the minimum 10 year period). This very striking difference in the severity of statutory penalties between premeditated and unplanned murder exists in most jurisdictions.

imposed. An impulsive offender can argue that the offence was an aberration: 'Had I reflected more, my personality would have asserted itself and I would have refrained from offending'. The offence was therefore 'out of character'. The offender who plans an offence can make no such appeal for leniency. Both conditions—premeditation and spontaneity—speak to the relationship between the offender and the offence, and to his or her mental state at the time of the offence. This is not a question of judging character; we are not inferring bad character on the basis that 'good' people may occasionally commit an assault, but would not go so far as to meticulously plan such conduct (although this seems very plausible). But when the act is premeditated we are more inclined, in the language of social psychology, to attribute the act to the actor rather than to his environment. We draw inferences about the mental state of the offender that are germane to the determination of culpability.

Justifying premeditation as an aggravating circumstance

Case law in many jurisdictions supports the position that offenders who plan their crimes are in some way more blameworthy although the justification for this practice is far from clear and reflects the underdeveloped nature of theories of aggravation. The earliest sentencing text in England simply notes that the first consideration in determining whether any mitigation is appropriate is whether the crime was 'a sudden impulse, or premeditated' (Cox 1877: 158). The author does not explain why premeditation should deprive the offender of any mitigation. Walker (1980) notes that 'a premeditated offence is usually regarded as morally worse than one committed on the spur of the moment' (p 47), and Smart (1969) subscribed to the same view: 'some crimes warrant sterner treatment than others because they are intrinsically worse (this is particularly so with premeditated crimes)' (p 215). These statements fail to clarify the grounds for considering one form of offending more morally wrong than another. After reviewing Canadian case law, Renaud (2004) offers the following account: 'That an offence is well planned is often quite aggravating in that it suggests that the offender's moral compass is non existent and only a significant attribution of correctional resources will remedy this situation' (p 125). This perspective suggests that an extraordinary state response is necessary to correct an offender who has wandered beyond the reach of the criminal law. Finally, Ashworth (2005, p 157) writes that 'A person who plans a crime is generally more culpable because the offence is premeditated and the offender is therefore more fully confirmed in his anti-social motivation than someone who acts on impulse'.[15] But the extent of the offender's commitment to crime requires more than simply evidence that he planned the offence.

Two avenues need to be pursued to understand why the existence of premeditation usually aggravates the sentence that should be imposed. One is normative, the other psychological. The latter explanation invokes intuitive judgments about sentencing which will be explored more fully in Chapter 9. However, it is necessary here to substantiate two points. The first is that premeditation is seen by the public to be an important aggravating circumstance. As with remorse, the public are concerned with the offender's relation to his offending, although in this case the concern is with his state of mind prior to committing the offence.

Empirical research on public attitudes to sentencing clearly demonstrates that people react more punitively towards offenders when there is evidence of premeditation. For example, when the Canadian Sentencing Commission asked members of the public to identify the factors that should be taken into account at sentencing, consensus was greatest with respect to this factor: premeditation was cited by more than four-fifths of the sample (Roberts 1988). Similar results are reported by researchers in England (Wilkins 1984) and Holland (Haas, de Keijser, and Vanderveen 2007; see also Thomas and Diver-Stamnes 1993). More recent research conducted for the Home Office Sentencing Review in England and Wales also demonstrates the importance of premeditation to public conceptions of sentencing. When asked to identify important sentencing factors, the three factors that attracted the highest level of support were the existence of previous convictions, the offender's likelihood of reoffending, and 'whether the offence was planned'. The three factors all attracted the support of more than two-thirds

[15] Ashworth (2005) offers some other justifications, namely that planned offending represents a greater threat to society since it 'betokens a considered attack on social values, with greater commitment and perhaps continuity than a spontaneous crime' (p 157). These seem less compelling grounds as the offender's level of premeditation may not necessarily be correlated with his level of commitment to crime.

of the sample and all were seen as being more important even than a factor such as the impact of the crime on the victim, which typically is perceived by the public to be very important (see Home Office 2001). The public clearly sees premeditation as a circumstance justifying a harsher punishment. Since premeditation does not affect the seriousness of the crime, the inference must be that members of the public see offenders who plan to commit crime as more culpable and worthy of a harsher punishment.

Why is this so? The research evidence suggests that increased attributions of responsibility have the effect of enhancing ascriptions of blame and hence the severity of assigned punishments. Evidence of premeditation will lead external observers to infer that the offender was more responsible for the offence than if the crime had been committed spontaneously. The same argument can be made for previous convictions. As the offender continues to reoffend, particularly if the offences form a pattern, we are more inclined to attribute the offending behaviour to the individual and this justifies a higher ascription of culpability, and consequently, a more severe penalty. The previous convictions disentitle the offender to mitigation based on the 'offence out of character' appeal, but they also speak to his state of mind with respect to the commission of the current offence. First offenders are less culpable while the degree of culpability ascribed to repeat offenders is influenced by the seriousness of their criminal history.

This analysis only takes us part of the way towards justifying a premeditation sentencing premium. Ascriptions of responsibility may become almost exclusively focused on the offender to the total exclusion of environmental forces, but this still does not tell us why this kind of conduct—premeditated crime—is more morally reprehensible and more worthy of condemnation than spontaneous offending. It may be that premeditation generates higher levels of blame for two reasons. First, an offender who plans the commission of an offence, particularly one with grave or fatal consequences, is assuming a total disregard for the law; he is effectively placing himself outside the community by his actions. This circumstance alone makes his actions more reprehensible.[16]

[16] The gravity of the consequent crime is clearly important: if the offence is likely to have severe consequences for the victim, the public expectation is even greater that the individual will refrain from committing the crime.

The second reason takes us back to the 'lapse' theory to account for the progressive loss of mitigation. That perspective acknowledges that the criminal law recognizes human frailty to the extent that people can forget their obligations to comply with the law. However, planning to commit a crime implies a level of moral turpitude beyond normal expectations.

Everyday conceptions of conduct include some sense of a norm; the further the conduct departs from an expected norm, the greater the degree of censure that is visited on the offender. Judgments of moral wrongfulness are affected by the degree to which the conduct flouts consensual values. Lacey (1988) observes that criminal penalties are 'instituted as a response to behaviour which directly violates socially acknowledged fundamental interests in such a way as to express rejection of or hostility to the values underlying those interests' (p 176). Premeditated crime constitutes an exceptional degree of impunity with respect to the community values enshrined in the criminal law.

Exceptions to the premeditation premium and gradations of aggravation

If premeditated crime is more heinous than unplanned offending, there are both exceptions to the rule as well as gradations of premeditation. Female offenders convicted of a premeditated crime of violence against an aggressive partner may not be perceived as more culpable since their premeditation springs from a need to avoid confronting a more powerful aggressor on an unequal basis. As the English Law Commission noted in its discussion of the aggravating effect of premeditation in a case of the killing of a violent abuser, 'it is not at all clear that the element of premeditation in such a case, motivated by fear, aggravates the offence' (Law Commission 2005: 35). Similarly, in a well-publicized case in recent Canadian legal history, a man was convicted of the murder of his severely disabled daughter. He claimed to have acted in order to terminate her protracted suffering. Robert Latimer openly acknowledged a significant degree of preparation regarding the crime, but few people would consider this premeditation to aggravate the seriousness of the crime.

Some offenders plan and premeditate their offences in order to receive benefit from others. Contract killers are perhaps the most egregious example of this category of offending. Singer (1979) for example notes that 'no offender is more consistently seen as deserving increased punishment as the one who commits crime for hire' (p 85).[17] Once again the mental state, or in this case, the motive of the offender, has an important impact on perceptions of his relative blameworthiness.

Public opinion and sentencing policies

An important normative question underlying this discussion is whether public views should play a role in shaping sentencing policy and practice. Should sentencing practices be influenced by whether the public feel leniency is due remorseful offenders or believe that premeditated crime and crime by repeat offenders should be punished more severely? Some scholars flatly reject any recourse to public opinion. Singer (1979) argues that 'sentencing by the state is not "ordinary moral discourse" by individuals' and that the 'innate reaction [to the use of prior convictions] should be rejected' (p 72).

In reality, public attitudes have for many years influenced the sentencing process. As noted in Chapter 1, sentencing commissions and councils in different jurisdictions have conducted surveys of the public to establish the relative seriousness of different crimes. The Sentencing Advisory Panel in England and Wales has also commissioned empirical investigations into public perceptions of the relative importance of specific mitigating and aggravating factors relevant to a number of offences (see discussion in Chapter 1). In a similar fashion, the Law Commission of England and Wales commissioned public opinion research to help establish the relative seriousness, in the public's mind, of different forms of culpable homicide (Law Commission 2005).[18]

[17] There is little doubt that if a sample of the public was asked to rate the seriousness of a list of offences, killing another person for profit would surely attract the highest ratings. Curiously, however, Singer (1979) argues that offenders who commit crimes for profit should be treated no differently from 'the typical criminal' (p 86).

[18] Consistent with the public opinion research cited here there was agreement among participants in the focus groups conducted for the Law Commission that

This research reflects the recognition that scales of sentence severity which were markedly different from public crime seriousness rankings would undermine public confidence in the sentencing process.[19] A desert-based model of sentencing cannot ignore public perceptions of the relative seriousness of different crimes, or community perceptions of the relative wrongfulness of specific criminal acts. In this sense a desert-based model of sentencing is tied more closely to community values than utilitarian accounts, where the severity of the sentence imposed reflects issues such as recidivism risk that are unrelated to public opinion. Indeed, this is one of the strengths of proportional sentencing. It would make little sense for the sentencing process to express censure on behalf of the community, yet pay no attention to public opinion regarding the kinds of offences and offenders which in the eyes of the community are seen as being most worthy of condemnation.

To summarize, the extent to which we consider offenders blameworthy is affected by their mental state at the time of the offence. A number of factors enhance culpability on this ground, including evidence of planning, and evidence that the offender has previously been convicted and punished. Evidence of premeditation reveals the offender's state of mind prior to the commission of the crime. Premeditation bespeaks a disregard for legality, and a commitment to offending that is not true of spontaneous offending. Having been charged, convicted, and punished, repeat offenders also share a state of mind that renders them more blameworthy than first-time offenders. Both considerations speak to the relationship between the offender and the offence and constitute legitimate grounds for aggravating the severity of sentence.

Communicating censure of repeat offending

The link between the issue of blameworthiness and the communicative purpose of sentencing is also relevant to this discussion. In

the existence of premeditation indicated a more serious form of homicide (see Law Commission 2005: 261).

[19] Imagine a statutory penalty structure for murder in which planned and premeditated murder was punished *less* severely than murder in which the offender intended to kill but engaged in no such planning. Public reaction to such an arrangement would be very negative. As Pillsbury (1998) notes, 'in ordinary talk about murder and in the formal rules of law, we find the idea that a cool and preconceived design to kill is the hallmark of the worst form of homicide' (p 100).

everyday life we censure people for a range of conduct of which we disapprove, and to the extent that we have a relationship with the target of our censure, we may consider elements of their character that have little direct relationship to the conduct giving rise to the censure. A parent may appeal to elements of a child's personality in an effort to induce attitude and subsequently behaviour change. The censure of the criminal law is more tightly focused on the offence of conviction. In theory at least, convicted offenders knew before being convicted and censured that the conduct giving rise to censure was illegal. Von Hirsch (1993) notes that 'unlike blame in everyday contexts, the criminal sanction announces in advance that specified categories of conduct are punishable. Because the prescribed sanction is one which expresses blame, this conveys the message that the conduct is reprehensible, and should be eschewed' (p 11). However, reoffending is also reprehensible, particularly if the offender continually reoffends. The sentencing process should not refrain from communicating a message about repetitive criminal conduct—but without losing sight of the principal reason for censure—the current conviction, the nature and seriousness of which should determine the degree of censure expressed.

It is now time to revisit the strongest argument against a recidivist sentencing premium from a retributive perspective, namely that it constitutes punishment of an offender's character, rather than his conduct.[20] According to this view, the recidivist is regarded as having a worse character and suffers accordingly, although his instant criminal conduct may be no more harmful or worthy of condemnation than crimes committed by first offenders. This carries clear dangers for a retributive account of sentencing. Singer (1979) states that 'the argument of character clearly raises the specter of bringing into the sentencing process all of that soft data upon which sentencing judges have relied for the last hundred years—the defendant's religion, his past unemployment, his relations with his spouse, his childhood history, whether he loves animals, and so forth' (p 70). Bagaric (2001) also shares this apprehension when he argues that considering

[20] Walker and Padfield (1996: 44) argue that the progressive loss of mitigation is also an example of allowing character considerations to enter the sentencing process: the reason why first offenders are offered a sentence reduction is to reflect their good character to this point in their lives.

previous convictions opens up an inquiry into all kinds of considerations 'as remote as what an offender got up to 20, 30 or 40 years ago' (p 245). He sees no logical way of excluding extraneous factors from entering the sentencing equation. Walker made the same point when he argued that considering such factors entails a 'leap into a bog without boundaries' (1985: 45).

These responses constitute a *reductio ad absurdum*. It is true that some sentencers may be tempted to judge the offender on elements of his past that reflect upon his current character. However, if the sentencing process articulates the way in which previous convictions—and only previous *convictions* enhance sentence severity, then the problem of punishing character will not arise.[21]

Similarly, if MacPherson's culpability model is adopted, in which previous convictions are taken into account because the offender has 'failed to respond to censure as would a rational moral agent' (2002: 200) the offender is not receiving additional punishment because of his character, or because he is considered defiant. Rather he is being punished for a specific series of moral decisions which subsequently resulted in criminal convictions.

If ascriptions of blameworthiness incorporate consideration of offender culpability, and if an evaluation of culpability includes the offender's previous convictions, does this approach not threaten proportional sentencing? It might, if the offender's culpability was weighed equally with the seriousness of the crime. Proportional sentencing requires a clear relationship between the severity of sentence imposed and the seriousness of the crime and the level of culpability. Little has been written about the relationship between crime seriousness and offender culpability, but a sentencing system concerned with condemning acts rather than actors must ensure that the influence of culpability considerations does not exceed, or even match, the seriousness of the offence as a determinant of sentence severity. An assault committed by the most culpable offender should not result in a more severe penalty than that which is imposed for rape, even if the latter crime is committed by a first offender.

[21] Some writers regard the offender's character as a legitimate source of aggravation. Charles Murray for example argues that 'are we not conflating the defendant's character with his guilt for the crime in question? In the case of defendants with many prior arrests and convictions, yes—and this is a virtue not a defect' (2005: 25).

Rational moral decision-making as a source of culpability

Before leaving the culpability-based justifications for a recidivist premium, it is important to note one other recent proposal. MacPherson (2002) argues that repeat offenders may be regarded as more culpable by virtue of their moral decisions. His rationale is 'the fact that a person has chosen not to react as a rational moral agent should' (p 213). Having been convicted and sentenced, a person should desist from offending; committing further offences is evidence that the offender has elected an alternate moral course to that of a law-abiding citizen. MacPherson notes that 'this idea supports a minor increase in culpability for recidivism' (p 213). By founding the justification in the moral decision-making of the offender, MacPherson's account ties it directly to the concept of culpability. However, the approach is very reminiscent of the view that having had their offending called to their attention, repeat offenders are more culpable because they have ignored this communication—a form of defiance. The practical implications of MacPherson's culpability-based justification for according harsher sentences for repeat offending will be explored in the last chapter of this volume.

To summarize, although previous convictions are excluded from a consideration of the seriousness of the offence, they should enter the sentencing equation through the determination of the offender's level of culpability as reflected in his state of mind at the time of the offending. But crime seriousness must always predominate as a determinant of the severity of sentence ultimately imposed.

Levels of aggravation

Consideration of a factor like premeditation enables us to better understand why previous convictions should aggravate the severity of the sentence. However, both premeditation and prior record need to be seen within the broader context of theories of aggravation and mitigation. The literature on mitigation and aggravation is theoretically underdeveloped. Most sentencing texts consist of little more than an inventory of factors that appellate review has sustained as relevant to the determination of sentence severity. Similarly, many sentencing guidelines manuals simply list the aggravating and mitigating factors to be considered by courts without providing any explanation of why they are relevant or any indication of the weight that should be ascribed to different factors.[22] Some commentary on the categories of sentencing factors is therefore in order here.

Sentencing factors may be conceptualized as falling into different categories reflecting different levels of importance. The primary category includes factors relating to the offence of current conviction. Premeditation, the use of unnecessary force, and the selection of vulnerable victims all fall into this category. Since these relate to the current offence—the specific act for which the offender is being judged—these are the most powerful aggravating circumstances. They should not be eclipsed by secondary aggravating factors, those that relate to the offender, such as the presence of previous convictions, or the fact that he was on probation or parole at the time of the latest offence. These offender-related factors must be subordinate to the offence factors within a retributive framework in which offence seriousness predominates. Allowing offender variables to carry the same or more weight at sentencing would shift the focus of sentencing away from the offence to the offender.[23]

Although limitations on space preclude a thorough exegesis of the issue, according to the culpability model proposed here, the difference in culpability between a first offender and an individual with two priors is much greater than that which differentiates an offender with two from another with four priors. Moreover, the recidivist sentencing premium cannot be reduced to the progressive ascription of a quantum of punishment for each prior; consideration of the offender's previous convictions requires a more multidimensional approach, one which incorporates the

[22] The 'sentencing user guide' published by the Missouri Sentencing Advisory Commission is an example of the few jurisdictions that distinguish between 'serious' and 'other' aggravating factors (see Missouri Sentencing Advisory Commission 2006), but this approach simply creates two lists instead of one.

[23] A third category could be added here: sentencing factors unrelated to either the offence or the offender which are nevertheless worthy of some consideration. This category includes considerations such as providing assistance to the state to prosecute other defendants. Some residual judicial discretion should be reserved for these matters, but they should carry much less weight and should be subject to careful scrutiny by the appellate process.

individual's efforts to achieve desistance, even if these efforts are ultimately unsuccessful.

Summary and conclusion

Table 4.1 summarizes the way that the principal sentencing theories use previous convictions at sentencing. The table makes it clear that previous convictions are relevant to the determination of sentence from almost all sentencing perspectives. The reaction of the general community and sentenced offenders to these different models will be explored in later chapters. Before then, it is important to understand how the different approaches to previous convictions are incorporated in contemporary sentencing systems. It is to those systems of justice that we turn in the next chapter.

Table 4.1 Summary of sentencing perspectives and use of previous convictions

Sentencing Perspective	Role of Previous Convictions	Sentencing Objective(s)
Individual deterrence	Each prior conviction results in an additional quantum of punishment	Preventing reoffending by the offender appearing before the court
General deterrence	Recidivist statutes aimed at potential offender population	Preventing offending in population of potential offenders
Incapacitation	Each prior conviction results in an additional quantum of punishment	Preventing reoffending by offender before court through detention
Rehabilitation (risk/ needs)	Rehabilitative intervention to vary (in part) according to extent and nature of previous convictions	To change the offender's attitudes, behaviour and lifestyle with a view to reducing reoffending
Defiance theory	Each additional conviction results in a harsher sentence	To punish repeat offenders for defying the criminal law; to encourage desistance from offending
Pedagogy of punishment	Harsher treatment justified for repeat offenders; not necessarily cumulative	To teach offenders the wrongfulness of criminal conduct; to encourage desistance

Table 4.1 *Continued*

Sentencing Perspective	Role of Previous Convictions	Sentencing Objective(s)
Restorative justice	Repeat offenders disentitled to restorative option after a number of convictions accumulated	Reconcile victim and offender where appropriate; achieve restoration and compensation if possible; encourage desistance
Prevent demoralization/ denunciation	Each additional conviction results in harsher punishment	Prevent members of public from becoming demoralized at the prospect of offending with impunity; to prevent retaliation against offender; to recognize the wrongfulness of repeat offending
Character-based sentencing theory	Severity increases with each additional conviction which offers evidence of bad character	To punish offenders for bad character
Pessimism/ optimism	Limited discount until optimism about offender dissipates; no record enhancement	Recognize possibility of desistance on part of offender
'Flat-rate' retributivism	No role for prior convictions at sentencing	Impose a sentence proportional to the seriousness of the crime and offender's level of culpability
Progressive loss of credit	Progressively mitigate severity response for offenders with five or fewer convictions	To recognize the good character of first offenders, or those who are nearly first offenders
Lapse theory	Progressive loss of mitigation: limited discount offered first offenders, no additional punishment for recidivism after three or four convictions	To recognize human frailty within a retributive model based on proportionality considerations; censure based approach
Penitential theory	Limited discount offered first offenders but no additional punishment for recidivism after two convictions	Achieve secular penitence

Table 4.1 *Continued*

Sentencing Perspective	Role of Previous Convictions	Sentencing Objective(s)
Enhanced seriousness	Each additional conviction results in a harsher sentence	To impose sentences the severity of which reflects the enhanced harm resulting from the offender's prior convictions
Mercy	First offenders receive an 'undeserved' mitigation in sentence; no mitigation after the first conviction	To partially forgive offenders for their first offence
Desert-based culpability model	Severity increases with each additional conviction, but the aggravating effect is restricted within a proportionality model	To impose a sentence that reflects the seriousness of the offence and the offender's level of culpability; censure of the offender

5

Role of Previous Convictions: Representative Sentencing Frameworks

As noted in Chapter 1, the focus of this volume is upon general sentencing provisions rather than habitual offender statutes which prescribe severe terms of custody for a carefully circumscribed category of repeat offender. The role of criminal record in the two-dimensional sentencing grids used in the US is well known. Generally speaking, the US guidelines ascribe a severity premium for each additional conviction or element of the offender's criminal record. The criminal history score is not a simple question of counting the previous convictions. An offender's criminal history score is often a compound of the number, nature, seriousness, recency, and relatedness of his or her previous convictions as can be seen from the sentencing guidelines manuals (eg, Minnesota Sentencing Guidelines Commission 2006a). Wherever possible, data are provided with respect to the nature of the premium imposed to reflect an offender's previous convictions.

Overview

The chapter reviews some of the different ways in which criminal history information influences sentencing decisions. Particular attention is paid to England and Wales since this jurisdiction has undergone a significant revolution in recent years. I then describe sentencing arrangements in a number of other common law jurisdictions, before concluding with illustrations of recidivist sentencing provisions from other countries. This selective review demonstrates that an offender's previous convictions are considered relevant to sentencing around the world, although the specific manner in which they are counted varies considerably. Before turning to these sentencing provisions it is worth noting

Table 5.1 Attitudes of criminal justice professionals toward the recidivist sentencing premium, Britain

	% of respondents supporting a recidivist sentencing premium
Police officers	94%
Prosecutors	90%
Magistrates	83%
Judges	78%
Prison officers	78%
Justices' clerks	72%
Barristers	63%
Solicitors	58%
Probation officers	51%

Source: adapted from Home Office (2001)

two findings which set the statutory sentencing provisions in some context.

Views of practitioners

Few surveys have explored the reaction of criminal justice professionals to a recidivist sentencing policy. One of the few such surveys was conducted by the Home Office Sentencing Review. Samples of criminal justice professionals were asked to identify the most important sentencing factors. Table 5.1 shows that with the exception of probation officers, large, and in many cases overwhelming, percentages of respondents support the imposition of harsher sentences to reflect an offender's previous convictions. Similarly, the limited literature on judicial perceptions of sentencing factors also reveals strong support for the relevance of previous convictions as a sentencing factor. A survey of the judiciary in New Zealand found that fully 95% of the sample rated an offender's previous convictions as important or very important to the sentencing decision (New Zealand Department of Justice 1982; see also Doob 2001[1]). Taken together these studies demonstrate that an offender's previous convictions are clearly a salient feature of the sentencing model to which most criminal justice professionals and sentencers subscribe.

[1] Doob (2001) conducted a survey of youth court judges in Canada and found that the second most often cited factor relevant to the imposition of custody was the offender's criminal record.

Table 5.2 Criminal history category of persons sentenced in England and Wales, 2005

	No previous convictions	1–4 previous convictions	5–9 previous convictions	10 or more previous convictions
Indictable offences	12%	31%	20%	37%
Summary conviction offences	24%	37%	18%	21%

Source: Home Office (2007)

The volume of recidivist offenders

The second preliminary observation concerns the caseload appearing for sentencing. Unlike some other sentencing policies, the practice of taking previous convictions into account affects a large proportion of offenders appearing for sentencing. This point can be readily made by examining criminal history data from a number of jurisdictions. As can be seen in Table 5.2, the vast majority of persons sentenced in England and Wales in 2005 had previous convictions. For the more serious (indictable) offences, criminal histories were particularly long—almost four out of ten offenders appearing for sentence had ten or more previous convictions (Home Office 2007). Historical trends are not easily available. However, in 1965 Nigel Walker described repeat offenders as constituting 'an interesting minority' of the offender population (p 311) suggesting that recidivists now account for a higher proportion of the sentenced caseload.

Recent data from New Zealand tell the same story: approximately three-quarters of all male offenders convicted in 2003 had previous convictions. Many of these offenders were quite prolific: over one-fifth had over ten prior convictions and 20% had over 20 priors. The average number of previous convictions for this cohort was 12 (Spier 2001). Comparisons with the United States are complicated by the fact that the guideline schemes conceptualize criminal history by counting many dimensions of a criminal record. However, recidivists clearly account for a high percentage of offenders at sentencing. For example, over 60% of offenders sentenced in 2005 in Minnesota had criminal histories, and almost one in five were sentenced in the three most severe criminal history categories (Minnesota Sentencing Guidelines Commission 2006b). Data from the state of Florida are comparable; three-quarters of all offenders sentenced in 2006 had a prior conviction (Florida Department of Corrections 2007). Similarly, across the United States approximately three-quarters of felony defendants sentenced in 2000 were repeat offenders (Bureau of Justice Statistics (2000).

Consequences for theoretical models of sentencing

These offender profile trends have consequences for the sentencing models discussed in previous chapters. Although the progressive loss of mitigation model and the 'flat-line' perspective appear to offer alternate perspectives on the use of previous convictions, once the first offender mitigation has expired, both models adopt an exclusionary approach. There is no consensus as to the number of previous convictions that may accumulate before the mitigation is exhausted but as Ashworth (2005) suggests, it is withdrawn after the offender has accumulated two convictions. If we accept this interpretation it is clear that the 'first offender discount' affects only a small percentage of offenders appearing for sentence. The previous conviction data are not broken down in a way that permits an exact estimate, but well over half the sentenced population in jurisdictions reporting these statistics have more than two prior convictions. For the majority of offenders then, the two retributive models are effectively the same; both approaches ignore any previous convictions after the offender has been twice convicted.

Use of previous convictions in the United States

An offender's previous convictions play an important role in the sentencing guideline systems found across the United States. Criminal history constitutes one of the dimensions in the two-dimensional grids found in states like Minnesota and also at the federal level (see US Sentencing Guidelines Commission 2006, and discussion in Roberts 1994, 1997b). Figure 5.1 contains the grid employed by the Minnesota Sentencing Commission. The importance of an offender's criminal record can be readily demonstrated by examining the sentences prescribed for a specific offence level. For an offence of seriousness level VIII, presumptive

Severity level of conviction offence		Criminal history score 0	1	2	3	4	5	6 or more
Murder, 2nd degree (intentional murder, drive-by shootings)	XI	306 261–367	326 278–391	346 295–415	366 312–439	386 329–463	406 346–480	426 363–480
Murder, 3rd degree Murder, 2nd degree (unintentional murder)	X	150 128–180	165 141–198	180 153–216	195 166–234	210 179–252	225 192–270	240 204–288
Assault, 1st degree Controlled substance Crime, 1st degree	IX	86 74–103	98 84–117	110 94–132	122 104–146	134 114–160	146 125–175	158 135–189
Aggravated robbery, 1st degree Controlled substance crime, 2nd degree	VIII	48 41–57	58 50–69	68 58–81	78 67–93	88 75–105	98 84–117	108 92–129
Felony DWI	VII	36	42	48	54 46–64	60 51–72	66 57–79	72 62–86
Assault, 2nd degree Felon in possession of a firearm	VI	21	27	33	39 34–46	45 39–54	51 44–61	57 49–68
Residential burglary Simple robbery	V	18	23	28	33 29–39	38 33–45	43 37–51	48 41–57
Nonresidential burglary	IV	12[1]	15	18	21	24 21–28	27 23–32	30 26–36
Theft crimes (over $2,500)	III	12[1]	13	15	17	19 17–22	21 18–25	23 20–27
Theft crimes ($2,500 or less) Check forgery ($200–$2,500)	II	12[1]	12[1]	13	15	17	19	21 18–25
Sale of simulated controlled substance	I	12[1]	12[1]	12[1]	13	15	17	19 17–22

Notes: [1] Presumptive sentence lengths in months; source: Minnesota Sentencing Commission (2006a).

Figure 5.1 Minnesota sentencing guidelines grid

sentence lengths range from 41 to 129 months. An offender sentenced for such an offence with no or only one criminal history points[2] is subject to an average sentence of 48 months. The average guideline range stipulated for the most serious criminal history

[2] Points are assigned for previous convictions or for aggravating characteristics of the offender's previous convictions such as the fact that the previous conviction was committed while the offender was on bail or under parole supervision (Minnesota Sentencing Guidelines Commission 2006a).

category is 108 months. Offenders in the most serious criminal history category are subject to sentence lengths more than double that prescribed for offenders with no previous convictions.

The formal sentencing guideline schemes used in the United States document another important feature of the recidivist sentencing premium: it increases the overall levels of punishment imposed. Returning to the Minnesota sentencing guidelines grid will illustrate this point. Consider first degree assault, an offence falling at seriousness level IX of the seriousness axis. If Minnesota followed a flat-rate approach to the use of previous convictions, offenders would be sentenced to an average of 86 months, regardless of any previous convictions that they may have accumulated. Over the six criminal history categories this would accumulate to 516 months of custody. However, the actual prescribed averages (which increase to reflect criminal record) results in a total of 854 months, an increase of 65% over the flat-rate model. Another way of evaluating the impact of previous convictions on sentence severity involves computing the recidivist range: the variability from the least severe sentence that may be imposed to the most severe sentence possible for offenders in the most serious criminal history category. Thus for example, using offence category IX generates a recidivist range of 88 months. However, the least severe sentence is 41 months while the most severe rises to 129.

Many states now employ a two-dimensional sentencing grid. The guidelines manuals provide judges in the United States with detailed guidance on the way in which previous convictions should be considered at sentencing. A criminal history score reflects a number of different dimensions (see Roberts 1997a for examples and discussion). Previous convictions have a direct influence on the 'in-out' decision—whether the offender is sentenced to custody—as well as the duration of any sentence of imprisonment.

England and Wales: statutory framework

England and Wales is a particularly interesting jurisdiction with respect to the recidivist sentencing premium, as the statutory framework has undergone a radical transformation in just a decade, from one relatively consistent with the flat-rate model to one which purports to be desert-driven but which in reality is closer to the cumulative model found in many US guideline schemes. This said, until recently there has been a lack of clarity regarding the statutory provisions relating to the use of previous convictions—the most obvious example being the 1991 Act (see below). The story is a somewhat complicated one, since the various statutory provisions relating to previous convictions must be considered in relation to the provisions regarding the use of custody, and proportionality. However, a good point of departure would be the Criminal Justice Act 1991.

Criminal Justice Act 1991

Section 1(2) and Section 2(2)(a) of the Act established a seriousness threshold for the imposition of a term of custody as well as the duration of any custodial term imposed:

> Subject to subsection (3) below, the court shall not pass a custodial sentence on the offender unless it is of the opinion—
>
> (a) that the offence, or the combination of the offence and one other offence associated with it, was so serious that only such a sentence can be justified for the offence; or
>
> (b) where the offence is a violent or sexual offence, that only such a sentence would be adequate to protect the public from serious harm from him.

Section 2(2)(a) states that:

> The custodial sentence shall be—
>
> (a) for such term (not exceeding the permitted maximum) as in the opinion of the court is commensurate with the seriousness of the offence, or the combination of the offence and other offences associated with it; or
>
> (b) where the offence is a violent or sexual offence, for such longer term (not exceeding that maximum) as in the opinion of the court is necessary to protect the public from serious harm from the offender.

Thus proportionality guides both the determination of sentence as well as the duration of any custodial term imposed, with the exception of violent and sexual offenders who represent a serious threat to the community. Section 29 is the critical provision which appears to restrict the role of previous convictions in a way consistent with the flat-rate approach:

> 29(1) An offence shall not be regarded as more serious for the purposes of any provision of this Part by reason of any previous convictions of the offender or any failure of his to respond to previous sentences.

Read in isolation, this provision would appear to exclude the offender's previous convictions from consideration in the judicial determination of crime seriousness or at least to reflect 'one part of the theory of progressive loss of mitigation' (Wasik and Taylor 1991: 28). However, as Wasik and von Hirsch (1994) noted, this is something of an oversimplification, as other sections of the Act allow courts to mitigate the sentence for first offenders, and to increase the severity of the sentence if examination of the offender's record revealed some factor which might aggravate the seriousness of the current offence. Despite this qualification, section 29(1) still represents the most ambitious attempt by any legislature to distance the sentencing process from a cumulative sentencing model. Commentators were divided regarding the likely impact of the legislation. Leng and Manchester (1991) for example concluded that it was 'hard to predict the extent to which previous convictions will be taken into account by the courts when sentencing offenders' (p 30). Statutory directions on such a critical issue should be clearer and inspire more confidence in predictions of their likely impact.

In the event, statutory amendments were not long in coming. A number of explanations have been offered for these reforms. It seems clear, however, that political, professional, and judicial[3] objections to what was perceived as a 'flat-rate' previous conviction model were largely responsible (see Ashworth 2000: 170; Thomas 2003). The Criminal Justice Act 1993 replaced the 1991 wording with a new provision, namely that:

> In considering the seriousness of any offence, the court may take into account any previous convictions of the offender or any failure of his to respond to previous convictions.

The revised provision represents an apparent reversal of policy, and accords courts the discretion to treat an offence as being more serious if the offender has previous convictions (see Thomas 2003). It would appear to grant sentencers considerable discretion to sentence offenders on the seriousness of their previous rather than current convictions (Henham 2005). Once again, though,

[3] A good example of judicial scepticism may be found in a speech by the Lord Chief Justice who noted in a speech that 'the court will approach the question of seriousness... by looking primarily at the instant offences... but looking at them not in a vacuum or blinkers, but against a previous history' (cited in Dunbar and Langdon 1998: 110).

Wasik and von Hirsch (1994) take a different view, arguing that the provision should be interpreted in the context of the seriousness threshold—which remained unamended from the 1991 to 1993 Acts (see also Ashworth 2000).

Whichever interpretation is preferred, it is clearly the case that the principle of the progressive loss of mitigation—which assigns no role to previous convictions once the mitigation is lost—carried less weight in England and Wales following the 1993 Act. A decade later, the pendulum swung even further away from the principle and towards the practice of cumulative sentencing, and the result was the Criminal Justice Act 2003. The source of this legislation was a review of sentencing policy and practice conducted by the Home Office in 2001 and motivated by a political desire to reform the sentencing process.

As noted in Chapter 1, the Home Office review and recommendations were guided by a desire to promote public confidence in the sentencing process. There was a clear message from the government that the sentencing process lacked 'sense'. The sentencing chapter of the White Paper that followed the sentencing review for example was titled 'Putting the Sense Back into Sentencing' (Secretary of State, 2002). The review concluded that the severity of sentence should be governed by three fundamental principles:

(i) the severity of punishment should reflect the seriousness of the offence and the offender's criminal history;
(ii) the seriousness of the offence should reflect its degree of harmfulness or risked harmfulness, and the offender's culpability in committing the offence;
(iii) in considering the offender's criminal history, the severity of the sentence should increase to reflect previous convictions, taking into account how recent and relevant they are. (Home Office 2001: 13).

The Home Office Sentencing Review was followed by a White Paper in 2002 (Secretary of State 2002), and, ultimately, the Criminal Justice Act 2003. The new act retains the proportionality constraints on the use of custody and the duration of custodial terms, but modifies the use of previous convictions by moving towards a cumulative model. Section 143(2) states that:

In considering the seriousness of an offence ('the current offence') committed by an offender who has one or more previous convictions, the court must treat each previous conviction as an aggravating factor if (in the case of that conviction) the court considers that it can reasonably be so treated having regard, in particular, to:

(a) the nature of the offence to which the conviction relates and its relevance to the current offence, and
(b) the time that has elapsed since the conviction.

The parallel with the US sentencing guideline schemes is unmistakable: each previous conviction must enhance the judicial determination of crime seriousness, and hence the severity of imposed sentence, if it can be reasonably so treated. This use of previous convictions is a long way from the formulation of the 1991 Act. The experience in England and Wales over the period 1991–2003 underlines the challenges confronting a sentencing model which attempts to limit consideration of previous convictions at sentencing.

Judicial practice in England and Wales

The statutory framework thus changed considerably over the period 1991–2003. How did sentencers react to the evolving policy environment? Figure 5.2 provides an indication of the magnitude and trajectory of the recidivist sentencing premium in England and Wales from 1993 to 2005. Several conclusions may be drawn from this figure. First, there is a remarkable degree of consistency over this period. Second, sentence severity rises to reflect the criminal history category of the offender. The average custodial rate for first offenders over the period was 15%, while the custody rate for the highest criminal history category (10 or more prior convictions) was 35% (see Figure 5.2). The pattern seen in Figure 5.2 is clearly inconsistent with the flat-rate approach to previous convictions or progressive loss of mitigation: first offenders appear to benefit from a modest degree of mitigation, but there is also clear separation between the higher categories of repeat offenders.

Earlier sentencing statistics from England and Wales confirm that the cumulative trend apparent in Figure 5.2 has existed for some time. Flood-Page and Mackie (1998) report a cumulative sentencing pattern for the magistrates' courts and the Crown Court throughout the 1990s. Fitzmaurice and Pease (1986) report the following incarceration rates as a function of criminal history category: no prior convictions: 3%; one prior: 12%; two to four priors; 26% and five or more priors: 47%.

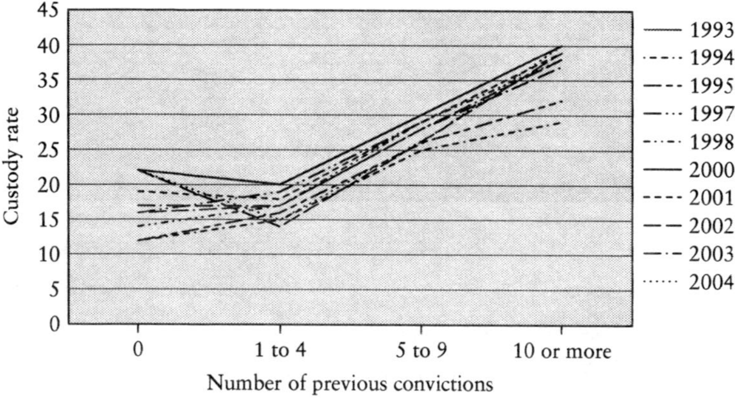

Figure 5.2 Custody rate by criminal history category, England and Wales, 1993–2005

Figure 5.3 presents sentencing trends for two triennia, 2000–2 and 2003–5. Separating the years in this manner might be expected to reveal some shifting in custodial rates as the previous conviction provisions of the new Act became known. However, as can be seen, the patterns for the two periods are remarkably similar. Taken together, these figures suggest a degree of judicial independence with respect to the statutory sentencing framework and directions from the Court of Appeal from which a number of judgments have emerged in support of the principle of the progressive loss of mitigation. In the much-quoted section from *Queen*, the Court stated that: 'The proper way to look at the matter is to decide a sentence which is appropriate for the [current] offence [...] Then in deciding whether that sentence should be imposed or whether the court can extend properly some leniency to the prisoner, the court must have regard to those matters which tell in his favour; and equally to those matters which tell against him, in particular his record of previous conviction.'[4] Thus prior convictions appear to be relevant only with respect to whether leniency may be extended, and not to aggravate the severity of the sentence.

[4] [1981] 3 Cr App R (S) 245.

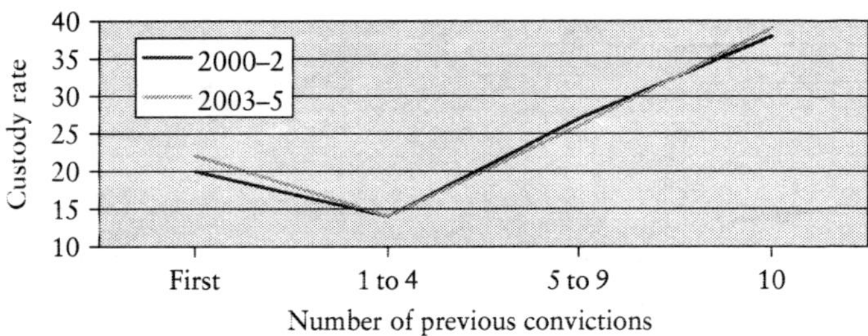

Figure 5.3 Custody rate by criminal history category, England and Wales, 2000–2 and 2003–5

Canada

Sentencing reform arrived in Canada in 1996, when Parliament approved a package of reforms to the sentencing process (see Roberts and Cole 1999; Roberts and von Hirsch 1995). Reflecting the universal importance of proportionality to which reference was made earlier in this volume, the Canadian Parliament codified the principle and designated it as fundamental, thereby assigning it a level of importance above other principles that were codified in the same statute.[5] In addition to taking this step, the sentencing reform of that year also created a number of statutory sentencing principles but curiously did not see the necessity to provide statutory guidance regarding the use of previous convictions.

Although there is no guidance with respect to the consideration of criminal history in the general sentencing provisions, for the purposes of sentencing drug offences defined under the Controlled Drugs and Substance Act, the fact that the offender 'was previously convicted of a designated substance offence' is designated as an aggravating factor (s 10(2)(b)). No specific direction is given with respect to the quantum of aggravation or dimensions such as recency and relevance. In addition, throughout the Criminal Code, many specific offences carry a recidivist sentencing structure. Perhaps the most well-known and frequently prosecuted are the mandatory minimum sentences for impaired driving offences. Thus a second conviction carries a term of imprisonment of at

[5] Section 718.1 of the Criminal Code states that: 'A sentence must be proportionate to the gravity of the offence and the degree of responsibility of the offender.'

least 14 days; subsequent convictions carry a term of imprisonment of not less than 90 days.[6]

The absence in Canada of any statutory direction with respect to the use of previous convictions at sentencing means that this jurisdiction is representative of one in which sentencers pursue their own sentencing philosophy, subject to the limited guidance offered by appellate courts. The case law supports a number of propositions consistent with sentencing practices in other jurisdictions, but stops far short of endorsing either the cumulative or retributive approaches to the use of previous convictions. For example, Renaud (2004) notes that: 'As a general rule, a measure of leniency is often extended to first offenders' (p 277). For many issues, sentencers in Canada have little guidance on which to draw. Thus Renaud observes that 'The impact on sentencing of an unrelated record is not an easy question to address' (2004: 293).

Canada is a good illustration of a jurisdiction in which the appellate courts have offered little direction regarding the application of such an important sentencing factor. The paucity of guidance for sentencers is well illustrated by the following quote from a recent judgment of the Canadian Supreme Court: 'The sentence imposed on a repeat offender may well be more severe, but this is not contrary to the offender's right not to be punished again. From the standpoint of proportionality, the sentence imposed in such a case is merely a reflection of the individualized sentencing process.'[7] The judgment subsequently makes repeated reference to the individualization of sentencing. Allowing—indeed encouraging—judges to exercise their discretion with respect to such an important sentencing factor is unlikely to foster consistent or principled sentencing.

Judicial Practice in Canada

Sentencing statistics published by the Law Reform Commission of Canada in 1976 revealed a clear cumulative trend: the custody rate for first offenders was 26% and this rate rose rapidly; offenders with only three prior convictions attracted a custody rate of 61% (Law Reform Commission of Canada 1976). No more recent statistical data are currently available with respect to the volume

[6] *Criminal Code*, s 255(1)(ii) and s 255(1)(iii).

[7] *R v Angelillo*, [2006] 2 SCR 728; 2006 SCC 55 at para 24.

Table 5.3 Custody rates by criminal history of offender, Canada

	No prior convictions	1 prior convictions	2 prior convictions	3+ convictions
Canada, all offences	12%	32%	47%	65%
Ontario, common assault	12%	39%	62%	71%
Ontario, assault with a weapon	26%	52%	76%	83%
Ontario, theft over $5,000	8%	26%	52%	64%
Ontario, burglary	23%	62%	76%	89%

Sources: national data derived from Kowalski and Caputo (1999); Ontario data from Doob and Cesaroni (2004).

of repeat offenders or the impact of previous convictions upon the severity of sentences imposed at the adult level.[8] However, sentencing statistics are available for the punishment of young offenders. Table 5.3 provides the custody rate for categories of offenders, from first offenders to those with three or more prior convictions. Data are provided for Canada as a whole (aggregated across offences) and also for specific offences in the country's most populous jurisdiction (Ontario).[9]

As can be seen, a clear linear relationship between the number of prior convictions and sentence severity emerges both for the aggregate database and for all the specific offences. Thus 65% of all cases with three or more previous convictions were committed to custody, compared to only 12% of the first offender group (see Table 5.3). Doob and Cesaroni summarize these data by noting that a youth's record of offending 'has a dramatic impact on the likelihood of a custodial sentence being imposed' (2004: 205). These statistics show that with respect to young offenders,

[8] Canada is therefore one of many jurisdictions which publish sentencing statistics from adult and youth courts annually but which fail to include the critical variable of the offender's previous convictions (see for example Thomas 2004; Calverly 2006; Birkenmayer and Besserer 1997; and discussion in Roberts 1999).

[9] In 2003 the Youth Criminal Justice Act was proclaimed into law. These data were collected under the previous regime, the Young Offenders Act (see Bala 2003; Doob and Cesaroni 2004).

sentencers in Canada conform to a cumulative sentencing model. There is no reason to believe that sentencing patterns are any different in adult court. The importance of previous convictions is also confirmed by research using a different methodological perspective. In Hogarth's study of sentencing practices the most significant predictor of sentence length (after the seriousness of the offence) was the number of previous convictions. Taken together, there seems little doubt that sentencers in Canada follow a cumulative model with respect to the use of previous convictions (Hogarth 1971).

New Zealand

Statutory sentencing reform took place in New Zealand in 2002 (see Roberts 2003b; Hall 2002). As with other common law jurisdictions, proportionality assumes an important role in the guiding statute, although unlike the Canadian statute, the New Zealand sentencing statute does not identify proportionality as a single primordial principle. Instead, proportionality is one of several interrelated principles, the first of which states that in sentencing a court 'must take into account the gravity of the offending in the particular case, including the degree of culpability of the offender'.[10]

The statute also provides a list of relevant aggravating and mitigating factors, and this list includes some direction with respect to the use of previous convictions. The language of the provision is quite directive. Courts 'must take into account the following factors...'. The list includes 'the number, seriousness, date, relevance, and nature of any previous convictions of the offender'.[11] In addition, section 9(2)(g) states that: 'In sentencing or otherwise dealing with an offender the court must take into account...any evidence of the offender's previous good character'. Thus New Zealand is an example of a jurisdiction in which the relevance of previous convictions is recognized by the same statute that establishes the importance of proportional sentencing.[12] If the

[10] Sentencing Act 2002; s 8(a).

[11] Sentencing Act 2002; s 9(1)(j).

[12] Spier (2001) provides a breakdown of prior conviction histories of offenders sentenced to custody which reveals the relationship between previous convictions and sentence severity: only 6% of offenders sentenced to custody were first offenders compared to one-third of those sentenced to a community penalty.

incorporation of previous convictions is inconsistent with a proportionality-based framework, this inconsistency clearly eluded the drafters of the New Zealand legislation.

Australia

Sentencing in Australia takes place at the state and federal levels. Considerable diversity exists with respect to the way in which criminal history information is considered at sentencing. The Crimes (Sentencing Procedure Act) 1999 in New South Wales provides guidance regarding sentencing factors in a symmetrical manner. Unlike the Canadian statute which specifies only aggravating factors, section 21A of the Crimes (Sentencing Procedure Act) 1999 specifies statutory aggravating, mitigating, and 'other factors' at sentencing which courts are directed to 'take into account'. The aggravating factors include 'a record of previous convictions'.[13] Under the list of mitigating factors, courts are directed to consider the fact that 'the offender does not have any record (or any significant record) of previous convictions'. It is interesting to note that another mitigating factor is the following: 'the offender is unlikely to reoffend'.[14] The addition of this mitigating factor may permit or encourage courts to ignore a number of previous convictions in the event that evidence is provided that the risk of reoffending is low.

Considering previous convictions in context

Three Australian jurisdictions place the consideration of the offender's previous convictions within a more general context of the defendant's life. This is accomplished by directing courts to consider the offender's previous character, and then articulating the factors to be weighed in determining character. Thus the Sentencing Act 1991 in the state of Victoria lists the factors that must be taken into account, including 'the offender's previous character'. Section 6 of the Act states the following:

In determining the character of an offender a court may consider (among other things)—

(a) the number, seriousness, date, relevance and nature of any previous findings of guilt or convictions of the offender; and

[13] Crimes (Sentencing Procedure Act) 1999, s 21A(2)(d).

[14] Crimes (Sentencing Procedure Act) 1999, s 21A(3)(e).

(b) the general reputation of the offender; and
(c) any significant contributions made to the community by the offender.

The Victoria Sentencing Manual makes the role of previous convictions crystal clear when it states that: 'Generally the decisive consideration in support of a finding of bad character is a history of prior convictions. The consequences of prior criminality are not however limited to a mere finding of bad character. As noted in the previous chapter, prior criminality is also relevant to the weight to be given to different sentencing purposes and to the assessment of the offender's moral culpability' (Victoria Department of Justice 2006).

The Penalties and Sentences Act 1992 in the state of Queensland incorporates consideration of rehabilitative efforts on the part of the offender. Section 9 of the Act identifies a number of guidelines for sentencers, to which courts must have regard. These include 'the past record of the offender, including any attempted rehabilitation and the number of previous offences of any type committed' (section 9(4)(g)). However, the statute includes a separate section articulating matters to be considered in determining the offender's character. There are three[15] important matters identified:

(a) the number, seriousness, date, relevance and nature of any previous convictions of the offender; and
(b) the general reputation of the offender; and
(c) any significant contributions made to the community by the offender.

Similarly in the Northern Territory, section 6 of the Sentencing Act contains a list of the factors to be considered including the three above as well as a fourth, namely 'the general reputation of the offender'.[16]

These statutes are silent with respect to the question of whether a significant contribution to the community may efface or discount an offender's previous convictions. Nevertheless, they represent the only examples in which the offender's previous conduct is evaluated for both positive and negative behaviours. The final chapter of this volume explores the ways in which positive

[15] In addition, there is a 'basket clause' which creates some residual judicial discretion; subsection 11(c) permits courts to consider 'such other matters as the court considers are relevant'.

[16] Section 6(b).

conduct on the part of the offender may counteract the effect of any previous convictions. For the present, however, it is worth noting two dangers associated with a broad provision of this nature. First, inviting courts to consider the offender's contributions surely leads to a social accounting model of sentencing in which considerations unrelated to the current offence or the previous convictions may affect sentence severity. Second, it creates a clear danger of inequitable treatment by privileging offenders with the means and opportunities to make a contribution to the community's welfare.

The Sentencing Act 1995 in Western Australia contains a section which articulates the principles of sentencing. The first of these identifies the principle of proportionality, albeit without any reference to the issue of offender culpability.[17] The statute also identifies a number of aggravating and mitigating factors. The absence of any previous convictions does not, unlike some other jurisdictions, constitute a mitigating circumstance. However, under the heading of aggravating factors the statute clearly prohibits courts from considering previous convictions in three ways:

Section 7(2) An offence is not aggravated by the fact that—

(a) the offender pleaded not guilty to it;
(b) the offender has a criminal record; or
(c) a previous sentence has not achieved the purpose for which it was imposed.

This provision is one of the rare examples in which a statute circumscribes the discretion of a sentencing court to impose a harsher sentence to reflect the offender's previous convictions.

In New South Wales, section 21A(2) of the statute identifies a number of aggravating factors at sentencing. One of these (d) is that 'the offender has a record of previous convictions'. In addition, section 21A(3)(e) of the same statute provides that the absence of any record (or any significant record) is a mitigating factor to be taken into account. Identifying the presence of a record as an aggravating factor and the absence of a record as a mitigating factor does not provide much guidance as to how previous convictions should be considered. For this judges in the state must turn to the appellate case law. The Court of Criminal Appeal has

[17] Section 6(1): 'A sentence imposed on an offender must be commensurate with the seriousness of the offence.'

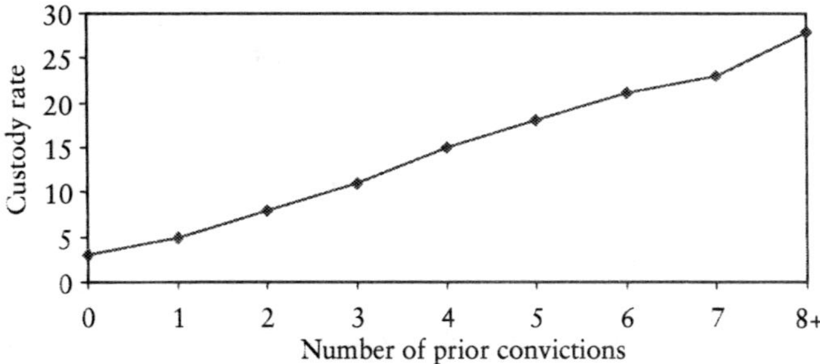

Source: Snowball and Weatherburn (2006)

Figure 5.4 Custody rate by number of prior convictions , New South Wales, 2005

taken a position consistent with the principle of the progressive loss of mitigation.[18] New South Wales is one of the few jurisdictions for which sentencing statistics are available broken down by criminal history. As can be seen from Figure 5.4, the cumulative model of the use of previous convictions emerges clearly.

Sentencing of federal offenders in Australia

In 2005, the Australian Law Reform Commission (ALRC) published a discussion paper regarding the sentencing of federal offenders. With respect to the principles of sentencing, the Commission recommended placing the principle of proportionality regarding the sentencing of federal offenders on a statutory footing.[19] In that publication the ALRC adopted the progressive loss of mitigation model. According to this view, the absence of a criminal record should constitute a mitigating factor at sentencing but the 'mere fact that the offender has an antecedent criminal history' should not be treated as an aggravating factor. The Commission recommended creating a legislative statement to this effect. In elaborating on the circumstances that might justify disregarding an offender's prior convictions, the Commission suggested that if the convictions were trivial, unrelated to the current

[18] *R v McNaughton* [2006] NSWCCA 242.

[19] The Commission proposed that proportionality be identified as one of five 'fundamental' sentencing principles (see Australian Law Reform Commission 2005: 113).

conviction, spent, or were acquired when the offender was a juvenile the aggravation of sentence on the basis of these convictions would 'serve no legitimate sentencing purpose' (Australian Law Reform Commission 2005: 138–9).

Although formulated in somewhat different language, this position is essentially consistent with that found in other jurisdictions such as England and Wales, where the analogous provision requires the court to determine whether the offender's prior convictions are sufficiently recent and relevant to the current sentencing proceedings (see above). By recommending a legislative statement the Commission hoped to discourage sentencers from automatically aggravating the sentence to reflect the offender's previous convictions. In cases in which the court used the offender's previous convictions to aggravate the severity of the sentence imposed, the Commission recommended that the severity of the disposition remain proportional to the seriousness of the offence—consistent with the Commission's emphasis on proportionality. It also hoped that such a statement would encourage more reflection on the part of judicial officers with respect to the question of whether an enhanced sentence to reflect previous convictions would promote the purposes of sentencing in the particular case before the court.

Other examples of sentencing provisions addressing previous convictions

The diversity of approaches to the use of previous convictions at sentencing is clear from even a cursory review of statutory arrangements. Many jurisdictions provide a definition of a recidivist and then specify an enhanced range of sentence.

Sentencing at the international level

Although the brief sentencing provision in the Rome Statute of the International Criminal Court (ICC) reflects proportionality considerations, there is no reference to previous violations: Article 78(1) states that: 'In determining the sentence, the Court shall, in accordance with the Rules of Procedure and Evidence, take into account such factors as the gravity of the crime and the individual circumstances of the convicted person.' However, previous convictions can be considered according to another provision. Rule

145(2)(b)(i) of the ICC Rules of Procedure and Evidence permits a court to consider previous convictions as an aggravating circumstance falling within the jurisdiction of the court (see Henham 2005). This provision identifies the following as an aggravating factor:

(i) Any relevant prior criminal convictions for crimes under the jurisdiction of the court or of a similar nature.

The sentencing provisions of the International Criminal Tribunal for Rwanda and Yugoslavia (ICTR and ICTY) are justifiably described by Beresford (2001) as 'laconic'. The only reference to aggravation is found in Rule 101(B) of the Procedure and Evidence of the ICTY: 'In determining the sentence, the Trial Chamber shall take into account the factors mentioned in Article 24, paragraph 2, of the Statute, as well as such factors as: (i) any aggravating circumstances;'. A similar provision exists with respect to the ICTR.

Finland

Chapter 6 of the Finnish Penal Code contains a number of general sentencing provisions, including statutory directions regarding the grounds for increasing the severity of punishment:

Section 5—*Grounds increasing the punishment*

The following are grounds for increasing the punishment:

(1) the criminal activity has been methodical;
(2) the offence has been committed as a member of a group organised for serious offences;
(3) the offence has been committed for remuneration;
(4) the offence has been directed at a person belonging to a national, racial, ethnic or other population group due to his/her membership in such a group; and
(5) the relation between the criminal history of the offender and the new offence, which as a result of the similarity between the offences or otherwise, shows that the offender is apparently heedless of the prohibitions and commands of the law.

This provision seems to reflect the defiance justification described in the previous chapter—the reappearance of the offender for sentencing justifies the imposition of a harsher sentence. In addition, previous convictions are relevant to the imposition of specific sanctions, for example, in determining whether a conditional sentence of imprisonment is imposed instead of a term of custody. According to Section 9, 'a sentence of imprisonment for a fixed period not exceeding two years may be conditional (*conditional imprisonment*), unless the seriousness of the offence, the guilt of the offender as manifest in the offence, or the criminal history of the offender requires the imposition of an unconditional sentence of imprisonment'.

Sweden

Sentencing in Sweden follows a proportionality-based model in which the severity of assigned punishments is supposed to reflect the relative seriousness of the criminal act (Jareborg 1995). Section 1 of the Swedish Criminal Code (1988) states that: 'The punishment shall be imposed within the statutory limits according to the penal value of the crime or crimes, and the interest of uniformity in sentencing shall be taken into consideration. The penal value is determined with special regard to the harm, offence, or risk which the conduct involved, what the accused realized or should have realized about it, and with the intentions and motives of the accused.' However, criminal history soon makes an appearance on the scene.

Section 4 of Chapter 29 of the Code states the following: 'Apart from the penal value, the court shall in measuring the punishment, to a reasonable extent take the accused's previous criminality into account, but only if this has not been appropriately done in the choice of sanction. In such cases, the extent of previous criminality and the time that has passed between the crimes shall be particularly considered, as well as whether the previous and the new criminality are similar or whether the criminality in both cases is especially serious.' The phrase 'to a reasonable extent' is the principal constraint upon the extent to which judges may allow previous convictions to influence sentence severity.

The Netherlands

Section 4, article 184 of the Dutch Penal Code (1983) places a specific limit on the recidivist sentencing premium. The section authorizes a court to impose a premium of up to one-third in the case of repeat offending involving similar conduct. Section 4 states that: 'Where, at the time the serious offense is committed, less than two years have passed since a previous conviction for a similar serious offense became final, the term of imprisonment may be increased by one third.' The provision is thus restricted to terms of custody. In addition, it is permissive rather than mandatory; courts are permitted but not required to increase the length of sentence to reflect the offender's previous convictions.

Italy

Article 99 of the Italian Penal Code adopts a similar structure. There is a premium of one-sixth for reoffending of any kind. However, this may rise to one-third if the new offence is: (i) of the same category as the previous offence, (ii) if the new offence was committed within five years of the previous conviction or (iii) if the new offence occurred during the execution of punishment or while the convicted offender was wilfully evading punishment. In addition, if more than one of these conditions obtains, the increase rises still further, from one-third to one-half.

Korea

Under Korean sentencing law, Article 35(1) of the Criminal Act specifies that 'A person who, having been punished with imprisonment without prison labor or more severe punishment within three years after the date on which the execution has been completed or remitted, commits such crimes as shall be punished with imprisonment without prison labor or more severe punishment shall be punished as a repeating offender.' Such offenders are then subject to the recidivist sentence range as specified in Section 35(2): 'Punishment for a repeated crime may be aggravated to twice the maximum term of that specified for such crime.'

Israel

The Sentencing Reform statute proposed in Israel in 2005[20] promotes proportionality as the central principle at sentencing. Article 40B(a) states that 'The guiding principle in punishment is the maintenance of a suitable correlation between the punishment on the one hand and the severity of the crime and the guilt of the accused on the other'. However, the statute also identifies a list of

[20] Amendment 92 of the Criminal Code (Constructing The Judicial Discretion in Sentencing) 2006.

mandatory aggravating factors that must be taken into account. One factor which carries a status apart and therefore presumably above the others is Article 40G(c): 'An additional factor to be weighed by the court in increasing the severity of the punishment is whether the accused has a criminal record with offenses of a similar nature or of a different nature which would justify a harsher sentence.' The statute also contains a provision which permits courts to impose a disproportionate sentence if the court deems the offender to be a danger to society 'in view of the type of offense and the past criminal record of the accused' (s 40C(a)).

Turkey

In Turkey, recidivism results in a proportional increase in the severity of any subsequent sentencing. Thus section 81 of the Criminal Code states that 'if a person commits a new crime within ten years of serving a sentence of more than five years and within five years in the case of other punishments, the punishment to be imposed for the new offence shall be increased by not more than one-sixth'. However, there is a premium imposed when the reoffending is of the same category as the first offence. Under these conditions, the punishment increases by one-third rather than one-sixth.

Summary and conclusions

This brief review of selected sentencing frameworks in a number of jurisdictions reveals both the prevalence and the diversity of criminal record provisions. Flat-rate penalty schemes may exist with respect to minor transgressions such as parking or speeding violations, but for more serious forms of offending, the offender's criminal history is almost always invoked as a relevant sentencing factor. Notwithstanding the diversity of criminal history provisions, a few common features emerge. First, although the statistical record is imperfect, even in jurisdictions adhering to the principle of progressive loss of mitigation, courts appear to go their own way and impose sentences according to a cumulative model. Second, statutes often invoke the concept of relevance, but leave the interpretation of this idea to sentencers to resolve. Many jurisdictions identify the issues of recency and relatedness, suggesting that previous convictions should weigh more heavily against the defendant when the priors are recent and similar to the current conviction.

We have now seen that previous convictions are relevant to almost all sentencing philosophies and are incorporated into sentencing frameworks around the world. The remaining chapters of this volume explore the reactions of convicted offenders and members of the public to the recidivist sentencing premium.

6

The View From the Dock: Perceptions of Sentenced Offenders

The legitimacy of the sentencing process cannot be established by legislative fiat; sentencing policies, principles, and practices need to reflect some degree of societal consensus—which in the main, they generally do. As noted in Chapter 1, the principle of proportionality reflects a fundamental consensus about the appropriate relationship that should exist between conduct and consequence. Sentencing patterns around the world reveal a direct relationship between the seriousness of the offence and the severity of the imposed punishment. A legal system which imposed disproportionate punishments—either disproportionately harsh or lenient—would undoubtedly attract public obloquy with adverse consequences for the criminal justice system. However, there is an even more important constituency to be considered: convicted offenders.

Overview

This chapter and the next draw upon interviews with a sample of repeat offenders conducted in 2007. The interviews explored convicted offenders' reactions to the sentencing process, and in particular, the recidivist sentencing premium. Chapter 6 summarizes findings from previous research and explores general perceptions of the sentencing process, specifically the issues of fairness, proportionality, and consistency. Chapter 7 describes the reactions of these individuals to the practice of imposing harsher sentences on repeat offenders.

Why are views of offenders important?

There are several reasons why offender perceptions of the sentencing process are important. First, if offenders do not accept the legitimacy of the sentencing process—or of a central feature such as a recidivist premium, they are unlikely to see the benefits of subsequent desistance from offending. If the imposition of progressively harsher sentences upon recidivists is perceived as being unfair, criminal sanctions will be regarded as unjust and this may fuel anger towards the sentencing process (Piquero, Gomez-Smith, and Langton 2004). Resentment of the legal system may thus impede or undermine efforts to desist from further offending. This point has been made repeatedly over the years (see for example, McTaggert 1896; Frank Pakenham (Lord Longford) 1961: 59). The Ouimet Report which examined the correctional system in Canada drew attention to the relationship between perceptions of unfairness and the likelihood of rehabilitation (Canadian Committee on Corrections 1969). The Committee noted that if prisoners feel 'aggrieved by apparent inequalities or inequities then their rehabilitation may present additional difficulties' (1969: 192).

A second reason to pay attention to the perspectives of sentenced offenders concerns compliance with court orders. There must be some degree of acceptance of the penal regime in order for offenders to be motivated to comply with judicial orders. If there is a link between attitudes to the sentencing process and compliance with court orders, the recidivist premium may be lowering the likelihood that offenders will comply with conditions imposed on them by the courts. In many cases these conditions are designed to promote rehabilitation and subsequent desistance.

A third reason for exploring offender perceptions is that attitudes towards legal authority may also be relevant to deterrence. To the extent that the recidivist premium deters crime by recidivists, this effect may well be diminished if offenders fail to acknowledge the legitimacy of such a sentencing practice. Criminologists have long asserted a link between a belief in justice and the effectiveness of the sanctioning process (eg, Schmideberg 1960) and a number of research studies have demonstrated a link between perceptions of legitimacy and the deterrent effect of sentencing (see Makkai and Braithwaite 1994). In short, the likelihood of an offender desisting from future offending may well be affected by his or her perceptions of the legitimacy of the justice system.

Defiance theory

Sherman (1993) proposed a number of conditions under which defiance of a lawful authority may arise from perceptions of unfairness. He suggests that sanctions may be perceived as unfair under two conditions, either of which is sufficient to generate defiance: '(1) The sanctioning agent behaves with disrespect for the offender, or for the group to which the offender belongs, regardless of how fair the sanction is on substantive grounds and (2) The sanction is substantively arbitrary, discriminatory, excessive, undeserved, or otherwise objectively unjust' (pp 460–1). The imposition of additional punishment to reflect criminal conduct for which punishment has already been imposed may well be perceived as excessive or unjust, and this may, as Sherman notes, undermine the offender's motives to return to a law-abiding lifestyle. Freeman, Liossis, and David (2006) report one of the few tests of this hypothesis. These researchers found that perceptions of fairness were not significantly related to intentions to reoffend. More support for the theory was found in recent work reported by Brownfield (2006) who found that defiance theory partially explained gang membership and participation in criminal activity (see also Hagan and McCarthy 1997).

Offender reactions to sentencing and sentencing reform

It is noteworthy and rather surprising that almost none of the sentencing reform initiatives conducted in recent years have explored offenders' perceptions of the sentencing system or their reactions to proposed reforms. Alpert and Hicks (1977) describe the subject of offender attitudes to sentencing as 'a relatively neglected area of inquiry' (p 461). Over a decade later Furnham and Alison (1994) noted the dearth of research upon this issue, and argued that it is 'not adequate to study the implementation of punishment without some knowledge of an offender's attitude towards it' (p 46).

The Home Office Sentencing Review of 2001 (which led ultimately to the Criminal Justice Act 2003) conducted a great deal of empirical research into the views of the public and of criminal justice practitioners (see Home Office 2001: Appendix 5), but did not explore the perceptions or experiences of offenders. Nor have the US Sentencing Commissions engaged with the population most directly affected by their policies. Two exceptions to this pattern are the Canadian Sentencing Commission and the Australian Law Reform Commission (1980).

The Canadian Sentencing Commission reviewed the sentencing process in Canada and ultimately published a report recommending sweeping changes to the sentencing of offenders in that jurisdiction (see Canadian Sentencing Commission 1987). As part of its research work plan, this Commission published three research reports that explored the views of convicted offenders (Landreville 1988; Ekstedt 1988; Morse and Lock 1988). Other Sentencing Commissions of that decade (eg, Victorian Sentencing Committee 1988) as well as more recent inquiries such as the Australian Law Reform Commission (2005) appear to have overlooked the importance of surveying convicted offenders.

The scant empirical scholarly literature on offender perceptions of the sentencing process sheds limited light on the issue of the recidivist sentencing premium. A number of issues have been explored, including perceptions of the relative severity of different sanctions (eg, Petersilia and Piper Deschenes 1994; Martinovic 2002) and the experience of imprisonment or specific community-based sanctions (eg, Blomberg, Bales, and Reed 1993; Heggie 1999; Roberts 2004). In addition, research in different jurisdictions has explored offenders' views of the legitimacy or fairness of the sentencing process. However, it is hard to draw conclusions about the attitudes of 'offenders in general' as views will vary greatly, depending on the degree and nature of the respondent's experiences with the criminal justice system. Moreover, many of the investigations into the attitudes of convicted offenders have used widely-varying samples of participants, thereby making it difficult to make comparisons between studies. Finally, the perceptions of people sentenced by the courts are likely to be more heterogeneous than public perceptions of sentencing since the latter are derived in large measure from mass media representations.

One finding which does seem to have some generalizability is that offenders hold negative views of the sentencing process.[1] This appears true for offenders in a range of jurisdictions and over a wide time period. For example, Indermaur (1994) reports

[1] Although the majority of studies find that offenders view sentencing as unfair, here too there are exceptions. Arcuri (1976) reports that over half the inmates interviewed for his research perceived sentencing as being fair.

that almost all (90%) of the Australian offenders in his study perceived the system to be unfair, and the principal reason for this perception was that sentencing outcomes were unpredictable. Indeed, when asked to define what they meant by the term 'fair', the most frequent response was 'consistency'. The offender survey reported by the Australian Law Reform Commission (1980) found similar results. The Commission noted that 'Among many submissions made to the Commission by offenders, no issue has been more recurrent than disparities in sentencing' (Australian Law Reform Commission 1980: 89). Krohn and Stratton (1980) found that less than half the inmates interviewed in their study viewed their sentence as being fair. McGinnis and Carlson (1982) report that offenders interviewed in their study conducted in Canada experienced considerable difficulty predicting the kind of sentence that would be imposed. If this is the case, they are unlikely to perceive the system as fair. Earlier research by Ekstedt (1988) found that fully 90% of the offenders interviewed disagreed with the statement that 'all judges are the same when it comes to sentencing'. Ekstedt concluded that 'offenders do not operate under the assumption that the judge is a neutral, objective arbiter, but instead they subscribe to him or her idiosyncratic decision-making' (p 21). Research in the United Kingdom has found comparable results. Bennett and Wright (1984) found that their sample of offenders convicted of burglary found sentences to be unpredictable. More recently Shute, Hood, and Seemungal (2005) summarize findings from a large survey of offenders processed in the Crown Court in England which found that the main complaint was that their sentence had been unfair.

Interviews with convicted offenders, England, 2007

The interviewees

The present research explored reactions of convicted offenders to the sentencing process in general and specifically the recidivist sentencing premium. It is important to stress that the description of sentencing and sentencers that follows is based upon offenders' perceptions. These may or may not accurately reflect the practice of the courts or the conduct of sentencers and it is therefore not possible to evaluate the professionals working in the courts on the basis of these interviews. However, as Ekstedt noted in his study 'the reality of their views is not at issue, but rather the perception itself' (1988: 21).

Participants were recruited with the assistance of probation authorities in the county of Oxfordshire in England. Recruitment signs describing the study were affixed in probation offices in the area. The signs asked for volunteers to participate in a study of offender perceptions of the sentencing system. However, no mention was made of the recidivist sentencing premium or repeat offending. The hope was to attract offenders or ex-offenders with a range of criminal histories, but in particular offenders with many previous convictions. The recidivist sentencing premium obviously falls most heavily on these individuals, who of all offenders, should be most keenly aware of its impact. To the extent that enhanced sentences for repeat offenders may be perceived to be unfair, these offenders may reasonably be expected to have the greatest sense of unfairness. These individuals would also have the most experience with the way in which courts use previous convictions to determine sentence severity.

The limited research into perceptions of fairness suggests that recidivists hold attitudes towards sentencing that are not appreciably different from first offenders. Indeed, some studies (eg, Alpert and Hicks 1977) show that prisoners with previous convictions held somewhat more positive attitudes towards sentencing. Mylonas and Reckless (1963) studied the attitudes of first and recidivist property offenders and found that first offenders expressed more favourable attitudes; however, the relationship between criminal record and expressed opinion was weak. Casper (1978b) also reports relatively small differences in perceptions as a function of the criminal record of the participant.

As it happens, most of the study participants had very lengthy criminal records. The number of self-reported previous convictions ranged from one to 105. Respondents were asked to disclose the extent of their criminal histories in categories of previous convictions and Table 6.1 provides a breakdown of the sample of 77 participants by the number of self-reported prior convictions.[2] As can be seen, over half the participants reported having at least ten previous convictions. In addition, all but two respondents had served a sentence of custody. Consistent with the general offender

[2] Although they had been asked to simply provide a category of prior offences, many participants stated the exact number of their previous convictions.

Table 6.1 Self-reported criminal history category of study participants

1 prior conviction	2–5 prior convictions	6–9 prior convictions	10 or more prior convictions	No response volunteered
11%	10%	17%	56%	6%

N = 77

population, the vast majority (80%) of participants were male. Ages ranged from 18 to 53, with an average of 32 years. While the sample cannot be described as random or necessarily representative of the larger population of offenders from which it is drawn, the consensual nature of responses to these issues in light of the diversity of participants is striking.

The interviews

The interviews followed a tightly-scripted protocol in which respondents were asked a series of questions about the following: their experiences in and perceptions of the sentencing process; their knowledge of and reaction to the recidivist sentencing premium; their awareness of the sentencing arrangements introduced in the Criminal Justice Act 2003; and their beliefs about the consequences of conviction. Some of these areas will be discussed in turn throughout this chapter. The interviews lasted almost an hour, and most were conducted in person, with the remainder conducted over the telephone. Almost all interviews were recorded and partially transcribed for analysis.

Emerging themes

Severity of the sentencing system

To begin the interview respondents were asked the following question: '*Based on your experience, how would you characterize the severity of the sentencing process. Would you say that people are treated much too harshly, too harshly, about right, or with too much leniency?*'. Surprisingly perhaps, a small number of participants were unwilling to express an opinion on the overall severity of the sentencing process. One participant noted that: 'I wouldn't like to characterize [sentencing] in such general terms; it really depends on the offence'. Similarly, another interviewee said that he could not give a general opinion because he made a distinction between categories of offending by observing that '[for] really important crimes—murder, sexual assault, violent crime—sentences aren't long enough—people are getting out when they never should.' Another participant responded in the following way: 'I can't judge across the whole spectrum of sentencing'. In general, however, excessive severity did not emerge as an important theme during the course of the subsequent discussions. Some individuals expressed anger at the sentence they had received, but usually because they had been led to expect another (more lenient) outcome by their legal counsel. On the issue of fairness, however, there was a clear consensus among participants.

Fairness and proportionality in sentencing

They say that British Justice is fair, but it isn't. (Interviewee 39)

Since the recidivist sentencing premium has long been discussed in terms of its potential to create inappropriate disparities between offenders based on the number and nature of their previous convictions, the interview explored perceptions of the fairness of the sentencing process in general: '*Based on your own personal experience how would you describe the fairness of the sentencing process: very fair, fair, not very fair, very unfair?*'.[3] This question was used to launch a discussion with the interviewees of the way in which the system may be unfair, in the event that the individual had expressed a perception of unfairness. Perceptions of a lack of fairness may spring from many circumstances; an offender may perceive that he has been unfairly treated because of the specific sentence he had received. On the other hand, offenders may see the system as being unfair because it is unpredictable, or because sentencers appear to employ extra-legal factors. We were particularly interested in whether a sample of people who had been sentenced on many occasions would perceive the recidivist sentencing premium as being unfair.

Most individuals held negative, and in many cases very hostile views of the sentencing process in England and Wales. These negative perceptions appeared to arise both from their direct experiences of sentencing and also from their observations of other sentencing hearings. It became clear during the course of the

[3] The phrase 'based on your own personal experience' was used to focus on participants' actual experiences rather than their general perceptions or what they had been told by other offenders although in the course of the interviews there was considerable discussion of this latter material.

interviews that by the term 'unfair' the interviewees meant sentencing lacked both consistency and proportionality—a finding consistent with participants in Indermaur's (1994) study involving offenders in Australia. Sentencing decisions were viewed as being unpredictable and lacking equity rather than, as might have been anticipated, simply being too harsh. Much of their commentary regarding fairness alluded to the unpredictable nature of disposals or the lack of proportionality in terms of the sentence imposed. Participants often made comments about the sentences that they had received in comparison to those imposed on other offenders convicted of crimes of comparable seriousness.

Consider the reaction of a 26-year old man with 15 previous convictions for a range of offences, mostly minor in nature. Just prior to participating in the study he had completed a 12 month custodial term for assault. Here is what he had to say about the issue of fairness:

Question: In your view, is the sentencing system fair?

Response: Is the system fair? No it's not fair at all. This offence—I defended myself[4] and at the end of the day they could have sentenced me to a suspended sentence but I got 12 months. I was employed [but] now I am without a job and my wife is four months pregnant. I think the sentencing system sucks. I know a person who's got previous convictions up to his eyeballs for burglary and stuff like that—quite nasty charges—and he just got sentenced for two common assaults. He basically broke into the place—forced the door and beat up two people. He got 60 days and he's got previous convictions for aggravated burglary. And I got 12 months for defending myself and my partner. It depends on what kind of day the judge had, whether he had a good day or bad. It's...what the word I'm looking for?...there's no...

Q: Justice?

R: No, not that. There's like no...

Q: Consistency?

R: Yeh, that's it—there's no consistency at all; they don't look at the actual facts. They just look at the charge and not the background. It could come down to what you look like or if they [the magistrates] had an argument with their missus...I don't feel there's any consistency in the sentencing system at all. Same with drugs. I know someone who was sentenced for nine ounces and he got 10 months. Another [was sentenced] for 18 ounces and he got six months. Just depends what judge you get.

[4] The individual in this interview stated that he had acted in self-defence in response to an unprovoked assault.

The following exchange from an interview with a 50-year old offender with considerable experience in the criminal justice system is also illustrative:

Question: In terms of the sentencing process how would you characterize the sentencing process: as very fair, fair, not very fair, or unfair?

Response: It's the luck of the draw. Some days you can go in there anticipating being, you know, harshly treated and yet you come out with a [positive] result. It depends on whether the magistrate has had his oats the night before. If he's had a bad day, if there have been a lot of similar cases that day, or if he just doesn't like you personally. To me it's not about matters of law.

Q: Earlier you have raised the issue of consistency—

R: —there is no consistency. There is no consistency. I'm talking from personal experience and there's no consistency at all.

R: Why do you think that is the case?

A: It depends on too many factors—whether the judge is in a good mood, whether you're first or last in court... You may go down [be sent to prison] even if you stole a chocolate. And you could rob a church and get away with it because you made the judge smile. It's totally ridiculous. And I'm speaking from experience. It's catch as catch can. It's a lottery. Consistency is nil. Nil.

The impact of perceptions of fairness was identified by several participants and most clearly by Interviewee 40:

They should have more guidelines. It causes an uproar when you're in jail and there's some black fellow or an Asian and he's doing two years and you've got four months for the same crime. It's unjust. This causes problems inside and carries on after you get out. You ask yourself: 'Why should I bother trying to toe the line and re-adjust because there is just no fairness in it'. It will have an effect on the rehabilitation of people in jail if you've got people in there for a lot less [serious offence] than you. People give up. They say: 'I'm not going to toe the line because it's not fair that he got less than me.' If all the criminals knew what they were going to get—not pot luck like it is now, depending on whether you get a good brief [lawyer] or whether the magistrates got laid the night before.

Influence of extra-legal factors on consistency and fairness

Some participants identified the extra-legal factors which in their view caused unfair outcomes at sentencing. A young man in his twenties held the view that variations in courtroom demeanor created disparate outcomes:

It depends on how you look, what you wear—how you speak. I went to court and got done for driving a car with [many mechanical problems]. Now I always go to court in a suit. I was speaking well, clean-shaven, had a smart appearance. So they [the magistrates] think 'Right, he's got a lot of money—whack him with a great big fine'. So I got an £800 fine. On the other hand some toe-rag goes in there wearing a scruffy pair of jeans, unshaven, grunting at the magistrates and he'll get a £30 fine for the same offence. Where's the justice in that?[5]

Another participant believed that he had received a harsher penalty because his partner—who was present in court at the sentencing hearing—had laughed aloud during the proceedings. The comments of Interviewee 48 are typical:

It's absolutely abysmal the way I have been treated...I really think it's a lottery, a bloody lottery. I got done [incarcerated] and I've seen far worse cases walk out the court...I really believe that they have a quota and they [the courts] have to fill the jails. In one day if they have 10 cases a proportion [of them] have to go to jail whatever [the circumstances]. If you are sentenced for property you are far more likely to go to prison than for crimes against the person.

Interviewee number 74 bluntly summarized his perspective:

It's totally unpredictable. I have been stood in court waiting [and seeing other cases come and go] and you get a different outcome. You don't get two judges doing the same thing in a similar case...I have been in prison and some of the people I have met there I said to myself 'I'm glad you're inside' while others I met I said 'What are you doing here in prison?' I think they [judges] decide on a personal matter; you don't get two judges making the same decision.

The following comments from nine other participants also reveal this perception of inconsistency in sentencing outcomes:

- [Sentencing] is very inconsistent, very unfair. Some people will get done for 20 burglaries and get one year. I got done for one burglary and got three years. It depends entirely on the individual judge.

[5] This interviewee subsequently added that 'I tried it one time myself—went in wearing a pair of jeans and t-shirt. They still gave me a massive fine and [this time] the magistrates said: "Do you not think you could have worn a suit and shown some respect for the court?"'.

- My mate got nicked [prosecuted] for stealing a can of beer and he got six months and there was this man messing with a kid and he could have got the same; and I thought that was unfair—that's always stuck in my head, I was shocked by that.
- My sentencing has always been really harsh while people [who have] done much more serious things than me and they're not going to prison.
- It's unfair. I have read in the newspaper of people who committed the same crime as mine but received a very reduced sentence from mine. I committed the same crime as several famous people who got one-sixth of the sentence I got—it's a very big difference.
- I can't really understand why...they're getting such sentences...the same offence, same background but some get longer and some get less. You've got judges and magistrates and they're all giving different sentences for the same crime. People who commit small crimes get big sentences—pedophiles get one year; selling crack gets 15 years. It seems anomalous if some people continually get away with things.
- [Let's imagine] I'm Robbie Williams. I get caught with an ounce of coke—[I'll be] let off but some poor little guy gets fucked. It [sentencing] changes with the times; like right now the prisons are full up and they [the courts] are sending [offenders] to the community and that's not fair.[6]
- The punishment doesn't fit the crime. You know what I mean? People murder and get five years and people do a lot less and get the same [time]. It all depends on the judge on the day. It should be the same but it isn't. Depends on the judge and whether you got previous [convictions].
- They send you to prison for silly things. Then people do some serious things and they go to court and they get a couple of months of probation. I think they need to concentrate not on people doing petty crimes.
- I know a lot of people who considerably reoffend and I know a lot of people that have done far worse than me, and they got six months while I got 15. I kind of think that is unfair...I can't get my head around that.

[6] At the time that this interview was conducted the news media in Britain were reporting that the prisons were overcrowded.

Person vs property offences

A number of participants asserted that the courts punished property crimes more seriously than crimes of violence and they considered this to constitute a violation of proportionality in sentencing. This view was captured by one individual in the following way: 'Some judges hate burglars and they sentence them harder, but all judges seem to value money more than life. You get caught for robbing a bank and you get 18 to 20 years. You get caught for raping a girl and you get two to three years. Now where's the justice in that?' The words of interviewee 76 represent the perspective expressed by many offenders. His words show that offenders can interpret a lack of proportionality to connote a lack of fairness. He compared the sentence he received for a substantial fraud to less severe sentences imposed for more serious crimes of violence:

> I received two and half years for fraud of 30,000 pounds. Which I thought was OK. But I have heard about people who have received two years for killing someone while they have been driving or someone who didn't even receive a custodial sentence for causing the death of a child or for sexually assaulting a baby. When I compare the sentences, the harshness of the sentences you know—I don't believe it is fair in that respect. If a crime has an economic effect, compare that to one that has a lifetime effect and consequences for the victim. The crime can cause the victim to commit offences of the same kind. In that respect I don't believe that the system's fair.
>
> Only recently there was this case in the news. There was a lady who caused the death of her baby by setting fire to her flat. She left the baby on the sofa and set fire to the flat in order to get back at the father of the baby. She didn't even get a sentence [of custody]. It doesn't seem to balance out to me. I don't think that's right. And manslaughter: I was in prison with a friend who had killed his ex-partner's boyfriend. He got two and a half years—same as me and he killed a man. If conning a business out of 30,000 pounds is worth two and a half years in prison, then fine. But that business will reimburse [customers] and the money can be replaced. If I am going to get two and a half years for taking money then surely someone who takes a life should get more than that?

Participants' perceptions of inconsistency also emerged from comments about their inability to predict outcomes when appearing for sentence. One 28-year old man who reported having approximately seven previous convictions noted that 'It's not predictable. You don't know what's going to happen—you're expecting a community order and then you appear before a court and you go to prison'. His partner who participated at the same interview stated that 'you don't really know—you haven't got a clue, you just don't know what to expect'.

It is important to note that the theme of inconsistent sentencing emerged even from participants who believed that they had been treated with undue leniency. This was the case with a 25-year old who reported 25 previous convictions:

> My sentence was too lenient. I know people in prison that done less than what I have and got three times as long. The way I see it there should be fixed sentences. When I was in the Crown Court I walked out with a sentence of three and a half [years of custody]. My list of previous convictions ranged between car theft, house burglary, assault, possession, and possession of offensive weapons—things like that. Then I am up [to be sentenced] for a section 18 Grievous Bodily Harm which is one under attempted murder and I walk off with three and a half years. There was another lad in prison and he got done for section 20 and he got five and half years. He's got to do two more years than me and I done something worse. To me that's not fair.

Several participants related the question about the fairness of the system to their own sentences: 'I got 17 years for armed robbery reduced to 14 on appeal. You can have a child abuser—they've done the same thing three or four times over and they're getting the same six-year sentence. The emphasis [in sentencing] is on property and money rather than people; they say "we're putting victims first", but it doesn't ring true at all.'

One respondent captured the sentiments expressed by many participants. He described the sentencing process in the following terms:

> I wouldn't say it's fair at all—by the time you get to sentencing everything has been decided. The barrister says we will present the case in the way that's most acceptable to the court—you're just going along for the ride. If you've got previous convictions the judge will already know and by the time you get to trial you're just a spectator at someone else's game. It's almost as if there's two different languages being spoken here—the one that people speak on the street and the one used in the court. When you try to interpret one into the other it gets lost in translation. No, I wouldn't say the system's fair at all.

The only respondent to express a positive view of the fairness of the system was Interviewee 69 who had accumulated more than ten previous convictions and who stated that 'It depends on the crime, but I have been treated fairly'.

Participants' views of sentencing in the news media

A number of the respondents' comments about proportional sentencing appeared to reflect recent media coverage of controversial sentencing decisions. Several alluded to sentencing decisions for driving offences causing death that had attracted newspaper headlines, as the following quotes from six individuals illustrate:

- If you [commit] a petty crime you get a stern punishment but you can kill a child on the street because they say if you knock someone over in a car it's classified as an accident.
- Death by dangerous driving—some people are getting away with being banned for two years but he's just killed a youngster—two years driving ban for killing someone. Death by dangerous driving sentencing should be stricter.
- Someone's done three burglaries and they're getting a life stretch—paedophiles only get six years; that's wrong; paedophiles are getting the same sentence every time and that's wrong; they get done again and that's another six years and that's wrong; judges are more lenient on paedophiles and I don't understand that.
- I was reading about the Home Secretary—he wants to bring down the sentencing [levels of severity] for killing on the roads. This will make it a road tax because at the end of the day it's a licence to kill again.
- It isn't totally fair. My co-defendant done exactly the same [crime] as what I done but he got a two-year drug order and I got five years in prison. So there is a severity of difference there isn't there? One person got custody the other no, exactly the same charge, same circumstance. He was from Brighton, I was from [omitted]. Exactly the same crime. That's why we appealed. But the Court of Appeal is the most corrupt court in the land. We didn't even go there; we got done in our absence.
- It's unfair, a lot of sex offenders, paedophiles, and asylum seekers they get the good fortune. A lot of sex offenders and even famous people—they get just a slap on the wrist. If it were me, I would get six months. And others get worse. I was at [omitted] and there was a lot of Somalis and Jamaicans, and they got done worse.

Professional judges versus lay magistrates

Most sentencing decisions taken in England and Wales are made by panels of lay magistrates who impose sentence guided by a legal advisor; fully 95% of sentences in England and Wales in 2005 were imposed in the magistrates' courts rather than in the Crown Courts (Home Office 2007). The more serious cases are sentenced in Crown Court by professional judges. In light of the fact that most interviewees were recidivists with long criminal histories, the vast majority had experience with both levels of court.

Magistrates were perceived more negatively than judges. For example, one participant bluntly observed that: 'They're just a lot of shopkeepers'. A number of participants noted that sentences were harsher in the Crown Court but conceded that they were fair. As one participant noted: 'judges have more experience; magistrates are just volunteers'. Another interviewee stated that: 'magistrates haven't got the experience to decide what sentence people should get'. And further: 'The magistrates are just three puppets on a string. It's the clerk who tells them what to do.' Interviewee 76 was a 50 year old repeat offender who had appeared many times in the magistrates' courts as well as before the Crown Court. Having made a pejorative comment about magistrates he was asked to compare the sentencing of magistrates and judges:

Question: Do you think that there is a difference between the Crown Court and the Magistrates? Is one better or more consistent than the other?

Response: Absolutely, absolutely. Absolutely.

Q: Why do you have that opinion?

R: You see, they [magistrates] don't have any legal training. The fact is that you've been charged with shoplifting and you're being tried by a greengrocer. You're not going to get a sentence that reflects the severity of the crime. It's not going to happen. And that's what magistrates are: greengrocers.

Finally, another interviewee complained that 'magistrates are useless because they're just normal people they're just following advice—it is the clerk who decides and that's wrong—they just look in that stupid book [magistrates' association guidelines]'.

These comments are consistent with research conducted by the Home Office into the perceptions of young offenders. Focus groups with these individuals revealed widespread dismissal of the magistrates' court. The magistrates were seen to possess neither the necessary legal qualifications nor the life experience necessary to judge offenders (see Lyon et al: 23–5).

Summary and Conclusion

To summarize responses in this phase of the interviews, many participants clearly perceived the sentencing process as unfair—and by this they meant lacking in proportionality, equity, and predictability. Somewhat surprisingly the perception of inconsistency was expressed by many participants, and assumed more importance than the view that the sentencing process was unfairly harsh towards offenders. This finding is consistent with the limited research literature on offender perceptions of the sentencing process in England and Wales as well as other jurisdictions. Nearly 30 years ago Casper (1978b) came to the same conclusion on the basis of his survey of convicted offenders in the US. Casper concluded that 'the data do not support the common image of a subculture of hardened criminals sitting around berating the ill-treatment they have received' (p 248). This conclusion applies equally to this sample of offenders and ex-offenders in Britain. While it is hard to make direct comparisons in light of the variable nature of samples of offenders, participants in the present research appeared to have more negative views than offenders interviewed in previous research studies. However, this may be explained by the fact that most participants in the current study were multiple recidivists. The perception of inconsistent and unfair sentencing held by most offenders is the backdrop against which to consider reactions to the specific policy of imposing harsher sentences on repeat offenders. This is the subject of the next chapter.

7

Sentenced Individuals' Reactions to the Recidivist Sentencing Premium

Having documented convicted offenders' perceptions of the fairness of sentencing, this chapter turns to the critical question of the practice of imposing harsher sentences on recidivists. The questions posed at this stage of the interviews 'funnelled'[1] participants' attention towards the specific issue of the recidivist sentencing premium. Discussion began with an exploration of the importance of an offender's previous convictions at sentencing. The interviews then explored the issue in considerable depth, and participants were asked to impose sentence in response to case scenarios.

Overview

This chapter describes participants' general reaction to the concept of harsher sentencing for repeat offenders and summarizes the sentences that they favoured in response to specific case scenarios. As will be seen, there was widespread acceptance of the recidivist sentencing premium, although many individuals took exception to the way in which the premium was imposed, and held the view that insufficient consideration had been given to their efforts to desist from offending. First, however, the chapter discusses findings from the limited previous research on this issue.

Research into offender perceptions of the recidivist sentencing premium

Few studies have explored offender perceptions of specific elements of sentencing such as the principle of proportionality or

[1] See discussion in Oppenheim (1992) of this approach to interviewing.

the recidivist premium.[2] Consistent with sentencing commissions (see previous chapter) the literature on the role of previous convictions has also overlooked the views of offenders, and has concentrated instead upon normative issues. One of the few references to offender reactions to the recidivist premium in the literature is made by Nigel Walker (1980) who noted that the use of previous convictions at sentencing 'is the feature of sentencing policy which offenders themselves most resent' (1980: 127; see also Walker 1999). However, Walker's observations were based on informal discussions with prisoners and university students, rather than on systematic research. This interpretation of offenders' views has passed into the literature, despite its anecdotal nature. For example, Bagaric (2000a) also describes the recidivist premium as 'the feature of sentencing practice which offenders resent most' (p 229) and cites Walker as the authority for this observation. The very limited research available prior to the study reported here suggests that Walker may have overstated convicted offenders' opposition to a recidivist premium.

Some insight into the issue can be gleaned from a recent study reported by Freeman, Liossis, and David (2006). These researchers describe findings from a survey of repeat offenders convicted of drinking and driving. Impaired driving offenders constitute an appropriate population to survey in light of the fact that impaired driving carries recidivist sentencing penalties in many jurisdictions. Freeman et al (2006) found that despite being subject to recidivist sentencing laws, almost three-quarters of the sample regarded their sentence as being fair. This is the only suggestion in the literature that convicted offenders may not necessarily regard a recidivist sentencing premium as being inappropriate.

Awareness of importance of previous convictions at sentencing

They make no bones about it; they sentence you on your previous. If you done that before it comes up to bite you.

The first question in this phase of the interview explored participants' perceptions of the importance of previous convictions—regardless

[2] One exception to this is the study by Benaquisto and Freed (1996). These researchers report findings from interviews with 40 inmates from a medium security institution in Massachusetts.

of their opinion of the propriety of the practice of counting prior offending at sentencing. The individuals seemed well aware of the importance of the recidivist sentencing premium; this is unsurprising in light of the fact that most had multiple previous convictions and had therefore appeared several times for sentencing. The participant who had accumulated over 100 prior convictions flatly observed that: 'If you've got loads [of priors] you know you're going to prison; that's how it is'. Another respondent with a lengthy criminal record noted that: 'As soon as they look at my previous convictions I'm done for'. Similarly, another individual stated: 'The first time you get a slap on the wrist; second time maybe a year, third time a heavy sentence'.

It was also clear that respondents believed that courts considered their criminal antecedents even if these were not formally placed before the court. Some individuals who had lived in the area for many years noted that the judge or the magistrates were well aware of their recidivist status having sentenced them before: 'A couple of magistrates...they recognized me though my priors [hadn't been] brought up'. Another participant, a 40-year old woman who had accumulated over ten convictions made the same point when she noted that: 'if you get the same judge twice then you're looking at more [time in prison], even if you done something petty'.

Knowledge of the new sentencing provisions in England and Wales

With one exception, all of the interviewees had been sentenced under the Criminal Justice Act 2003, as well as under the previous sentencing arrangements. Accordingly they were asked whether they knew of the provisions relating to the use of previous convictions or had heard any talk of a changed role for priors at sentencing. Only two respondents stated that they had heard about the criminal record provisions of the 2003 Act. However, when pressed for details, could provide none. One other participant believed that previous convictions now played a greater role in court but he was unaware of any change at sentencing. It was clear that none of the interviewees—many of whom who had been sentenced on numerous occasions and almost all of whom who had appeared for sentencing since 2003—were aware of the statutory provisions regarding previous convictions. This suggests that little attempt had been made by legal professionals to educate the offenders about a critical element of sentencing reform of direct relevance to their current sentencing proceedings. The absence of explanation may simply reflect the self-evident nature—from the perspective of these professionals—of the recidivist sentencing premium. Counsel may have simply assumed that section 143 reflects such a fundamental feature of sentencing that explanation of its function or purpose is unnecessary.

Magnitude of the recidivist sentencing premium

Chapter 1 noted that the impact of an offender's criminal record on the sentence imposed was usually obscured by the imposition of a sentence that reflected all the characteristics of the case, including all mitigating and aggravating factors. This issue arose during the interviews and it was clear that the interviewees had no specific idea of the magnitude of the premium imposed in their case although a small number of individuals believed that the impact of their previous convictions had been to move them from consideration of a non-custodial sentence to a term of custody. When probed with respect to this issue, there was general agreement that greater clarity would be desirable regarding the impact of previous convictions.

Attitudes to the recidivist sentencing premium

If you commit the crime twice you should pay for it twice.

Even though almost all the participants were recidivists who had been repeatedly subject to harsher punishments as a result of their criminal histories, most offenders seemed to accept the premium without demur:[3] 'it's obvious' said one participant in response to a question which asked whether previous convictions should count

[3] Some readers may interpret this tacit acceptance of the recidivist premium as reflecting a desire to conform to the expectations of the interviewer—a well-known phenomenon in social science research (eg, Orne 1969; Rosenberg 1969). Yet it should be recalled from the material discussed in the previous chapter that most interviewees were highly critical of, and very blunt in their comments about, sentencers and the sentencing process. If 'interviewer effects' explained responses to the recidivist premium, they also would have produced more positive evaluations of the courts.

against a defendant. Responding to the same question others said: 'Absolutely. Absolutely' and 'I think they [courts] should definitely take [previous convictions] into consideration and if people are reoffending they should get longer sentences. They should gradually [incrementally] get longer and longer sentences until they have learned their lesson.' The following exchange captures the sentiments of a number of participants:

Interviewee: She's a repeat offender—the law gives you a couple of chances and then they give you a piece [ie, a very punitive sentence].

Question: And you agree with that?

Response: Yeh, you haven't learned your lesson.

Q: So your sentences have gotten longer as your record got worse. Do you agree with that?

R: Yes.

The following comments are also illustrative of the nature of the reactions of these offenders to the recidivist sentencing premium.

- If [an offender] goes up for shoplifting his first offence and then [another offender] it's their fifth, obviously there's going to be a difference in sentencing. If a judge gave the same sentence [in these two cases] that really wouldn't be fair.
- I can understand [previous offences being taken into account]. If you've got one offender with 30 previous and the other is a first offence.
- I would do the same [as the courts]—you've been done for the same crime and it's about time that you had a statement that you can't do this kind of thing.
- At the end of the day if you keep doing burglaries you deserve a harsher penalty—you're not learning from your mistakes.
- I'd be sentencing her for the previous as well—to teach her a lesson; she might be thinking about this in her cell—she's not learning her lesson. If I were the judge I would tell her 'you're not learning at all'—same as anyone who keeps reoffending.
- It's a judgment isn't it? Everyone gets judged—on what they are wearing [for example]. The courts are judging by what you have done in the past. They've got to hold that against you.
- I don't think it's wrong myself; if someone keeps doing street robbery then yeh, they [the courts] should get really harsh; if someone's fucking doing it and doing it then they deserve it.

Repetition as a justification for greater intervention

Participants expressed various opinions as to *why* previous convictions should be considered at sentencing. While there was no evident consensus that sentences should reflect the recidivist sentencing premium for reasons of deterrence, some respondents suggested that evidence of repetition justified greater intervention in the life of the offender. For example, Interviewee 48 stated that as previous convictions accumulated, the need to intervene in the life of the offender became more pressing: 'if someone's doing the same crime again and again, there's got to be a reason and the court can look into this.' When asked whether he thought that cumulatively harsher sentences could be justified in terms of deterrence he rejected this justification: 'no, all they are doing [when imposing progressively harsher sentences] is creating an institutionalized person.'

An important theme emerging from the comments of several participants was that the use of previous convictions was necessary in part at least to determine the offender's needs: 'I think that your previous convictions are very important. Because the person can get support—the sentence can be aimed at his particular problem.' These offenders saw previous convictions as relevant to sentencing as a means of helping the offender rather than simply increasing the severity of the sentence for reasons of enhanced risk or ascribed culpability. The existence of priors might therefore change the nature of the sentence, but not in a mechanical way of simply enhancing severity. Finally, in light of the strong consensus with respect to the legitimacy of using previous convictions, it is not surprising that the extent of the criminal record was unrelated to the degree to which respondents accepted the recidivist premium. Thus one of the very few participants with a single previous conviction affirmed that it was very important to know and consider previous convictions at the time of sentencing—using words that were very similar to those employed by the offender with the longest criminal history (in excess of 100 previous convictions).

Ambivalent respondents

Despite the consensus surrounding the legitimacy of the practice, a small number of individuals appeared ambivalent with respect to the role of previous convictions or endorsed a more nuanced repeat offender premium. One participant began by expressing the view that previous convictions should play no part at all at sentencing. In his words 'each crime should be judged on its merits'. However, when asked to impose sentence in response to the scenarios (to be discussed later in this chapter), he offered the following account:

> If you've got previous [convictions] you're going to get a longer sentence. And I would say that's right. Because if people know what is going to happen to them, everyone can make a mistake. Once. You make a mistake and you do your time. If you keep doing it that should be taken into account at sentencing. Take robbery. First time you get one year. Second time you get two years because you take into account the previous conviction. The third time you get three years, and so on. It just keeps adding up. And if people knew that they were going to be sentenced in that way, there would be more of a deterrent.

One of the ways in which some people departed from expressing clear support for the premium involved the way in which it was conceived. Several respondents articulated their support for a restricted sentencing premium that would apply only to offenders with particularly long criminal records. For example, an individual with 15 prior convictions noted that:

> Previous convictions do count at sentencing. They're part of your past and they can judge you on your past. But there are repeat offenders and prolific offenders. If you're a prolific offender it means you're getting worse as you go along. Each crime is getting worse. Then, yes, you should be punished more for that because at the end of the day you're not getting any better. It's the same as [going to] the doctor. You can go there once and get some medicine and if you don't get better you keep going back for more medicine.

Another individual expressed opposition to the recidivist sentencing premium but added that 'it depends on the severity of the priors whether they should be brought into play'. He took the view that it was legitimate to consider serious priors or related priors but that unrelated or less serious priors should be ignored.

One young woman in her twenties with a history of drug dependency and offending expressed her views with respect to the premium in the following way: 'I think it depends on the person's circumstances, how well they have been doing. Someone might be doing really well and they [the courts] are not taking that into consideration. It is important that they take into account how you're doing and not necessarily just your criminal past.' Her partner, who had participated in the study, also saw merit in a recidivist premium, but only if the context of the previous offending was considered. He began his comments by affirming the importance of the premium: 'Yeh, it's important because otherwise you will keep doing it, you'll be offending all the time.' But he then continued by saying: 'I think [previous convictions] are quite relevant but it depends on the circumstances. My first offence was an assault causing bodily harm which occurred a few weeks after my mother died. I was celebrating my 18th birthday and I was in no state of mind to get drunk but I went out and got drunk and with all the badness, the bereavement, and loss—I went out and hit a stranger for no reason whatever.'

This individual clearly wanted the context of the previous conviction to be taken into account on the grounds that it arose from the exceptional and tragic circumstances that existed at the time, and not as a result of any violent proclivities. He was making an important distinction between prior convictions that spoke to the character of the individual offender and other priors that reflected the circumstances in which he had found himself at the time. Simply counting the previous convictions with a view to increasing the severity of sentence was in this individual's view an inappropriate use of a record of prior offending.

A single participant appeared to endorse a reverse recidivist premium approach. His preferred sentences for the offenders with more serious records were less, not more severe. For these cases this interviewee favoured the imposition of some form of community-based programme with the purpose of addressing the offender's needs. When asked to explain his pattern of sentences it appeared that the logic underlying this participant's atypical response was that repetition connoted an individual in need of intervention rather than mere punishment. He added: 'I would look at what has made them reoffend; maybe a six month custodial and then an offending programme to sort out what he's reoffending. Maybe house arrest with a curfew.'

Offender sentencing expectations and preferences

An alternate and more direct way of exploring offenders' reactions to the recidivist sentencing premium is to ask them to impose sentence in specific cases. During the interview participants were presented with three scenarios describing a crime and the offender responsible for the offence. Participants were then asked to estimate the sentence that courts *would* impose in such a case, and second, to state the sentence that they *should* impose.

A number of questions of interest arise within this sentencing exercise: (i) Do offenders expect sentence severity to increase in response to increments in the seriousness of the offender's previous convictions? (ii) Do the sentences imposed by these offenders rise in severity to match the increase in the number of previous convictions? (iii) To what extent do offenders' sentencing preferences correspond to the sentences that they believe would be imposed by courts in response to the scenarios? Even if a recidivist premium emerges from the sentences favoured by respondents, it may be significantly more modest than the premium that they anticipate will be imposed by the courts.

Case scenarios

The offence was the same for all scenarios: the offender had been convicted of a street robbery, namely, stealing a person's wallet and a mobile phone by means of threats. The number of previous convictions was manipulated: one offender was described as having a single previous conviction for an unrelated offence (fraud). The second offender was described as having three prior convictions, two for the same offence (robbery) and one for theft. The third scenario was the most serious: the offender was now being sentenced for his fourth robbery. Thus the latter two offenders had the same number of prior convictions, but were differentiated on the number of previous crimes similar to the current conviction.

Before considering these data, however, it is worth noting that a number of respondents had difficulty providing a response on the basis of minimal information. Others provided a sentence for only one of the scenarios—the most serious—in which the predicted and favoured sentence was presumably more obvious. Some interviewees declined to respond to these questions for a variety of reasons. Many felt that they needed more information about the offence and the offender. They often asked whether the offender described in the scenario was on drugs or whether the victim had sustained injury. One stated that 'a judge would have all the details [about the offence and the offender]. I can't do a hypothetical.' This reluctance on the part of many respondents to provide a sentence for some scenarios is consistent with another theme emerging from the interviews. Offenders adopted a nuanced and multidimensional approach to sentencing, one that incorporates many factors and which explores the etiology of the offending as well as the seriousness of the offence. Some participants returned to the theme of change, expressing a need to know whether the offender had made any attempts to change his or her lifestyle. One participant said that 'I would have to get more information to find out whether she's making an effort to change. I want more background information about that—no matter how many previous convictions [she has accumulated].' Other participants simply declined to assign a punishment. Interviewee 40 for example stated that 'I'm being honest with you; I don't think any sentence will help an offender or society.' Finally, a very few interviewees assigned non-custodial sanctions. The data summarized in Table 7.1 are therefore based upon the participants who assigned a custodial sentence for at least two of the three scenarios. Table 7.1 summarizes the sentencing expectations and preferences of participants in response to the three case scenarios.

As can be seen from Table 7.1, with regard to the first question measuring sentencing expectations, respondents clearly anticipated that courts would impose harsher sentences upon offenders with previous convictions. This outcome is consistent with the free responses of participants during the interviews reported earlier

Table 7.1 Expectations of sentencing outcomes and sentencing preferences, sentenced offenders

	Scenario A: offender has one prior conviction for fraud	Scenario A: offender has three prior convictions: one for theft, two for robbery	Scenario C: offender has three prior convictions for robbery
Average expected sentence (in months)	11.1	31.5	35.1
Average preferred sentence (in months)	25.2	54.0	69.0

Note: all means significantly different, p.<.001

in this chapter. The average anticipated sentence rose from 11.1 to 31.5 to 35.1 months across the three scenarios. The sentence anticipated for the offender with the most serious record was thus more than three times longer than the sentence anticipated for the offender with the single previous conviction, and all three means are significantly different from each other. In terms of the magnitude of the premium, slightly more than two-thirds of the average sentence anticipated for the third case was accounted for by the previous offending.[4] Moreover, the model emerging from the expected sentences conforms clearly to the cumulative sentencing model rather than either retributive scheme. The second important finding is that the sentencing preferences of these offenders also matched the same cumulative sentencing model. Thus their preferred sentences also rose in severity to reflect the seriousness of the offender's previous convictions. This finding is consistent with Benaquisto and Freed's interviews with 40 inmates in the state of Massachusetts.[5]

With respect to the magnitude of the premium, just under two-thirds of the preferred sentence for the third case was accounted for by the previous offending. In both cases—expected and preferred sentences—the linear equation was highly significant[6]—confirmation that responses to both questions were consistent with the cumulative model of sentencing. This conclusion is also confirmed by the high correlations between the expected and assigned sentences: the average correlation between the responses was +.81 ($\underline{p}$. $<.001$). A difference did emerge between the expected and preferred responses in terms of the magnitude of the recidivist sentencing premium, and the variability of responses to the two questions. As can be seen in Table 7.1 the severity of anticipated

[4] The recidivist premium is defined here as the proportion of the third scenario average sentence accounted for by the average sentence in response to the first scenario.

[5] Participants in that study were asked to sentence offenders with criminal histories ranging from no previous convictions to a record of having served seven years in prison. The average number of months of prison assigned rose from 13 months for the first offender to 77 months when the offender was described as having previously served seven years in custody (see Benaquisto and Freed 1996: Table 1).

[6] Both linear equations were highly significant: expected sentence: $\underline{F}(2,44) = 43.3$. $\underline{p}. < 01$; assigned sentence: ($\underline{F}$ $(2, 44) = 18.2$; $\underline{p}. < .01$; all pair-wise comparisons of the means (eg, 1 prior versus 3 priors) were also significant.

sentences rose somewhat more sharply than the severity of imposed sentences. This suggests that offenders ascribe less importance to the recidivist premium than they expect the courts to employ.

This sentencing exercise provides a useful validity check on participants' expressed views with respect to the recidivist sentencing premium. Thus, one of the few participants who, during the course of being interviewed, seemed to oppose a premium for persistence nevertheless chose sentences in a manner consistent with cumulative sentencing. When the interviewer brought the inconsistency to his attention the following exchange took place:

> *Question*: But doesn't this [the respondent's preferred sentencing patterns] contradict something that you were saying earlier that people *shouldn't* be given harsher sentences because of their previous convictions because they were being punished twice?
>
> *Response*: Yeh, but at the end of the day he [the repeat offender described in the scenario] has been done for it three times—so why hasn't he learned from it? I would consider that he's taking the mickey. If he's done it three times he's kicking dirt in your face. You fed him a bit of rope and now he's hung himself.

In light of this response it is hard to classify this individual as being opposed to the recidivist premium.

Similarly, in his comments responding to related questions, Interviewee number 40 appeared to endorse a flat-rate approach to sentencing repeat offenders. However, it became clear that he believed previous convictions were relevant, but only in the case of serious crimes:

> In certain circumstances, yes [taking previous convictions into account was appropriate]. If someone goes out and mugs an old lady and then ten days later goes out and does it again...murders and more serious crimes yes [then] you've got to look at an offender's previous convictions. But for the [less serious] crimes that I committed, I have paid for the crime, and why should I be punished again for that offence? I just don't think that's right at all.

One interviewee was asked why he had prescribed harsher punishments for the repeat offenders. His response was clear: 'Criminal history is what it is. This chap's got four convictions and the sentences they imposed before clearly aren't working. So he needs to learn. Yeh, that's why. Why he's up for a really hefty stretch now. Yeh, it's because of his previous—give him a harsh sentence to teach him a lesson'.

One last somewhat striking feature of the data requires comment. Table 7.1 makes it clear that the sentences 'imposed' by the offenders were significantly harsher than the sentences that they expected the courts to impose. Thus the participants seemed to favour harsher sentences than they believed the courts would impose. This finding may be explained by comments that many made about the offenders described in the scenarios. These comments were quite negative; participants appeared to be distancing themselves from the offenders that they were being asked to sentence. Their comments focused on the criminal histories of the offenders described in the scenarios. It is possible that the participants wished to distinguish between their own offending histories and the offenders described in the scenarios, and one way of underlining this point was to respond in a quite punitive fashion. Once it became clear that participants were imposing sentences in excess of the predicted court sentence, this was raised in the interview, but the offenders with whom this issue was discussed offered no commentary on this fact.

Justifying the Premium

Pedagogical Function of Recidivist Premium

How do convicted offenders who see some legitimacy in the practice of harsher sentencing for recidivists justify the practice? When asked to justify the policy one respondent answered: 'Obviously the punishment wasn't hard enough the first time. You have got to stop someone from reoffending. Whatever's happened before [the previous sentence] had no effect whatever.' This perspective is consistent with one of the few previous studies exploring offenders' perceptions of the sentencing process. Ekstedt (1988) found that two-thirds of his sample of convicted offenders agreed that prison should be used if an offender continued to reoffend after having been sentenced to a non-custodial sentence.

Generally speaking, participants in the present study had little to say regarding the justifications offered to them at sentencing for a recidivist sentencing premium. It was clearly not an issue that had been discussed by the court or had come up in conversations with their solicitors. When asked whether a court had explained why previous convictions should be taken into account, an offender with many convictions answered: 'No, no, never.'

A number of explanations were offered by the participants in response to the question about why the courts consider previous convictions. The most frequent justification involved the need to arrest the offender's criminal career by teaching them the wrongfulness of offending:

Comments about sentencing as a learning experience

- He needs to be punished [more]—he hasn't learned, has he?
- It's not unfair—if they have gone back again, then six month's didn't work for that person and the courts have to try something else.
- Because you did the crime again. You didn't learn about it.
- Quite frankly I do [agree with the recidivist premium]. If they are going to continue to offend they must be punished more harshly than first offenders.
- Definitely. They have got to learn—let them know that they're bang out of order.
- I assume that if you have been convicted you would be aware of the implications and should have adjusted your life accordingly.
- Obviously it [criminal history] gives you an idea of the offender. The nature of the crime is different if he's done previous. Otherwise it looks like they're [repeat offenders] walking over the system.
- A harsher sentence is correct; they [repeat offenders] obviously didn't learn the first time that the more you do something the more you get [punished].
- I do think that people who have been in trouble before and have been convicted before should get harsher sentences—at least until they have learned their lesson.
- He's taking the piss. He keeps doing it. If they keep doing the same thing, they haven't learned.

Double punishment for the same offence?

Not a single interviewee in the current study involving repeat offenders spontaneously mentioned the 'double punishment for the same offence' objection to a recidivist sentencing premium.[7]

[7] One participant did disagree with the cumulative sentencing model, and stated that it was unfair. However, later in the interview he changed his position and

However, the interview schedule included a section where this argument against the premium was made explicit and presented to participants. Interviewees were asked the following question: '*Some people argue that courts should punish offenders with previous convictions more harshly. Others say that this is unfair, and that these people have already been punished for their earlier crimes. Which of these two views come closest to your own?*'.

Even when the counter argument to the recidivist premium was made salient in this way and put directly to the interviewee to consider, only a few participants seemed in agreement. One individual who did agree stated the following: 'I don't think it's fair. Whatever sentence they give you it should be the be all and end all. It [the previous conviction] should not rear its ugly head every year because they do that—they never get scrubbed. If you have done your time you should be given a new chance; what you did before should be wiped. It's done.'

Another individual conceded that as the interval between episodes of offending increased the double punishment argument had some merit: 'it was a valid point if the time lapse was, say, five years'. By this he meant that a harsher sentence for a conviction acquired as long as five years ago seemed unfair, whereas if the previous conviction occurred just a few months ago, it was appropriate to impose a harsher sentence. Another individual noted that: 'It's a fair argument; you have done the time and it shouldn't be brought up again, but it's not a fair world.' Finally, there was also some cynicism expressed with respect to the double punishment argument. For example, one respondent stated: 'fair enough, I've pulled that one too....'

Alternative views regarding the recidivist premium

A number of participants expressed the view that the sentencing process was too mechanical and needed to make a greater effort to understand why the offender was being re-sentenced, rather than simply punishing him or her for the repeat offending. Unsurprisingly, perhaps, they were interested in the relationship between offenders' needs and the response of the court at the time

expressed clear support for a 'three strikes' sentencing law. In addition, when asked to impose sentence in response to the sentencing scenarios he imposed sentences that rose in severity to reflect the seriousness of the offender's criminal history.

of sentencing. One stated that: 'If somebody's committing a crime over and over then they [the courts] need to be looking at other options—what the person's needs are...'. Another participant noted that 'it depends on the nature of the second crime—if it were the same as the first then he might be a risk; but jail is not always the answer'. This same respondent assigned a five year sentence in response to the third vignette, but added mandatory therapy to 'see why [the offender] was doing it'. One participant in his thirties had accumulated over ten convictions. He expected that the offender in the third vignette would get six years, and assigned the same sentence himself but added that: 'I would want to know why he was doing so many robberies. I think that they should do it another way—they can't keep sending you back to prison every time they need to start thinking about what else to do'.

Another individual highlighted the importance of considering the origin of offending and reoffending: 'I would take a look at the gentleman's background and try and get an explanation as to why the offence occurred. If it was drug related I would sentence him to a drug rehabilitation order because even though it was a severe offence [street robbery] he needs to be more structured in his way of life. I wouldn't just send him to prison.' However even this participant imposed a more punitive custodial sentence in the second and third offending scenarios: 'If she's done it before she's not actually learned so what I would do is give a short prison sentence...'. With respect to the offender with the worst criminal record this participant favoured imposing two years imprisonment: 'he's carried on thinking he can get away with it'.

Dimensions of criminal record

Despite their lack of awareness of the statutory sentencing provisions relating to recency and relevance, participants were clearly sensitive to these dimensions of an offender's previous convictions. Thus in response to a question about the importance of previous convictions, an individual with more then ten previous convictions stated that 'it depends on the period of time since the last offence and whether the new offence is the same [as the previous offence]'. It is interesting to note, however, that none of the participants evinced any awareness of the provision in the Act that places the concepts of recency and relevance on a statutory footing. Another interviewee observed that 'everyone deserves a chance to change' to support his position that previous convictions should lose their significance more rapidly than was, in his experience at least, currently the case.

Interviewee 20 stated that 'even though they're five years down the road [ie, in the past] they're still bringing them up which isn't right; I might have previous convictions seven years ago and they are still bringing it up and holding it against me; they say "look at your criminal record". In some ways they [previous convictions] should be considered but not when they're so far down the line [in the past]'. Some interviewees objected to the inferences that they thought were being drawn by courts when hearing about previous convictions: 'If it's five years [since the last conviction] and you've kept your nose clean then it's spent [irrelevant]. But they bring it up again like you've been doing that all through the past five years.' One participant objected to the longevity of a criminal record. He gave the example of a caution he had received: 'I was cautioned for asking for money five years ago and that caution is on record for eternity.'

Other participants stated that the length of time between episodes of offending would influence whether he would favour a harsher sentence. In the words of one interviewee: 'it depends how long [it's been] from his last conviction; if he has been out of trouble for a while'. Another interviewee also took issue with what he perceived as a rather mechanical application of the premium when he stated: 'they shouldn't just have an extra six months for a crime you did six months ago'.

An individual with many previous convictions was asked 'How would you feel if down the road, say five years down the line, you are reconvicted and these convictions came up again?' He responded in the following way: 'I suppose that depends on what I will have done. If I was done again for a violent offence [after having previously been convicted of a violent offence] I suppose that's fair [but] I wouldn't find it fair if I had been good for a long time.' Similarly, other interviewees noted that: 'If the previous [conviction] was two years ago they should let it go and start again. The way that I look at it, what's in the past is in the past. I can understand if it's a rapist then a judge has a right to bring it up. But when it's just petty things I don't think they should judge you on that' and 'A lot of people should be given more help for the drugs—if you keep sentencing them they will become institutionalized.' A significant number of the participants clearly resented what they perceived to be a mechanistic application of the recidivist sentencing premium. However, their views were consistent with the statute and judicial practice regarding the significance of two principal dimensions of criminal history: recency and relevance.

Of the two dimensions there was more support for the relevance dimension. By relevance the participants appeared to mean relatedness. A number of participants argued that previous convictions should count at sentencing only when they revealed a pattern of similar criminal conduct over a number of sentencing occasions. Although the nature of the interviewees' criminal histories was not explored in the interviews,[8] their spontaneous comments suggested that consistent with research on criminal histories, they contained a variety of offences. The relatively punitive responses of participants when asked to sentence the scenarios and their spontaneous comments suggested that many subscribed to a perception of 'specialists'—individuals who were committed to a specific criminal lifestyle which involved repeat offending of a similar nature. This label seemed to be one that they were eager to use to distinguish themselves from consideration as specialists. With respect to the temporal dimension, two general themes emerged. First, the 'inclusion' period was according to many to be too long. A number of participants expressed resentment at what they perceived to be the automatic invocation of previous convictions that had been acquired years before. Their argument was that in the time since the previous sentencing they had changed their lives sufficiently so that the previous convictions were no longer relevant to their current circumstances.

Distinguishing among offenders

Some participants made a distinction between categories of repeat offenders. Thus one individual affirmed that:

> You've got the criminals who go out and constantly reoffend and they know why they're doing it—money, drugs or whatever. Then you've got the other side of the coin. Criminals who commit crimes through circumstances—like I kept my nose clean for five years then I had a bad year and

[8] In light of the volume of priors disclosed by participants, asking them to identify the nature of their previous convictions would have been time consuming, and some individuals might not have wanted to discuss their previous offending.

this happened. Now if that bad year hadn't happened I wouldn't be here now. It wasn't as if the offence was premeditated.

Interviewee 40 had accumulated over ten previous convictions, all but one of which was for speeding offences. He resented what he perceived to be an implication that he was a persistent offender because of the one other previous conviction for public damage:

> You go to court now and they bring up stuff from 1989 [the year of the previous damage conviction]. They say that it's a habit—you're a persistent offender. But 1989! How can that be a pattern? This was public damage—but all my previous [convictions] are for driving offences. And, as they are talking about me, I'm thinking: 'Am I in the right room here? Are they getting me mixed up with someone else?' They try to make you out like you are a repeat criminal. If I break a window in 1989 and a fence in 2006 I would hardly say that's a repeat offender. Things happen in life. I wouldn't say it was a regular occurrence and to be re-punished for it—well it's a bit harsh.

Another way that participants decided whether the recidivist sentencing premium was appropriate invoked the theme of change in a person's life. One interviewee captured an opinion expressed by others when he said the following (in response to the question of whether the recidivist premium was fair): 'It depends if they have made an effort to change. If they haven't, if they are constantly doing it, then there's no intention of changing in which case it [the recidivist sentencing premium] is fair.'

A number of offenders expressed dismay at the asymmetry of the use of previous convictions when sentencing offenders. Courts looked back to learn about the offender, but did not look past the negative elements, namely the previous convictions:

> It's a bit judgmental really. People can change. Previous convictions are taken from the past and I think they should take into account how the person changes in the past. In some way it's fair [considering previous convictions]. You have to find out who the person [before the court for sentencing] is, but previous convictions just tell you about the bad side of a person. It paints a bad picture.

Interviewee 54 reflected the perspective held by many others that the seriousness of the prior convictions was important. She did not think that prior convictions should be taken into account unless 'they [the offenders] were hurting people; well then yes—why shouldn't they be punished more?' But she opposed the use of prior convictions if they were minor 'for shoplifting or whatever'.

Scepticism about deterrent value of a recidivist sentencing premium

While many respondents expressed the view that the recidivist sentencing premium was designed to 'teach offenders not to reoffend' there was widespread scepticism expressed about the deterrent effect of such a sentencing policy, particularly when the recidivist premium simply resulted in the imposition of longer prison terms. This is consistent with earlier research involving sentenced offenders in other jurisdictions (eg, Arcuri 1976; Australian Law Reform Commission 1980;[9] Lyon et al 2000[10]). Arcuri's interviews with inmates revealed that by a margin of more than two to one participants rejected the position that harsher sentences were an effective deterrent to offending (Arcuri 1976). In response to a question about the effectiveness of deterrent sentencing another respondent observed: 'No it doesn't work. The jail's not a deterrent. Doesn't matter how long you're going to be put away. [If] someone's done a £60,000 robbery they know they're going to jail; it doesn't matter how long.' One participant expressed his view about a policy of imposing progressively harsher sentences in the following way: 'We hit him with a stick last time and it didn't work, so we'll hit him again—but harder this time. I am not sure that this [policy] will do what the people behind it assume it will do.' Others concurred with this view, as the following comments illustrate:

- To be honest I can't say it does [deter]. I know people with long records and they still go out and do it.
- There's a whiplash effect. If you have loads and loads of prison you come out without a job, without a place to live. It destroys your life. All they want to do is go back to prison. For people who go back to prison it is not a deterrent.
- [Deterrence] just doesn't happen. I know a lot of people and they have offended and offended; it just doesn't seem to work.

[9] In its report the Commission concluded that 'Consistently, respondents felt tough sentences were not likely to prevent serious crime'. (p 31). Over four-fifths of the offenders surveyed disagreed with the proposition that 'if you want to lower the crime rate you've got to make sentences tougher' (p 31).

[10] The young offenders interviewed for the Home Office research reported by Lyon et al used remarkably similar language to describe the failure of prisons to deter: 'prison doesn't work. It's the fear of coming to prison that works…[but] once you're here it doesn't work.' (2000: 43).

- They [repeat offenders] still haven't learned a lesson; but it doesn't work. You get used to prison and then it's not a big thing anymore.
- Jail's not a deterrent for me. The people I met in there—it wasn't a deterrent for them to be honest. You go inside right—so who are you in there with? Other criminals. So what do you talk about? 'We'll do this or that.' You learn a lot of things.
- Deterrence doesn't work—a lot of them [prisoners] just get out and reoffend.
- I don't think it is true [that deterrence works] there are people who are going to reoffend no matter what. I don't think [harsher sentences for recidivists] is a deterrent.
- No I don't think it is [a deterrent]. Prison is a bit scary—but after 20 minutes there I said to myself: 'It's not so bad.' It should be more punishing. It's not that bad.
- No it's no deterrent. If they have been back and forth in the courts for a similar crime then obviously it's not working. If they have been to prison and they're back again it's not worked.
- Does it deter? Not at all, not in the slightest. Prisons are too easy—not like in other countries. You've got everything you need. Some homeless people get [themselves] sent to prison in winter.

Attitudes to the use of custody as a sanction

In addition to the scepticism about deterrence voiced by most participants there was clear opposition to the use of imprisonment: a significant majority expressed the view that the repetitive imposition of prison sentences was counterproductive as the following examples illustrate:

- Then they go to prison again, it's a school of crime—why don't they teach them something? They come out and do the same old crime, same old drugs and reoffend again. Why the hell are they sending them back into prison, into schools of crime and at £500 a week? Why don't they spend half that money educating the geezer?
- If you're a repeat offender obviously jail's doing you no good... At the end of the day if you have done it again the judicial system should look at why they are doing it again. Jail's

a deterrent until you've been there—I know a lot of criminals what would prefer to go to prison than do community work.

- Prison's not a deterrent; it's more of a destructive force in the life of the individual.
- I don't believe that [it works]. You just get into a routine in prison where your responsibility for your life is taken away from you. You get a roof over your head (even though it's not a great one). You get three meals and you do your time. It doesn't rectify anything. For me prison didn't make me think 'I better not do another crime.' I just thought 'How much time do I have left?' [on my prison term].
- It makes more sense if somebody has more previous convictions, then they do deserve to be sentenced more harshly but it doesn't necessarily mean locking them up in a little metal box. I don't think prison works.

Excessive focus of the court on the crime

Many participants held the view that courts often failed to consider more than just the seriousness of the crime and the number of previous convictions. This is part of a more general view of many offenders that courts and criminal justice professionals paid insufficient attention to them as individuals.[11] One respondent noted that: 'They only see the crime, they don't take into account the circumstances.' Another individual concurred, saying that: 'The judge at the end of the day is not seeing a person.' A recurrent theme in the interviews was that courts adopted a relatively simplistic approach to sentencing, meting out sentences to reflect the seriousness of the crime and the number of previous convictions, but little more. Few comments were made about pre-sentence reports (PSR), although when they were they tended to be positive; offenders saw the PSR as an example of a more individualized approach. Thus: 'Pre-sentence reports were meticulous, but the problem is that [sentencing] is too formulaic.' Not surprisingly perhaps, respondents seemed far more sensitive to

[11] Indeed the very positive response of participants—far in excess of the modest remuneration they received for participating in the research—is evidence that many offenders wish to be heard, having spent more time listening than speaking in their careers through the courts. A number of participants seemed astonished that their views were being solicited, even in the context of a research project.

the complexities of offending, to the many pressures that may provoke offending, as well as to the circumstances that would promote desistance.

Participant 66 had considerable experience with sentencing, having accumulated more than 30 convictions. He noted that:

> They don't actually look at you as a person or if you've changed since your last conviction. Quite a lot of people change. They just look at your record and go by that. The prosecution and the judge just see you as a persistent offender, look at you more as a persistent offender—someone who goes out to offend on purpose. When I've been in court [for sentencing] they have just looked at my record, they see how many previous offences I've got and go by that. They need to look more at what the person's achieved as well as what bad things he's done. The good things are never recognized in court.

When asked to consider imposing sentence themselves (see earlier sections of this chapter) many of the interviewees often stressed the need to look beyond the crime and the offender's previous convictions to consider the circumstances that may have given rise to the offending. One particularly thoughtful respondent noted that: 'Again I would go back to the reason for the offending—I would want to know why the person is doing this and that, and I would [impose] counselling or training. You've got to ask the questions "Why?" "What is the point?" You've got to address the reasons why [the offence occurred]. Was it drugs?'

One interviewee contrasted his experience with two different judges. According to this individual, the first judge had simply imposed sentence without much apparent reflection while the second had, in this respondent's view at least, taken some time to consider the reasons for his offending. In his words: 'He listened to the reasons for the crime. The other didn't give any thought to the circumstances at the time...It's not just a case of punishing you.' Another individual asserted that 'for many people it's a cry for help; so you have to look at the reasons for why these offences occurred'. Finally, one participant argued that being sentenced following a guilty plea prevented the court from hearing the offender's side of events, and he regarded this as unfair: 'Sentencing is not fair if you plead guilty because then it's over and done with. If you plead not guilty then there's a chance for you to say something and for witnesses to say something.' This perspective of offenders resonates with findings from previous research. Lyon et al (2000) found that young offenders held the same view, as expressed by one individual who observed that 'They [the courts] should take more notice of your pre-sentence reports as well because they don't. I got a pre-sentence report [but] they just turn a blind eye don't they? They don't look at your background or anything' (Lyon et al 2000: 27).

In general, offenders objected to what they perceived to be a mechanical application of the recidivist sentencing premium, particularly when it resulted in longer terms of custody. While they mostly appeared to accept the principle of progressively more severe sanctions to reflect the accumulation of convictions, they clearly saw the need for a more thoughtful judicial application of the principle, one which would consider more carefully the causes of the repeat offending, as well as one which would weigh against the fresh offences any substantial intervals of desistance.

Summary and conclusions

The interviews conducted during this research generated a number of counter-intuitive findings. The sentencing preferences of the offenders followed a recidivist sentencing model: the participants assigned harsher punishments when the scenario described a repeat offender. There was also a high degree of concordance between participants' expectations of sentencing patterns and their own sentencing preferences. Moreover, since three levels of criminal history were employed in the scenarios it was possible to demonstrate that offender sentencing preferences did not conform to a progressive loss of mitigation model: in their sentences the participants distinguished between recidivist offenders with criminal histories of varying seriousness. However, a clear schism emerged with respect to the way that previous convictions should be used at sentencing. A number of participants were of the view that the court should do more than simply record the previous convictions and adjust the sentence accordingly. To many participants, the previous convictions represented a source of information for the court that indicated the offender had a problem that should be addressed. In their view however, the courts failed to take the opportunity to consider this information, preferring instead to simply impose harsher punishments to reflect the prior offending.

The narratives emerging from the interviews with repeat offenders throw into stark relief the fissure between the sentencer and the sentenced. The courts' attempt to impose consistent sentencing seemed invisible to those appearing for sentencing. To people being sentenced, the imposition of punishment was perceived as an almost random event in which extra-legal factors are highly predictive of the sanction ultimately imposed. The offenders clearly regarded judges and magistrates as lacking what might be termed 'penal imagination', in the sense that they appeared to make few or limited attempts to understand the origin of the criminal behaviour for which the offenders were being sentenced. In the concluding chapter of this volume I consider the implications of these views for the way that previous convictions are currently conceptualized and considered at sentencing. For the present however, it seems clear that the progressive escalation of punishments to reflect the increase in previous convictions is generally consistent with the views of the offenders on whom the practice is imposed. Although these individuals took issue with some aspects of the way the principle is applied in practice, they accepted the legitimacy of the recidivist sentencing premium. The extent to which this principle is consistent with the views of the 'intuitive sentencer' will be the subject of the next two chapters.

8

The *Intuitive Sentencer*: Public Attitudes to Prior Offending

Questions of fairness and justice are not the exclusive property of the victim, offender, judge or legislator but can be asked from the broader perspective of justice in the community. (Davies 1993: 16).

Where does the *intuitive sentencer* stand with respect to the use of previous convictions at sentencing? At first glance the answer would seem straightforward. As Tonry (2004) notes, 'many people have an intuition that offenders who have previously been convicted of a crime should be dealt with more harshly' (2004: 117). In 2003, The *Observer* newspaper in Britain commissioned a survey of the general public which contained the following question: '*Would you support or oppose the introduction of a "three strikes and you're out" scheme whereby offenders automatically receive a prison sentence if they are convicted of any three crimes?*' Four-fifths of the polled public endorsed this tough recidivist sentencing proposal (*Observer*, 2003). A decade earlier exactly the same proportion of American respondents expressed support for a law that imposed life imprisonment on offenders convicted of a serious felony for the third time (see Roberts 1996, 2003c). These results suggest that public support for cumulative sentencing is overwhelming—and for an offender convicted for only the third time. In reality, community reaction to the punishment of repeat offenders is more nuanced. This is one of many instances in which polls conceal more than they reveal about public attitudes to criminal justice issues, particularly in the area of sentencing (for other examples and discussion, see Roberts and Hough 2005).

Overview

This chapter and the next explore the nature of public reaction to the sentencing of repeat offenders. First I discuss related research in the field of public attitudes to sentencing. This is followed by a description of findings from original research drawing upon a survey of the public in Britain. Having established that the public believes that previous convictions should be considered at sentencing—albeit within limits—Chapter 9 explores the reasons for public attitudes towards this issue.

Public attitudes towards an offender's previous convictions

A wealth of research has accumulated upon the subject of public attitudes to sentencing—both in Britain and elsewhere (see Walker and Hough 1988; Roberts 1992; Flanagan and Longmire 1996; Roberts and Stalans 1997; Cullen et al 2000; Roberts and Hough 2005; Wood and Viki 2004, for reviews) although attitudes to the role of previous convictions at sentencing remain unexplored. Before reviewing the relevant research, it is worth noting that the relevance of previous criminal misconduct for public opinion is not restricted to the sentencing process.

Impact of previous criminal misconduct at other stages of the criminal process

The public regard previous convictions as being relevant to decisions taken throughout the criminal process, both before and after conviction. The importance of antecedent criminal conduct also emerges from research in which members of the public are asked about alternatives to prosecution. A recent study conducted by the MORI organization in Britain is illustrative. A representative sample of the public was asked to identify the most appropriate resolution to a case in which an adult had admitted speeding (driving at 40 miles per hour in a 30 mph zone). When this transgression was the individual's first offence, 45% of the sample favoured imposing a caution or doing 'nothing at all'. When the incident was the individual's second speeding offence only 5% chose this response (Office for Criminal Justice Reform 2006). The number of previous convictions also influences the level of public support for the transfer of juveniles to criminal court. Applegate, Davis, and Cullen (2007) found that there was a clear tendency towards favouring transfer when the juvenile suspect had multiple contacts with the juvenile justice system.

Cumberland and Zamble (1992) measured the impact of previous convictions upon public decisions regarding release on parole. Members of the Canadian public were given a series of parole applications to consider. Each file included a description of a prisoner who was applying for parole having served part of a sentence of imprisonment for aggravated assault, robbery, or burglary. Participants were asked to choose from a range of responses to the application, including granting, denying, or deferring release on parole. Unsurprisingly, study participants were less likely to grant parole if the prisoners were serving time for a serious offence or had refused to participate in institutional programmes. However, the presence of previous convictions also resulted in much lower parole grant rates from members of the public (Cumberland and Zamble 1992). More recently, a survey of Massachusetts residents found that repetitive non-compliance with parole conditions provokes a more punitive response from the public. Respondents were asked what should happen to a parolee who had failed a routine drug test. If it was the first such occurrence only 17% of the sample supported returning the offender to prison; however, half the respondents favoured reincarceration if the violation was his second such transgression (Roberts, Clawson, Doble, Selton, and Briker 2005).

Public models of sentencing

Insight into public reaction to sentencing repeat offenders can be gleaned from research exploring public models of sentencing. Members of the public are eclectic sentencers; they align themselves behind different sentencing objectives according to key case characteristics such as the nature and seriousness of the offence. Polling from Canada, New Zealand, and elsewhere has demonstrated that public support for different sentencing purposes varies according to the seriousness of the case under consideration. For example, a representative sample of the public in Canada was asked to identify the most important purpose for sentencing minor and serious offenders. The purposes chosen by the public were quite different for the two categories of offenders. Individual deterrence and general deterrence were identified as most important for minor offenders; proportional sentencing and incapacitation were most important when sentencing serious cases (Canadian Sentencing Commission 1987; Roberts 1988).

More recent data from New Zealand sustain the same pattern of public sentencing preferences, but this time for specific offences. For example, 39% of respondents support rehabilitation as the primary purpose for offenders convicted of cannabis possession, while only 8% support this goal when sentencing offenders convicted of fraud (see Paulin, Searle, and Knaggs 2003).

These data on public support for sentencing objectives make it clear that with respect to sentencing philosophies the public cannot be easily categorized as endorsing one perspective to the exclusion of all others. In fact, members of the public respond in complex ways to questions about sentencing, and in this respect they are no different from professional judges. Despite this propensity on the part of the public to select different sentencing objectives for different crimes, some general lessons may be drawn about community support for competing sentencing philosophies. One such lesson is that there is widespread popular support for proportionality in sentencing across all jurisdictions in which polls have been conducted.

Public support for proportional sentencing

Support for proportional sentencing emerges from a number of public opinion surveys conducted in a variety of jurisdictions over the past 20 years.[1] For example, Darley, Carlsmith, and Robinson (2000) asked subjects to assign penalties to offenders described in brief scenarios. The crimes varied in seriousness and the offenders varied in terms of their likelihood of reoffending. Darley et al (2000) report that participants were influenced primarily by just deserts considerations and far less by the offender's likelihood of rehabilitation. Carlsmith, Darley, and Robinson (2002) found that although subjects expressed strong support for deterrence theory, when asked to sentence offenders they followed a

[1] Sharp and Otto (1909) report the earliest empirical demonstration of public support for retributive sentencing. University students were given a description of the sentencing problem attributed to Kant in which, just prior to being disbanded due to rescue, an island society is confronted with dealing with an offender convicted of murder and who has been sentenced to death. Utilitarian sentencers would see no purpose to executing the offender since the island society is about to dissolve. However, the majority of participants in the study approved of the execution of the offender despite there being no utilitarian purpose to carrying out the sentence.

retributive approach. Gebotys and Roberts (1987) demonstrated the same phenomenon using a sample of Canadian subjects (see also Hamilton and Rytina 1980). Sentences derived from members of the public were highly related to the seriousness of the crime. Most recently a national survey conducted in the United States found that ensuring proportional punishments emerged as being as important to the public as 'keeping violent offenders in prison' (see Princeton Survey Research Associates International 2006). These trends may suggest that the public align themselves behind one of the two desert-based approaches to the use of previous convictions at sentencing. However, the public appear to reject both these models, in favour of a third possibility which incorporates previous convictions albeit with proportional limits.

Public support for sentencing factors

Clear evidence of the public's interest in an offender's previous convictions comes from surveys in which respondents are asked about factors relevant to sentencing. For example, Russell and Morgan (2001) report findings from a survey conducted for the Sentencing Advisory Panel in England and Wales. Respondents were asked to spontaneously identify aggravating factors relevant to the offence of burglary. After the presence of injury to the victim, the existence of previous convictions was the most frequently mentioned factor. As one individual noted in a subsequent interview, 'If they are a persistent offender then other punishments have not worked so they should get a higher sentence...so if the typical burglar should get three years [a repeat offender] should get four years' (Russell and Morgan 2001: 50). Similarly, when the individual had no previous convictions there was less support among respondents for the imprisonment of the offender. Comparable findings emerge from the British Crime Survey. For example, the 1992 administration asked respondents to identify the factors which aggravate a sentence. As Hough notes, 'the most striking example involved criminal history' (1992: 7).

In older studies conducted in Canada, Australia, and the United States, representative surveys of the public were also asked to identify the factors that a judge should generally consider at sentencing. In Canada, the offender's criminal record and the seriousness of the offence were identified as being the most important variable by the same percentage of respondents (Doob and Roberts 1983).

Indermaur (1990) reports findings from an Australian survey that found that criminal history was the second most frequently-cited sentencing factor (after the seriousness of the offence). A survey of US respondents found that 88% of the sample held the view that sentencing should be tougher if the accused 'has previously been convicted of the same crime' (National Centre for State Courts 1978). When respondents were asked to consider an offender with a record in which the offence was not similar, almost as many people (81%) agreed that the sentence should be tougher, suggesting that similarity of past to present offending was not critical to justify a recidivist sentencing premium.

Studies conducted in a number of other jurisdictions (including Belgium and South Africa) have generated the same finding. In a survey of the Belgian public respondents were given a list of factors and asked to identify those factors that they would take into account at sentencing. Approximately equal percentages of respondents chose the seriousness of the crime (73%) and the criminal record of the offender (70%; see Versele, Goffin, Tsamadou, Legros, and Van Haecht 1972; see also Glanz 1994).

A compelling demonstration of public support for the use of previous convictions as a sentencing factor comes from research conducted by the Home Office Sentencing Review in 2001 (Home Office 2001). Members of the British public were asked to identify the factors that 'should have a great deal of influence on a sentence'. (Respondents were allowed to identify more than a single factor.) Table 8.1 summarizes the sentencing factors that were endorsed by at least 25% of the sample. As can be seen, the most popular factor by far was the offender's criminal record, endorsed by almost nine out of ten respondents. This level of support is far higher than even the impact of the crime on the victim, a factor that is usually very important for members of the public.[2]

The most recent study of public opinion and sentencing factors confirms previous findings. In research for the Sentencing Advisory Panel (in England and Wales) Hough et al (2007) manipulated the presence or absence of a number of mitigating and aggravating factors in crime scenarios presented to a representative sample of

[2] Researchers also posed this question to a sub-sample of members of the public who were given information about crime and punishment. The views of this 'informed' group were the same: 92% of respondents endorsed the use of previous convictions as a sentencing factor (see Home Office 2001: 109).

Table 8.1 Public support for sentencing factors, Britain

Factor	Percentage of sample endorsing factor
Previous convictions	86%
Likelihood of reoffending	72%
Whether crime was planned	68%
Impact of crime upon the victim	54%
Whether offender was mentally ill at the time of the offending	53%
Whether the particular crime is a problem in the area	47%
Whether offender has made amends to the crime victim	28%

Source: adapted from Home Office (2001)

the British public. The most powerful sentencing factor by far was the presence of previous convictions.[3] The public interest in the offender's past was also clear from discussions in the course of focus groups conducted as part of the same research project (see Hough et al 2007).

Impact of previous convictions on public sentencing preferences[4]

Further evidence of the importance that the public ascribes to previous convictions can be found in another branch of public opinion research. A common research strategy over the last 40 years consists of providing people with brief scenarios describing criminal cases (eg, Knight 1965; Doob and Roberts 1983). Respondents are then asked to impose a sentence, with or without a 'menu' of sentencing options. In several such studies the extent of the offender's previous convictions has been manipulated. One

[3] For example, when the offender had previous convictions the average term of imprisonment imposed by respondents rose by from 21 to 34 months. (The crime involved causing death through careless driving.) To place this increase in context, if the offender had fled the scene—a very important aggravating circumstance—the average sentence increased by only seven months.

[4] This chapter explores findings from public opinion polls. When laypersons sentence as lay magistrates they also impose harsher sentences on repeat offenders (see Diamond 1990: Table 8).

of the most robust findings from this literature is that members of the public assign harsher penalties to repeat offenders.

In research by Tufts and Roberts (2002) respondents to a nationwide survey were asked to sentence first offenders and recidivists who were either juveniles or adults and who had been convicted of burglary or minor assault. The incarceration rates derived from public sentencing preferences were significantly higher for the adult offenders and for the more serious crime of burglary than for minor assault. However, the offender's criminal history also proved to be a highly significant predictor of whether the respondent favoured incarcerating the offender. In fact, the odds of choosing a prison sentence were five times higher if the offender was a repeat rather than a first offender (Tufts and Roberts 2002). Data from the British Crime Survey make the same point. When respondents were asked to sentence a first time juvenile, 9% of respondents favoured custody. If the juvenile was being sentenced for the third time, 59% of the sample imposed imprisonment (Mattinson and Mirrlees-Black 2000). Finally, the aggravating effect of previous convictions on public sentencing preferences emerges in a diversity of countries. Sanders and Hamilton (1992) report findings from surveys of the public in Japan and Russia and found the same pattern in both locations: respondents assigned a significantly higher average number of years when sentencing an offender with a criminal record.

This finding alone establishes that the 'flat-rate' desert model is inconsistent with public opinion but fails to resolve the question of whether the public endorse the progressive loss of mitigation model or an overt cumulative sentencing position. What is needed is a study in which the number of priors is systematically varied, to see whether this generates a monotonic rise in sentence severity—as predicted by the cumulative model. A good example of such a study can found in public opinion research conducted by John Doble in the United States (Doble Research Associates 1995).

Respondents were asked to sentence an offender convicted of shoplifting $300 of clothing. The offender was described as holding a steady job and having three young children. The number of his previous convictions was manipulated, with different groups of subjects being told that he had one, two, or six previous convictions for the same offence within the past five years. Subjects were then asked to sentence the offender. Support for incarcerating the individual rose in direct relation to the number of prior convictions. When the offender was described as having one prior conviction, 37% of the sample favoured incarceration. This rose to 45% when he had two previous convictions and 83% when he had accumulated six priors (Doble Research Associates 1995). Studies in several other states have demonstrated this escalating incarceration rate associated with more extensive criminal histories and with a variety of criminal offences (eg, see Doble and Klein 1989; English, Crouch, and Pullen 1988; Gandy and Galaway 1980; Mande and English 1989; Mande and Butler 1982; Zimmerman, Van Alstyne, and Dunn 1988).

In all these experiments public respondents react more punitively when sentencing repeat offenders. Recidivists are more likely to be imprisoned, and for longer periods, in direct response to the number of their prior convictions. Several studies have also manipulated the relationship between the previous and current offending. When this occurs the public appear very sensitive to this relationship: related priors enhance the recidivist premium. In this way a critical element of the sentencing process in many jurisdictions finds support among members of the community.

Applegate, Cullen, Link, Richards, and Lanza-Kaduce (1996) explored the role of criminal history in a survey of public attitudes to drink-driving. Some predictable findings emerged: the amount of harm caused by a drunk driver was highly predictive of public punitiveness. However, the number of *related* prior arrests was an equally significant predictor of the severity of responses. Applegate et al (1996) report that: 'the number of previous arrests for [drink-driving] was significantly related to increases in punitive attitudes' (p 74). This finding is consistent with earlier research into public sentencing preferences in cases of drink-driving. Applegate et al concluded that the impaired driving laws across the United States that prescribed significantly harsher penalties to reflect the defendant's number of previous convictions are 'largely consistent with the public will' (p 75).

Finally, support for the consideration of prior convictions as a sentencing factor remains strong even when respondents are sensitized to a potentially adverse consequence of such a policy. In research conducted in the United States, respondents were asked whether they supported or opposed 'judges taking into consideration an offender's record...even if this means that those convicted of identical crimes may receive quite different sentences'

(Doble Research Associates 1998). Fully 70% of the sample responded in favour of this proposition.[5]

Public justifications for a recidivist sentencing premium

Do members of the public see a recidivist premium as being justified on grounds of desert or dangerousness? Are assigned sentences harsher for repeat offenders in order to prevent future offending or to reflect enhanced culpability? The studies summarized so far fail to tell us whether members of the public see crime seriousness and criminal history as two separate categories, or whether, like the Home Office Sentencing Review, they take the view that seriousness ratings may be influenced by the offender's previous convictions.

One small-scale study has attempted to disentangle the relationship between crime seriousness and the offender's likelihood of reoffending. Subjects in the research were provided with a brief description of a criminal case and were also asked a series of questions about the sentence that should be imposed. Participants were asked how much prison time the offender 'morally deserves' for the offence, as well as how much time was necessary to protect society from future offending. These responses were designated the *deserved* sentence and the *utilitarian* sentence (see Monahan and Ruggiero 1980; Monahan 1982). In this way researchers hoped to compare the amount of punishment which subjects wished to impose for retributive reasons with the amount they thought was necessary to prevent further offending. The researchers manipulated the criminal record of the offenders described in the scenarios: some offenders had prior convictions while some were first offenders. In addition, the offenders were described as being either low or high risk to reoffend.

The existence of prior convictions increased the severity of sentence imposed upon the offender. Unsurprisingly, both variables (number of previous convictions; recidivism risk) also affected the utilitarian sentence imposed. Subjects were more punitive towards offenders with previous convictions and offenders who were rated as highly likely to reoffend. The researchers also found that these

[5] Thirty-three per cent were strongly in favour, 37% somewhat in favour, 14% somewhat opposed and 14% strongly opposed.

variables exercised a significant impact on the severity of sentence that subjects believed the offender deserved. Moreover, the effect was very striking: subjects perceived the low risk offender (20% chance of reoffending) as deserving a one-year sentence while an offender with a high (80%) likelihood of reoffending was perceived as deserving a six-year term of custody (Monahan and Ruggiero 1980). The results of this experimental study suggest that public conceptions of deserved punishment do not conform to either retributive model.

Public judgments of crime seriousness

The Criminal Justice Act 2003 in England and Wales requires courts to consider an offender's prior history in the determination of crime seriousness. The Act appears to assume that criminal history is an element of offence seriousness. As noted elsewhere (von Hirsch and Roberts 2004), this represents a different version of desert theory, at least as defined in the scholarly literature. Desert theorists argue that an offender's previous convictions have no relevance to the seriousness of the crime. For example, Bagaric argues that 'one hundred burglaries committed by a single offender cause exactly the same amount of harm as one hundred first timers committing a burglary each' (2001: 17).

Retributive theories may regard crime seriousness and offender culpability as independent concepts but the public do not see matters this way.[6] Three small-scale studies have manipulated the criminal history of the offender and asked members of the public to rate the seriousness of their crimes and the findings suggest that public perceptions of crime seriousness are affected by the offender's previous convictions. For example, Hilton (1993) asked a small, convenience sample of members of the public to rate the seriousness of a case of assault. Tellingly, the crime itself was rated as being more serious when the offender had a criminal history. Higginbottom and Zamble (1988) also found that seriousness

[6] Curiously, the literature on perceptions of crime seriousness (eg, Levi and Jones 1985; Parton, Hansel, and Stratton 1991) fails to test the hypothesis. For example, one of the largest crime seriousness investigations—the national survey of crime severity conducted in 1985—explored many aspects of a wide range of crimes, but not the criminal history of the offender (see Wolfgang, Figlio, Tracy, and Singer 1985).

ratings of homicide made by college students were significantly affected by the criminal history of the offender. The same homicide description was rated as being more serious if the offender had a criminal record. Finally, Klein, Newman, Weis, and Bobner (1983) asked a small number of college students to rate the seriousness of a number of crimes and found that for some offences at least, subjects rated the crime itself as being more serious when the offender had a prior arrest.

These findings suggest a clear divergence between lay and professional theories of crime seriousness. Desert theorists see no link between previous convictions and offender culpability. The mitigation allowed first offenders according to the doctrine of progressive loss of mitigation is not extended because they are less culpable but for other reasons (see Chapter 3). And no amount of *previous* offending can change the seriousness of the *current* offence. However, the public appear to be sentencing to reflect a global judgment of the case. This judgment includes an evaluation of the culpability of the offender based in part on his previous conduct. In addition, the concepts of offender culpability and crime seriousness are not, from the public's perspective, independent. A crime committed by a multiple recidivist is viewed as being more serious than the same offence committed by a first offender.

Public attitudes to the recidivist sentencing premium: 2007 study

Previous studies have used small, convenience samples, often college students, who are not necessarily representative of the general public. It is important, when attempting to establish the reactions of the intuitive sentencer, to employ representative samples of respondents. In order to conduct a direct exploration of public attitudes to the recidivist premium, questions were placed on a representative survey of residents of the United Kingdom conducted by the MORI survey company in 2007.[7] The sample

[7] The Ipsos MORI Omnibus survey employs a nationally representative sample of 2,000 adults in Great Britain aged 15 years old or more. The sample reflects the British population in terms of region and area types as well as informant demographics such as gender and age. In order to correct minor deviations from population statistics, a rim weighting system is used which applies weights to defined profiles for age, social grade, region, and working status, all within gender. All

was divided at random into three groups. Each group was asked to consider a different crime scenario, although the three questions posed were common to all. There were thus three conditions in which the number of the offender's previous convictions was manipulated. The offender was described as having no, two or five previous convictions:

a. The crime is a robbery in which £500 worth of property was stolen from the victim. A robbery is a crime where things are taken from a person by force or threats of force—it is also known as mugging. The offender is an adult who has never been convicted of a crime before.
b. The crime is a robbery in which £500 worth of property was stolen from the victim. A robbery is a crime where things are taken from a person by force or threats of force—it is also known as mugging. The offender is an adult who has already been convicted of two crimes before this one.
c. The crime is a robbery in which £500 worth of property was stolen from the victim. A robbery is a crime where things are taken from a person by force or threats of force—it is also known as mugging. The offender is an adult who has already been convicted of five crimes before this one.

The three questions posed to all respondents measured perceptions of: crime seriousness, the probability that the offender would reoffend, and the severity of the sentence that should be imposed.

1. Can you please tell me, on a scale of 1 to 10, where 1 is the least serious crime and 10 is the most serious crime imaginable, how serious you think this crime is?
2. Can you please tell me, on a scale of 1 to 10, where 1 is not at all likely, and 10 is almost certain, how likely you think it is that this individual will commit another crime?
3. Finally, punishment for this crime in this country would probably be a prison sentence. If you were the judge setting the sentence in this case, for how long would you sentence this offender to prison?[8]

interviews are carried out in the respondent's home using the computer assisted personal interviewing (CAPI) technique.

[8] Respondents were steered towards imposing a custodial sentence in order to facilitate statistical analysis and to permit a quantification of the magnitude of

Ratings of crime seriousness and perceptions of risk of reoffending

As can be seen in Table 8.2, public perceptions of the seriousness of the same criminal offence were significantly affected by the criminal record of the offender.[9] The same crime was rated as being significantly more serious when the offender had a criminal record. In addition, a clear cumulative pattern emerged with statistically significant differences among mean scores for all three conditions. The increasing number of previous convictions made a difference to average seriousness ratings between the conditions in which the offender had previous convictions. This finding demonstrates the inherent link in the public mind between the criminal record of the offender and the seriousness of the crime.

Table 8.2 also reveals that respondents rated the offender as more significantly likely to reoffend if he was described as having previous convictions.[10] Moreover, a statistically significant linear trend[11] emerges across the three levels of criminal history convictions: respondents assigned a higher risk of reoffending score to the repeat offenders (see Figure 8.1).[12]

Additional analyses demonstrate the intrinsic relationship between previous offending and crime seriousness. Ratings of crime seriousness were significantly correlated with perceptions of crime risk: if the respondent believed that the offender was likely to reoffend, they tended to rate the crime of which he had just been convicted as a more serious offence ($r = .422$, $\underline{p} < .01$,

the recidivist premium. Despite the wording of the question a small percentage of respondents (less than 3%) provided a community penalty; their responses have not been included in the analysis reported here.

[9] Anova: $\underline{F}\ (2, 1{,}958) = 19.80$, $\underline{p} < .001$; all means were significantly different using the bonferroni multiple comparison method.

[10] Anova: $\underline{F}\ (2, 1{,}958) = 95.94$, $\underline{p} < .001$ all means were significantly different using the bonferroni multiple comparison method.

[11] Anova: $\underline{F}\ (1, 1{,}958) = 171.5$, $\underline{p} < .001$.

[12] Not surprisingly, although both effects reached a high level of statistical significance, the impact of previous convictions was greater upon ratings of recidivism risk than crime seriousness.

Table 8.2 Average ratings of crime seriousness, recidivism risk, and severity of assigned sentence

	First offender	Two previous convictions	Five previous convictions
Seriousness of crime (10 point scale)	7.45_a	7.76_b	8.13_c
Likelihood of reoffending (10 point scale)	7.66_a	8.71_b	8.98_c
Severity of prison sentence (in months)	28.63_a	40.95_b	46.22_c

Note: means with different subscripts are significantly different, p.<.001

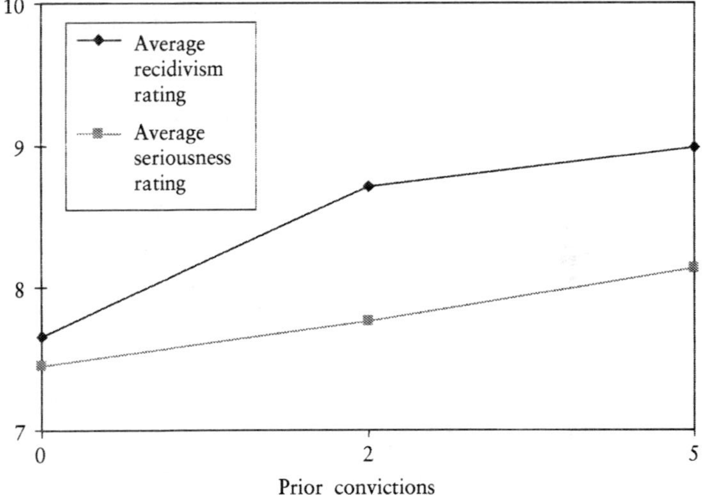

Figure 8.1 Public opinion: average crime seriousness and recidivism risk scores

two-tailed test).[13] Both variables were also significantly correlated with the severity of sentence, although the magnitude of the associations was lower.[14]

[13] Hilton (1993) also found a correlation between ratings of crime seriousness and likelihood of reoffending in her study using a convenience sample of the public.

[14] Crime Seriousness and Sentence Severity: r = +.110; Recidivism Risk and Sentence Severity: r = +.09; both correlations significant at .001 level, two-tailed tests.

Public sentencing preferences

A version of the cumulative sentencing model emerges from these public sentencing preferences. The clearest distinction can be seen between the first and the second scenarios. Respondents sentencing the first offender assigned, on average, a sentence of 28.6 months, compared to 40.9 months for the offender with only two priors. The magnitude of the recidivist premium can be expressed in a number of ways. One method is by calculating how much higher the sentence length imposed in the second scenario is as a function of the average sentence length for the first offender (43%). Thus sentence lengths increased by almost half once the scenario moved from a first offender to an offender with two prior convictions. It is interesting to note, however, that the increment between the second and third scenarios was only 12% (from 40.95 to 46.22 months). The fact that the magnitude of the recidivist premium is far more modest between the more serious cases is significant. The relationship between number of previous convictions and the severity of assigned sentences is presented in Figure 8.2.

Two possible explanations may be offered for this departure from a purely cumulative sentencing model.[15] First, it may be the case that public support for a recidivist premium declines as the policy threatens a more fundamental sentencing principle: proportionality. Second, the limited difference between the two recidivist conditions in light of a large difference between the first offender condition and the offender with two priors may suggest that the public wish to make a clearer distinction between first and repeat offenders than between categories of repeat offenders. The latter explanation is consistent with the previous literature on sentencing preferences which reveals a great difference between first and repeat offenders: the first offender discount

[15] Since the US sentencing guideline systems count more than simply the number of previous convictions, direct comparisons with these public sentencing data are not possible. However, the increments in severity are usually linear as offenders move across the criminal history categories. For example, under the Minnesota sentencing guidelines, first offenders convicted of a category VIII offence are sentenced to an average of 48 months. This average rises 42% to 68 months for offenders with two criminal history points, and the matrix average for offenders with five criminal history points is 44% higher at 98 months (Minnesota Sentencing Guidelines Commission 2006a).

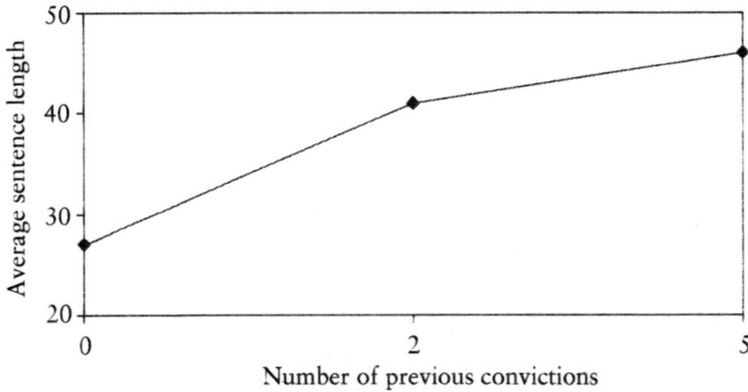

Figure 8.2 Average sentence length (in months) imposed by number of offender's previous convictions

finds considerable support among members of the public,[16] even if they also endorse a policy of progressively escalating penalties for recidivists. Similarly, research into public perceptions of repeat offenders (to be reviewed in the next chapter) demonstrates that people tend to stereotype offenders as recidivists.

This experimental study, using a representative sample of the public, reveals the importance of prior convictions to public perceptions. Crime seriousness ratings were strongly influenced by the prior record of the offender, and the severity of assigned sentences rose to reflect the number of previous convictions. It is worth noting that these effects emerged with a relatively mild manipulation of criminal history. In England and Wales, approximately half the offenders appearing for sentencing in 2003 had more than five previous convictions (Home Office 2007). The data reported here therefore reflect public attitudes to the least serious repeat offenders. The experiment also shows that the public employ criminal history information in a way that is inconsistent with the flat-rate

[16] Although the hypothesis has not been fully explored in the current or previous research, it seems likely that the strong public support for a first offender sentencing discount will be absent when the offender is convicted of a very serious violent crime. In the research conducted by Doble Research Associates (1995) there was almost no support for reduced sentence for an offender convicted of rape. If this failure to offer a discount for first offenders convicted of the most serious crimes can be generalized, members of the public would respond in a way consistent with judicial practice. As noted earlier, the first offender discount is of little benefit to offenders convicted of the most serious offences.

or progressive loss of mitigation model. However, these findings must be seen in the context of other research that demonstrates important limits on public support for a punitive recidivist premium.

Limits on public support for the recidivist sentencing premium

At what point would the public baulk at imposing progressively harsher penalties on repeat offenders? It is tempting to infer, on the basis of the research, that public support for a recidivist sentencing premium has no limits. This inference would be an overstatement. A number of research studies have found that as the recidivist sentencing premium results in increasingly disproportionate punishments, public support declines. Finkel, Maloney, Valbuena, and Groscup (1996) demonstrated the limits of public support in this context. Subjects in this research were asked to assign sentence in one of a number of cases, some of which involved first offenders, others recidivists. The pattern of responses suggested that people sentenced according to a proportionality-based model which assigned some limited role to the offender's previous convictions. The researchers concluded that 'past priors matter and are taken into account in a punishment calculus: Participants did not limit their punishment to the last [ie, instant] offence when they knew there were six priors, but neither did they dramatically, geometrically, or exponentially escalate their punishments because of priors. What we did find is that they sentence in an additive way, with retribution and proportionalism in mind, but refraining from excess' (pp 481–2; see also Applegate, Cullen, Turner, and Sundt (1996) for research showing the limits on public support for recidivist statutes).

Sentencing offenders convicted of multiple offences

Further evidence of the proportionality-based limits on public opinion can be found in research upon attitudes to multiple offence sentencing. Offenders who commit multiple offences over a relatively brief space of time create a challenge for the sentencing process. If the offences are treated as being independent of each other, the overall penalty imposed will be severe. To avoid excessively punishing the offender, sentencers often resort to concurrent sentencing, without which the sentence imposed would be disproportionately severe. For example, an offender sentenced to a year for each of ten burglaries committed over the course of a single night might receive ten concurrent one-year sentences, rather than the ten-year term that a strict accounting of convictions would require.

When viewed in the context of the recidivist sentencing premium, this 'bulk discount' practice creates a clear penological paradox. Consider the recidivist offender versus the offender facing sentencing for multiple offences. The former commits five offences over a two-year period with the result that the fifth and final sentence in the sequence is significantly harsher as a result of the previous four offences. The multiple offence offender commits his five offences within the same twenty-four hour period, but four of the offences are effectively ignored through the imposition of concurrent sentences, or have a modest inflationary effect constrained by the totality sentencing principle.

It is unclear why the impact of the individual offences is discounted in this way; the harm occasioned by a single burglary is surely not diminished by virtue of the fact that it was the fifth in a run of ten—any more than the presence of four previous robberies years ago enhances the seriousness of the current conviction.[17] Concurrent sentencing is an imperfect solution to the problem of sentencing an offender convicted of multiple offences. It creates a legal fiction—that an offender may discharge two or more sentences contemporaneously—and one which offends many crime victims who see the sentence imposed for the harm inflicted upon them effectively erased by means of this sentencing policy.

Public reaction to the problem of sentencing multiple offence cases

If the public follow a cumulative sentencing model, they might be expected to reject the concept of concurrent sentencing in favour

[17] Some models of sentencing may regard the multiple offender convicted of, say, four offences as being less blameworthy than the recidivist convicted of the same number of offences. According to a pedagogical or defiance-based approach, the state has repeatedly brought the recidivist's offending to his attention by means of repeated sentencing decisions; the person convicted of multiple offences has had no such experience on which to draw. The multiple offences may be evidence of greater commitment to the criminal project but they cannot be interpreted as multiple examples of an attempt to defy legal authority.

of the imposition of an independent sentence for each of the multiple offences. The intuitive sentencer's reaction to this sentencing problem was put to the empirical test in research reported by Robinson and Darley (1995). Respondents were asked to assign liability (using a scale) to offenders described in scenarios. In this context liability may serve as a reasonable proxy for sentence severity.[18] Respondents in one experiment were asked to consider the case of offenders convicted of assaults against one, two, four or seven victims over the same day. If respondents were following a cumulative liability model, the offender convicted of assaulting seven victims within a single day would receive a sentence seven times the length of the sentence imposed for an assault of a single victim.

Respondents did assign harsher punishments when multiple assaults were committed. However, as with the pattern of severity described in Figure 8.2 of this chapter, the slope of the line of severity as a function of number of offences did not rise monotonically. Thus the single victim scenario resulted in a liability score of 5.85. However, the average assigned liability in the two victim case was only marginally higher at 6.17, and even the seven victim case attracted an average sentence in the range of seven years—a far cry from the value that would be predicted if subjects were following a cumulative model (see Robinson and Darley 1995: Table 6.12). Robinson and Darley summarize the phenomenon in the following way: 'The greater the number of offenses, the greater the sentence grows... but it does not do so in a linear fashion. Instead it follows the general rule of adding a decreasing increment for each additional offense' (1995: 191–3). As with sentencing the recidivist offender, when sentencing the multiple offender, members of the public seek to avoid a strictly cumulative sentence which would be disproportionate.

Summary and conclusions

The public opinion research reviewed here makes it clear that an offender's criminal antecedents are highly relevant to public

[18] The scale used the following points: 0 = liability but no punishment; 1 = one day; 2 = 2 weeks; 3 = two months; 4 = six months; 5 = one year; 6 = three years; 7 = seven years; 8 = fifteen years; 9 = thirty years; 10 = life imprisonment; 11 = death penalty.

reactions to decision-making at all stages of the criminal process, and particularly at sentencing. This conclusion finds support in public perceptions of sentencing factors, ratings of crime seriousness, and sentencing preferences. It is clear that members of the public are concerned about the mitigating as well as the aggravating power of criminal record. A number of surveys have demonstrated strong support for the imposition of mitigated punishments for first offenders. As one participant noted in the context of a Home Office research study, 'For your first offence you shouldn't really get a lot... everyone's allowed one chance' (Office for Criminal Justice Reform, 2006). Similarly, an individual participating in a focus group discussing the sentencing of driving offences resulting in death made the following distinction between first offenders and recidivists: 'We said it was bad luck in the first instance, didn't we—but if he's got other convictions he is making a habit of it' (Hough et al, 2007).

What lessons should the sentencing process draw from this research? It is clear that the flat-line perspective espoused by some retributivists finds no support among members of the public. If a flat-line sentencing policy were to be implemented, it would surely encounter great public resistance.[19] The progressive loss of mitigation model also seems inconsistent with the views of the public who see a continued relevance to previous convictions beyond the point at which the mitigation afforded first offenders has been lost. Thirty years ago, George Fletcher characterized contemporary support for a recidivist sentencing premium as reflecting a 'theory of social protection rather than a theory of deserved punishment' (1978: 466). The empirical research into community views suggests that this unidimensional interpretation is incorrect.

Public support for the recidivist sentencing premium rests principally on three branches: first, repeat offenders are perceived as being more culpable; second, crime by recidivists is perceived as being more serious than the same offending by novice offenders; and third, repeat offenders are seen as being more likely to reoffend. Public endorsement of the recidivist sentencing premium reflects all three issues. Despite all this, the public never entirely lose sight of proportionality; as consideration of previous

[19] Some sentencing theorists readily acknowledge that it is unlikely that either of these models of the use of previous convictions could be implemented (see for example, Frase 2005: 13).

convictions swamp the seriousness of the crime, public support will decline.

Although this chapter has demonstrated robust public support for a policy of taking previous convictions into consideration at sentencing, we have yet to understand why this is so. Is it the case that they simply wish to inflict harsher punishment upon the category of offender for whom they have least sympathy—a form of reflexive punitiveness? I think not. Rather, the answer lies in more fundamental judgments about social behaviour and intuitive explanations of criminal conduct. These issues will be explored in greater depth in the next chapter.

9

Explaining Public Attitudes: The *Intuitive Sentencer* and the *Intuitive Psychologist*

There is a strong feeling that those who continue to repeat their offences are somehow more deserving of more severe punishment than those who do not repeat. (Newman 1983: 54).

The preceding chapter demonstrated that the public is keenly interested in an individual's criminal antecedents and consider previous convictions to be highly relevant to sentencing decisions. But why is this the case? Can it be ascribed to mere punitiveness, a desire to punish people who offend repeatedly more harshly out of pure vindictiveness for unsympathetic offenders? Or is a part of a more complex—and possibly fundamental—reaction to judging the actions of other people? Establishing that the public reject a policy which excludes consideration of an offender's previous convictions at sentencing is insufficient; we need to better understand the psychology and knowledge base of the intuitive sentencer.

Overview

This chapter explores the reasons for public support for the use of criminal history information at sentencing. The explanations for public support for a recidivist sentencing premium will take us in a number of directions. The point of departure for understanding the public's position is public knowledge of reoffending patterns and laypersons' expectations of sentencing outcomes. Having established the level of public knowledge the chapter presents a discussion of the social psychology of causal inferences.

Public knowledge of repeat offenders

Persistent offenders in the public mind

When most people think about offenders in general—or the sentencing process—an image of repeat offenders often comes to mind. Even the terms used in everyday language to describe people convicted of a criminal offence—'offenders' and 'criminals'—imply persistence or at least repetition; people who repeatedly offend rather than people who have committed a crime. A number of empirical studies have explored public perceptions regarding the 'average offender', or have asked subjects to specify who they have in mind when answering questions about the sentencing process. When probed in this way, most people identify repeat offenders. This stereotype of the offender helps to explain public criticism of sentencing practices—people are thinking of repeat offenders.

In a survey reported by Doob and Roberts (1983) for example, respondents were asked two questions: first, whether sentencing was too harsh, too lenient, or about right; and second, 'What type of criminal were you thinking about when you answered the last question?' In response to the first question, four-fifths of the sample expressed the view that sentences were too lenient (Doob and Roberts 1983; see also Brillon, Louis-Guerin, and Lamarche 1984). When asked to specify who they had in mind when offering this judgment on the sentencing process, respondents were four times more likely to say they had been thinking of repeat offenders than first offenders.

Public estimates of criminal recidivism rates

Public attitudes towards the use of criminal history information at sentencing must be seen in the context of knowledge of the prevalence of previous convictions. Knowledge of patterns of recidivism has been explored in two ways: by asking respondents to predict categorical rates of reoffending and also by asking people to estimate the number of prior convictions of defendants appearing for sentencing. Research in Canada, Spain, and the United States has shown that people overestimate criminal recidivism rates and underestimate the proportion of offenders who appear for sentencing for the first time (see Stalans and Diamond 1990; Roberts 1996; Roberts and White 1986; Doob and Roberts 1982; Redondo, Luque, and Funes 1996). For example, survey research has shown that public estimates of the recidivism rate of property offenders in Spain were more than double the official rates (Redondo et al 1996). When asked to estimate the rates of recidivism for violent offenders, the gap between public estimates and official rates was even greater.

Although criminal recidivism rates tend to be higher in the US, Americans also hold overly-pessimistic views of reoffending rates. Stalans and Diamond (1990) found that a majority of the public believed that the typical burglar had committed at least four prior crimes although court statistics from the respondents' area revealed that only a quarter of the offenders convicted of this offence had such an extensive record (see also Stalans and Lurigio 1990). A representative sample of Florida residents was asked about the effects of legal punishment on recidivism rates. Specifically, they were asked whether they believed that ex-offenders were more, less, or as likely to reoffend after having been punished. Most people believed that offenders would be more, not less likely to reoffend after having been punished. Statistics published by the Florida Department of Corrections demonstrate that only 18% of ex-offenders had reoffended within two years of expiry of the sentence (Florida Department of Corrections 1997).[1] These trends reveal considerable public scepticism about the ability of the sentencing process to reduce reoffending.

Public overestimates of criminal recidivism rates are particularly striking for offenders still serving their sentences. One of the most difficult challenges of correctional authorities around the world is to convince a sceptical public that prisoners released on parole are unlikely to commit further offences while being supervised in the community. Parole failure rates—defined as the proportion of parolees who are returned to prison for allegations of fresh offending—vary across jurisdictions, but are generally significantly lower than members of the public believe. Most parolees complete their sentences in the community without incident; the individuals that are returned to prison are usually brought back to custody as a result of a technical violation of one of the conditions of release. In 2004, only one federal parolee in ten in Canada was returned to prison as a result of an allegation of fresh offending

[1] It is possible that respondents to the survey had a longer term in mind than two years; however, most reoffending will occur within this period. Even if one doubles the recidivism rate it still means that approximately two-thirds of the ex-offender sample was not rearrested.

(Public Safety Canada 2004). That is not how the public generally sees matters. According to a public opinion survey conducted the same year, public estimates of recidivism rates by parolees were much higher. Thus only one-fifth of the public sample was accurate in estimating the parole recidivism rate; approximately one-third of respondents estimated a recidivism rate of between 41% and 60% (Public Safety Canada 2004). These results are consistent with earlier surveys of the public which found that most people greatly overestimate reoffending rates of parolees and ex-offenders in general (Doob and Roberts 1983; Roberts 1988).

Criminal specialization and the duration of criminal careers

The public perceives repeat offenders as criminal specialists—violent offenders, property offenders, and so forth (O'Connor 1984; Conklin 1975). In reality, most repeat offenders have general criminal histories; this means that the offence of conviction is an unreliable guide to the offence of reconviction (see Cunliffe and Shepherd 2007). This reality has been repeatedly demonstrated by reoffending studies in a number of countries. For example, Farrington (1991) reported limited specialization in his research involving British offenders. Bottomley and Pease (1986) demonstrated that when reconviction occurred it was more likely to involve a dissimilar than a similar offence. Recidivism statistics published by the Washington State Sentencing Guidelines Commission (1992) reveal that offenders convicted of a crime of violence were more likely to have a non-violent than a violent previous conviction. More recent data reveal that offenders convicted of homicide, robbery, or sexual violence were the least likely to have a current criminal conviction that was in the same category as their previous offending (Washington State Sentencing Guidelines Commission (2005: Figure 6)). The absence of specialization, in conjunction with the reality that the volume of property crime is much higher than violent crime, means that regardless of the offence of conviction, offenders who are reconvicted are likely to be convicted of a property crime.

In all likelihood the public are also unaware of the brief duration of many offenders' criminal 'careers'. Fully 60% of male offenders and an even higher percentage of female offenders in England and Wales born between 1953 and 1978 had criminal 'careers' that were over in under a year (see Prime, White, Liriano, and Patel 2001). Such duration may be more reasonably described as a brief apprenticeship than a career per se. If the public was asked to estimate this statistic, it seems likely that they would predict a much longer period of 'active' criminal service.

Naïve expectations of desistance

There are other reasons related to public knowledge that may explain why the public endorse a sentencing model which prescribes harsher penalties for repeat offenders. Members of the public in all probability subscribe to a naïve expectation that the imposition of punishment should result in subsequent desistance. When this expectation is not met, the public may assume that the offender's reappearance before the court is evidence that the previous sentence was insufficiently harsh and that a more rigorous disposition is now appropriate. Desistance is thus considered the norm; reoffending an aberration reflecting the individual's criminal disposition. Indeed, the public may well consider the imposition of sentence to constitute a kind of contract with the offender: the offending has resulted in the imposition of punishment, and this should in turn result in a return to law-abiding behaviour. When the offender desists from offending he or she regains his or her standing in the community—hence the strong public support for pardon legislation (except for the most serious forms of offending). But if the offender reoffends, the subsequent sentence should reflect the seriousness of the new crime, as well as an additional penalty for breaching the contract arising from the previous crime. As noted in Chapter 2, the empirical research on deterrence in recent years has demonstrated important limits on the ability of harsher sentencing to deter crime. In all probability, however, deterrence theory still holds great intuitive appeal. The public may also have sympathy with a model which punishes defiance of the law. Both of these considerations will inflate public support for a recidivist sentencing premium.

Summary

Misperceptions about reoffending patterns help to explain support for the recidivist sentencing premium and indeed punitive attitudes towards offenders in general. These findings suggest that people ascribe more predictive power to criminal record than is warranted empirically. Finally, if most defendants appearing before the courts are recidivists, the intuitive sentencer may well infer that punishment levels are insufficiently harsh—otherwise recidivism rates would be lower.

Role of the news media

Media representations of crime generally focus on the seriousness of the offence—particularly when violence is involved. Content analyses of print and electronic media have focused on the relationship between the crime stories in the news media compared to crime statistics. These studies repeatedly find a strong correlation between the seriousness of a crime and the amount of attention it receives from the news media. The most serious crimes, particularly murder, account for a disproportionate percentage of media crime stories (eg, Graber 1980; O'Connell 1999; Beckett and Sasson 2000; see Reiner 2007, for a review). However, there has been very little attention to the characteristics of offenders described in the news media.[2]

Crime by recidivists and news values

Anecdotal evidence suggests that media coverage of sentencing decisions is sensitive to the existence of an offender's previous convictions. Crime stories by repeat offenders fulfill a number of news values thus making them 'good copy'. First, they confirm the public stereotype of an offender: an individual who offends as a result of a moral failure rather than someone who has committed a crime in partial response to environmental pressures and life circumstances. Second, crimes by recidivists convey the message that the criminal justice system has failed to achieve one of its most basic objectives, and failed repeatedly in the case of offenders with long criminal histories.[3] This failure is often linked to judicial leniency towards convicted offenders—another favourite

[2] In the content analysis reported by Reiner, Livingstone, and Allen (2003) the offender's previous offending status was not one of the variables coded. Earlier media research by Graber also explored a number of demographic variables of offenders, but not criminal history. One exception to this generalization is the multiple regression analysis reported by Chermak (1998) although it sheds little light on the current issue.

[3] In his analysis of media coverage of crime, O'Connell (1999) found that the image of crime and criminal justice projected in the media was negative; crime by repeat offenders certainly conforms to this image.

theme of the news media, particularly tabloid newspapers in Britain.

There are clear parallels with news media coverage of crime involving offenders on parole. The news media represent an important source of pressure on parole authorities. This is true in all countries in which the discretionary release on parole is an element of the correctional environment. In Canada, news reports periodically note the number of crimes committed by parolees over a number of years—usually without providing any indication of the number of individuals released on parole annually. In Britain in 2006 the *Sun* newspaper[4] devoted a number of headline stories drawing attention to the '200 Murders by Yobs Freed Early' (*Sun* 2006). Crime by parolees is particularly likely to arouse public ire in light of stories such as these, but it is a short step to crime by recidivists. The public is likely to regard judicial leniency as the cause of the reoffending.

Another tabloid story in 2006 carried the headline that 'The Killers Were Freed Just Hours Earlier' (*Daily Express* 2006). The front page article began by quoting a crime control advocate who 'repeatedly criticized the soft sentences handed to violent criminals'. The individual tied lenient sentencing explicitly to reoffending when he stated that 'criminals given soft sentences often reoffend time and time again' (*Daily Express* 2006). The same year the *Daily Mail* ran a story under the headline 'Justice Denied... Violent Serial Offenders Walk Free.' (*Daily Mail* 2006).

Newspaper stories involving repeat offenders often establish a link between the offender's previous convictions and his attitude to the offence and victim. An example of this appeared in the *Sun* which ran a lengthy story under the following banner headline: 'Laughing Hit-Run Driver With Long Record. Maniac Got Just 6 MONTHS Jail.' (*Sun* 2004a, emphasis in original). Such stories encourage cynicism on the part of the public who will associate reoffending with an attitude of defiance to the court.[5] Other stories

[4] I focus on newspapers here because Russell and Morgan (2001) found that respondents to their survey were more likely to cite national newspapers than any other source of information about sentencing.

[5] Another story in the same newspaper contained a picture of an individual convicted of drink-driving standing outside a court provocatively waving a can of beer at the press photographer (Sun 2004b).

place psychological and legal professionals in conflict when the former predict reoffending while the latter release an offender. The *Daily Record* carried the following banner headline: 'Warning. All the Experts Say This Rape Monster Will Strike Again...but the System Has Set Him Free.' (*Daily Record* 2005). The article went on to describe how 'police, psychologists, social workers and doctors all say that the muscle-bound beast will reoffend. But the legal system has no power to hold MacLeod beyond the end of his fixed 10-year sentence' (*Daily Record* 2005, p 1).

Thus when a serious crime is committed by an individual with a record of previous offences the incident is likely to generate newspaper headlines.[6] Crime stories involving repeat offenders will therefore account for a disproportionate number of crime stories, in the same way that serious violent crimes account for a disproportionate volume of stories relative to their incidence in official crime statistics. This over-representation is likely to affect the public consciousness. Estimates of recidivism rates will reflect media coverage, rather than official rates, in the same way that public estimates of the volume of violent crime reflect disproportionate coverage of this form of offending.[7]

Intuitive explanations of criminal behaviour

Perhaps the most powerful explanations for attitudes towards repeat offenders emerge from the field of social psychology. Earlier in this volume, I speculated that public support for the recidivism sentencing premium reflects a model of culpability or moral blameworthiness which incorporates prior offending in the equation. Here research and theory in social psychology is used to explain how attributions of the cause of criminal behaviour underpin this model of culpability. This requires an exploration of the phenomenology of the intuitive sentencer.

[6] This is particularly the case when the crime involves sexual aggression. Indeed, the widespread media coverage of the perpetrator responsible for the sexual assault and murder of Polly Klaas in California precipitated passage of the repeat offender ('three strikes') statute in that state. Public outrage focused on the failure of the system to prevent the offender reoffending (Gest 2001).

[7] Surveys conducted in a number of jurisdictions have consistently demonstrated that members of the public overestimate the proportion of recorded crime that involves violence (see Roberts and Hough 2005).

Dispositional versus situational explanations of behaviour

Naïve explanations for human behaviour have been the subject of theorizing and empirical research in social psychology for at least 70 years. Much of this scholarship is the result of pioneering work by Fritz Heider (1944) who popularized an intuitive distinction between internal and external factors, and subsequent publications by Jones and Davis (eg 1965). We constantly make judgments about the conduct of others, and speculate about the causes of, and influences upon that conduct. The intuitive psychologist seeks explanations for human behaviour in order to predict future conduct.

Factors explaining human behaviour may be classified in two broad categories: those arising from the environment and those associated with the individual's personality. Observers will hold a person responsible for an act to the extent that the act can reasonably be attributed to the actor rather than his or her environment. Repetition of an act increases the tendency of observers to attribute actions to the actor rather than the environment.[8] An individual who repeatedly commits an offence—particularly the same offence—will become more closely aligned in the public's mind with the act itself. The action will increasingly define the individual. External explanations such as provocation or drunkenness become increasingly implausible explanations of the act.

The relationship between repetition and ascriptions of responsibility can be represented graphically by two ring Venn diagrams with one ring representing the offender and the other the offence. The first offender's rings are slightly overlapping; the crime invokes a minor involvement of the offender's life, which to that point has revealed no wrongdoing (Figure 9.1). As convictions accumulate, the offender and the offence are viewed as increasingly united—as in Figure 9.2. The speed with which the two rings fuse is greatly accelerated if the convictions are for similar offences as

[8] Repetition of the act would appear to enhance ascriptions of culpability or blame. One of the elements of the killing of the toddler James Bulger in England in 1993 that explains the punitive response on the part of the public was the fact that the young killers had rehearsed the kidnapping on a number of occasions. The rehearsal of the crime also confirms the existence of premeditation, which is a powerful source of aggravation in the public's view.

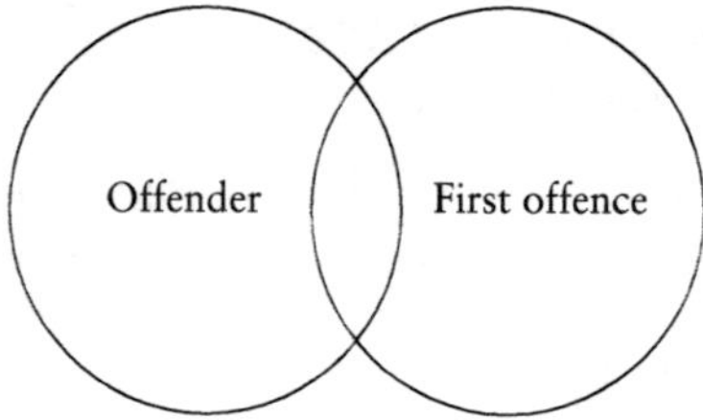

Figure 9.1 Relationship between offender and offence: first offender

Figure 9.2 Relationship between offender and offence: repeat offender

this enhances still further the attribution to the individual rather than his environment.

Jones and Davis (1965) proposed a model of correspondent inferences, according to which people attempt to make attributions about the character of other individuals. This creates a tendency to seek explanations for behaviour that reside in the wilful decisions of the actor rather than the influences of the environment. According to Jones and Davis, people will ascribe intentionality and attribute responsibility when they believe that an actor had the capacity and freedom to act as well as sufficient awareness of the consequences of his or her conduct. Violent crimes—especially when they occur in public spaces—come most readily to the public mind and are most often the subject of public discussion; they are also the crimes covered most often by the news media. Most people see the perpetrators as having as much freedom to act as themselves; accordingly they will infer intentionality and ascribe responsibility without much thought about environmental influences.

Apply this analysis to the first offender sentencing discount. Except for the most serious offences or those which carry a mandatory penalty, all jurisdictions extend a discount to offenders who have been convicted for the first time. This principle is accepted by all sentencing schemes and theories, whether retributive or utilitarian. There is widespread acceptance of the first offender discount at sentencing, although members of the public (and crime victims) may resist the application of the principle to serious crimes. Crime by a first offender may plausibly be attributed to external factors—temptations or pressures to which all of us are subject and to which many may succumb. Once, at least. External forces offer increasingly implausible explanations in light of repeated criminal conduct. An offender who commits a violent offence becomes in the popular imagination a 'violent offender'. This analysis appears to hold true regardless of the valence of the conduct in question. The altruist who repeatedly makes a humanitarian gesture is viewed very differently from the individual who acts in a similar way—but for the first time in his life. In short, repetition changes perceptions of an individual, both in terms of attributions of blame and ascriptions of virtue. And these judgments in turn influence the allocation of legal punishments and the distribution of rewards.

Freedom of action

As noted, the naïve psychologist explains the cause of behaviour by reference to the degree of choice available to the actor. Behaviour that emerges from a context in which the actor is highly constrained is less likely to be attributed to the individual.[9] This is an obvious finding, perhaps, but one which has particular relevance to explanations of criminal behaviour. A common reaction of many members of the public to pleas for mitigation is one of initial scepticism. This arises in a number of contexts. For example, Hough et al (2007) report findings from focus groups in which people were asked to consider the sentencing of offenders convicted of driving offences resulting in death. Discussions revealed very little public sympathy for offenders convicted of these offences; in large

[9] A number of attributional theories incorporate this notion of freedom of action. Another leading attribution theorist (Weiner 1980) identified 'controllability' as one of the three principal dimensions determining whether attributions of personal causality are made: the extent to which the behaviour was under the actor's control will affect causal attributions. Members of the public are likely to see desistance as within the offender's control, and they will therefore attribute subsequent offending to the offender's character.

part this reaction probably reflects an attribution of the crime to the individual offender's character. People who were involved in a fatal accident caused in some degree by their careless driving were seen as having no 'excuse' for such conduct; environmental factors which might explain why the offender was behind the wheel or why they drove with an unacceptable standard of care were given short shrift by focus group participants.[10]

The exception to this generalization emerged when the scenario stated that the offender had been rushing to hospital when the accident occurred. If this was the case respondents in the study expressed some limited sympathy—as evidenced by the less punitive sentence imposed (see Hough et al 2007). This finding underscores the attributional model underlying public judgments; the offender with a medical emergency requiring hospital care was seen as having a restricted range of options. Similarly, the public generally have little sympathy for social adversity considerations at sentencing, unless the adverse conditions to which the offender was exposed were sufficiently debilitating as to deprive him or her of the freedom to act in a particular way. As with other issues this may be interpreted as mere penal impatience—members of the public being disinclined to hear such arguments prior to sentencing. More likely it reflects cognitive biases: people fail to appreciate the constraints upon the individual's freedom of action.

Frequency, valence, or social desirability of behaviour

Research on attributions of causality reveals that behaviour that is exceptional or unusual in some respect is more likely to trigger a personal rather than an environmental attribution on the part of observers. People are more likely to conclude that atypical behaviour is a consequence of the character of the actor, rather than a result of his environment. Criminal acts, particularly the more serious forms of offending, clearly fall within this definition, and this helps to explain the tendency to perceive criminality as

[10] This research finding also raises another branch of inquiry in social psychology, namely the belief in a so-called 'just world'. Members of the public have a tendency to attribute consequences to actors in part out of a belief that people deserve their misfortune. Offenders will be perceived to deserve the adverse consequences (whether legal or not) associated with their offending (see Lerner 1980, for further information).

an individual decision, and hence an act that is likely to reoccur across different contexts.

In addition, the *valence* of the behaviour in question also influences whether observers attribute the behaviour to disposition rather than environment. Socially undesirable actions such as crimes are more likely to be attributed to the character of the actor rather than environmental causes. In their review of research exploring attribution theories, Fiske and Taylor argue that 'when people are willing to break with norms or conventions...one can be reasonably certain that their behaviour reflects their true beliefs because by so doing they are risking socially aversive consequences' (1991: 29). This may be an overly simple inferential model to apply to criminal behaviour; nevertheless it helps explain why members of the public attribute criminal actions to the offender rather than his environment—and assign punishments accordingly.

There is also a tendency for people to attribute more personal responsibility for actions that result in serious rather than mild consequences. Individuals will be more likely to be held responsible for an action that has serious rather than trivial consequences—even when information about their actual level of responsibility is held constant (Gebotys and DasGupta 1988). If two individuals are convicted of the same offence, under exactly the same set of conditions, they will be seen as being differentially responsible if the consequences are fortuitously more severe in one case. This reflects a cognitive bias that in the legal domain translates to an analysis based almost exclusively on harm; members of the public tend to punish according to the level of harm rather than fault.[11]

Explaining behaviour: actor-observer differences and the intuitive sentencer

A great deal of research in social psychology has documented the differences in causal accounts of behaviour made by actors

[11] Driving offences resulting in serious harm or death are a good example. An offender who causes an accident by driving while impaired carries the same level of fault as one who is convicted of impaired driving having been stopped by the police as a result of a random check. The only difference is the harm inflicted; both offenders are equally culpable for the offence of impaired driving but when sentencing offenders, the public tends to focus on the harm, and overlooks the issue of fault.

compared to observers. This is referred to as the 'actor-observer' effect. Actors tend to explain their actions by reference to external factors—those found in the environment in which the individual functions. Observers on the other hand are more likely to explain behaviour by reference to dispositional (ie personal) factors. The different perspectives of actors and observers have been repeatedly demonstrated in laboratory and field research (see Fiske and Taylor 1991). In the present context offenders represent the 'actors' and the public constitute the 'observers'.

Differences in attributional perspectives clearly emerged from the comments of the offenders interviewed for the present volume. A theme that repeatedly emerged was that courts failed to take environmental influences into account. The offenders perceived themselves as being labelled as 'offenders' on the basis of their previous convictions when they believed that their current offending arose as much or more from a range of situational factors. One participant noted that 'very few people are malicious—but they can do bad things'. This perspective is consistent with the 'actor-observer' effect; judges and magistrates were perceived by offenders as making dispositional attributions about the causes of the offenders' behaviour—and relying heavily on the existence of previous convictions in so doing. The actors in this context—the offenders themselves—were more sensitive to accounts of offending that invoked environmental factors.

It is hard to make generalizations about the weight that the public assign to internal versus external factors when asked to explain criminal behaviour. Members of the public consider a multiplicity of explanations for criminality, some internal, some external. In all likelihood the balance or ratio of internal to external will be influenced by variables such as the nature and seriousness of the offence. Many surveys have asked people to identify the causes of crime, and these may then be grouped into personal or internal compared to external or environmental.[12] In his review of the early research Flanagan (1987) noted an increased tendency, beginning in the 1980s, for the public to blame the criminal justice

[12] There is a parallel between public explanations for offending and support for sentencing purposes. Research has shown that to a degree both are offence-specific (eg, Hollin and Howells 1987). People draw upon different explanations for offending depending on the nature and seriousness of the crime, and this presumably leads them to pursue different sentencing objectives.

system for crime.[13] This shift may explain the increasing salience of deterrence-based responses to crime: the public believed that by becoming tougher the system could reduce crime.

Other writers (eg, Cullen et al 1985) have also noted a trend among members of the public to attribute crime to the individual offender. The media may have played a role here. Reiner, Livingstone, and Allen (2003) argue that news media coverage of crime and justice has become more polarized in recent decades. Today, crime is more likely to be attributed to pathological personalities. Environmental factors associated with the offence remain invisible, although they may well emerge at trial or sentencing. The etiology of criminal behaviour in the public mind will fail to incorporate, or inadequately reflect, environmental influences. When the public are made aware of environmental factors, or are explicitly asked to consider the causes of crime, they acknowledge the importance of social and economic factors (see Roberts and Hastings 2007, for a review). However, this balanced evaluation is unlikely to take place when people casually read about crime in the newspapers. Whatever the cause, the shifting emphasis from internal to external explanations for offending will have consequences for repeat offenders. The public will become increasingly oriented to an explanatory model that ascribes offending to the individual offender.

The 'fundamental attribution error'

When attempting to determine whether the behaviour of other people reflects situational or individual factors, we can often be wrong. Another important and often-replicated finding from the field of attribution research over the past 30 years is that an asymmetry emerges with respect to laypersons' explanations of the causes of behaviour (see Jones and Nisbett 1972). The public is more likely to ascribe others' actions to personal factors than is empirically justifiable. Nisbett and Ross (1980) argue that

[13] The changing nature of the questions posed on surveys complicates any attempt to draw firm conclusions about historical trends in the extent to which people attribute crime to individuals or environments. However, even a cursory examination of polls in the 1960s and 1970s shows that the public was more interested in environmental explanations for offending (see Erskine (1974) for examples).

western culture in particular exhibits a bias in favour of dispositional rather than environmental explanations for behaviour. This may explain why the American subjects in research reported by Hamilton and Sanders (1992) assigned greater importance to an offender's previous convictions than did Japanese subjects. The actor-observer phenomenon results from a well-documented tendency for 'observers' to use personal accounts to explain the behaviour of another individual. When asked about their own behaviour, however, 'actors' tend to rely on external explanations. This gives rise to the *fundamental attribution error*.

Aronson describes this cognitive error in the following way: 'The term Fundamental Attribution Error refers to a general human tendency to overestimate the importance of personality or dispositional factors relative to situational influences when describing the causes of behaviour' (1999: 164). This cognitive tendency or error (in the language of cognitive social psychology)[14] has a clear application to public responses to repeat offenders. Situational factors that emerge from the criminological literature as being powerful predictors of reoffending will be discounted by members of the public in favour of personal choice explanations. As criminal convictions accumulate, the external causal attributions will decline still further, giving rise to a perspective in which the individual is seen as an offender making independent moral decisions to reoffend, regardless of environmental influences. The fundamental attribution error helps to explain why public estimates of recidivism rates are higher than the official rates. People are more likely to attribute offending to the individual rather than the situation in which the individual finds himself.

The fundamental attribution error is particularly likely to emerge when people are asked to make relatively quick 'snap' judgments or are asked to infer causality on the basis of a relatively small amount of information. Such is the nature of many judgments that people make about crime, offenders, and sentencing—in response to brief news media accounts or during casual conversations about crime. When people have more information to consider, or more time to respond to the question

[14] This cognitive error is one of many shortcomings identified by researchers in the field of psychology. These errors all represent departures from rational inferential attributions that would be drawn by a scientist (see Ross 1977, for a review).

posed, they are less prone to overlook the importance of environmental factors. This tendency explains why people tend to be more punitive in response to polls that pose simplistic questions and require an instantaneous response from the respondent. Public judgment is more nuanced, less punitive when people are given more time to arrive at an opinion (see Green 2005, for discussion).[15]

How does the so-called fundamental attribution error arise? Research suggests it occurs as a result of the salience of specific behaviours compared to less visible background factors that may nevertheless have played an important causal role. Serious criminal behaviour is highly salient when brought to the attention of the public by the media. Some causes of this kind of offending, such as drug or alcohol addiction, social deprivation, or other factors remain in the background—hence the observer's tendency to overlook their influence. This is referred to as an example of the behaviour 'engulfing the field' to return to Heider's earlier writings (1958). Even a cursory examination of media stories will reveal that environmental explanations of criminal acts seldom make their way into the newspapers. Graber (1980) for example found that only 4% of the media stories in her analysis discussed the causes of crime. Finally, the news media also present a one-sided discussion on the origins of criminal behaviour. In discussing news media values relating to crime and justice, Jewkes (2004) notes that 'individual definitions of crime, and rationalizations which highlight individual responses are privileged at the expense of more complex social explanations' (p 40). The natural inclination of members of the public to overlook environmental explanations of crime is exacerbated by what people read and hear about criminal behaviour in the news media.

Moreover, as Fiske and Taylor note, 'dispositional attribution is a relatively spontaneous and simple process, whereas the use of situational information to qualify or discount the role

[15] The obvious illustration concerns public punitiveness. Polls routinely find that respondents decry the leniency of the system. When provided with actual case scenarios to consider, members of the public become less punitive, in part, presumably because the role of external influences upon the offender becomes more salient (see Doob and Roberts 1983; Roberts and Hough 2005; Justice 1 Committee 2002, for research examples). This also helps to explain why people become less punitive when serving as a juror, than when simply making judgments in response to an opinion poll (see Roberts 2002b, for discussion).

of dispositional factors is a more complex process, requiring a greater commitment of cognitive resources' (1991: 71–2).

To summarize, there are a number of explanations, all supported by the findings of empirical research from the field of cognitive social psychology, why members of the public are likely to attribute criminal behaviour to the individual offender rather than to external influences. As he accumulates additional criminal convictions the actor becomes increasingly associated with his actions, and is more likely to be seen as an offender rather than a person who has committed a criminal act. When criminal conduct is attributed to internal rather than external factors people making the attributions are more likely to impose punitive sentences (Carroll and Payne 1977; Hawkins 1981). The consequences for repeat offenders are clear; their offending is attributable to their personal characteristics (an internal factor) and the result is that the public favour harsher sentences for such people—crime is a result of offenders' moral decisions rather than external forces. They are accordingly more to blame for this conduct.

The final point about the attributional biases described here and applied to naïve explanations of criminal behaviour is that they help drive and explain neoconservative approaches to crime control which have become more popular in recent years in many western nations. If crime is explained in terms of individual disposition rather than on environmental forces, crime control policies naturally focus on offenders rather than circumstances that give rise to or foster offending. There is empirical support for this assertion. Ewart and Pennington (1987) found that when people attribute behaviour to internal causes they are more likely to favour deterrence as a sentencing purpose, and more likely to choose incarceration as a sentencing option. This shifting from rehabilitative to deterrent sentencing and from community to custody is consistent with the recidivist sentencing premium.

The offender as outsider

Stereotyping processes also play a role in explaining public attitudes to repeat offenders. One of the most robust findings in the literature about public perceptions is the tendency of members of the public to see offenders as stereotypical 'outsiders'. This stereotyping is also likely to create pressure for more punitive recidivist laws. As Pratt (2007) has observed, 'populist responses to crime are strongest and would seem most likely to influence policy when they are presaged around a common enemy, a group of criminals who seem utterly different from the rest of the population.' (p 5). From the public's perspective, crime is a deviant activity committed by a relatively small group of individuals that are—or should be—easily identifiable. Over the years, a number of person perception studies have demonstrated that many people subscribe to a relatively distinct stereotype about offenders. Social distance studies support the proposition that these stereotypes have behavioural consequences for interpersonal relations. For example, the European Values Study collects survey data from residents of over 30 European countries. In the third wave of this survey, respondents were provided with a list of groups to consider and asked to identify the groups that they would prefer 'not to have as neighbours'. On average, slightly over half the total sample identified a person 'with a criminal record'. Ex-offenders were perceived to be less desirable neighbours than political extremists. Heavy drinkers and drug addicts were the only groups seen by respondents as being less desirable neighbours (Halman 2002).

Assumptions and intuitive theories about the etiology of crime are responsible for creating the out-group of the offender. The existence of this out-group then affects communications about the group (see Ruscher 1998). Members of the out-group are seen as being more homogenous than in-group members—another cognitive error in the sense that it is without empirical foundation. When many people talk about crime and 'criminals' the discourse reflects this tendency to classify the offender as an out-group member. Stereotype-congruent information is privileged while information which is inconsistent with the stereotype is less likely to be transmitted or assimilated. Ruscher (1998) notes that 'When people communicate about outgroup members, they develop and affirm their shared understanding of them.' (p 285). She refers to stereotyping in general, but the generalization certainly holds true for conversations about crime (Hough 1996). Finally, research on stereotyping also reveals that expressing an opinion about a target group ('violent offenders'; 'sex offenders') strengthens the stereotype in the mind of the communicator (eg, Greenberg and Pyszczynski 1985).

The social psychology of attributions explains how many members of the public see a clear dichotomy between law-abiding persons and offenders. A wealth of empirical research has demonstrated the widespread prevalence of offending. Self-report surveys have shown that offending behaviour is found throughout society rather than concentrated in a small number of individuals. It is unlikely that many people will be aware of the prevalence of offending. Over one-third of the British male population born in 1953 had acquired a conviction for a standard list offence before the age of 40 (Home Office 1999). Such findings would surprise many people and highlight the importance of environmental factors. They are, however, overlooked by the intuitive sentencer who is more likely to see offenders as a group apart.

Once the public perceives offenders as being a group apart from law abiding individuals (like themselves), laypersons' explanations of behaviour are affected. Another well-documented phenomenon in social psychology is known as 'defensive attribution' (Shaver 1970). The essential idea here is that people ascribe less responsibility and blame to other people who are similar to themselves. Shaver asked subjects to assign blame for an accident in cases in which the person causing the accident was similar or dissimilar to the subjects in the research. Results demonstrated that subjects assign more blame if the perpetrator of the accident is dissimilar to themselves even though the level of responsibility is constant.[16] Once offenders come to be viewed as a homogenous group unlike the majority of citizens, their involvement in criminal behaviour will more likely be attributed to personality rather than environmental factors.

Punishing disposition

When the public act as 'observers' and explain the behaviour of offenders, they will be inclined to attribute offending to the individual's personality. Compelling evidence of the importance of ascriptions of criminality to character can be found in the research by Robinson and Darley (1995). In one of their experiments using members of the public as subjects, Robinson and Darley studied

[16] As with a number of concepts in social psychology, this concept echoes intuitive explanations: we are generally less punitive towards people like ourselves, and this diminished punitiveness reflects the belief that someone like us could not have acted in such a fashion—so there must have been extenuating, ie, environmental influences on their behaviour.

laypersons' reactions to the criminal law defences of duress and entrapment. Participants were asked to read about a case in which one of these defences was raised. One scenario described an individual with no prior record who was approached and pressured by an undercover government agent to transport drugs—a classic entrapment scenario. In another condition the same scenario was used except that the person was now described as having acquired two convictions for transporting drugs. An analysis concerned with the professional conduct of the agent would have little regard to the characteristics of the individual alleged to have been entrapped. Yet the liability assigned to the 'entrapped' driver in these circumstances was significantly higher when he was described as having previous convictions.[17]

Summary and conclusions

Research reviewed in this and the preceding chapter reveals several explanations for the public's views regarding the sentencing of recidivist offenders. First, people subscribe to a model of culpability best represented by a continuum, much like crime seriousness (rather than the 'capped' model advocated by Fletcher). Second, members of the public do not make a clear distinction between the seriousness of the crime and the legally-relevant characteristics of the offender. Rather, they appear to arrive at global judgments in which their rating of case seriousness is directly affected by the criminal record of the defendant. The defendant's previous convictions provide a context in which to judge the seriousness of his current offending. Third, the public may well have unrealistic expectations regarding the crime prevention potential of a recidivist sentencing premium. By overestimating the recidivism rate of offenders they hold an overly-optimistic view about the volume of crime that may be prevented by imposing harsher sentences on repeat offenders. Fourth, the public probably make the assumption—refuted by a great deal of deterrence research—that harsher sentencing will have an important impact on aggregate crime

[17] The average assigned sentence in the prior record condition was approximately four years, compared to about four weeks for the offender with no previous convictions for transporting drugs. The existence of previous convictions had the effect of largely washing out the force of an exculpatory argument based on entrapment (see Robinson and Darley 1995).

rates. Fifth, many people subscribe to an unrealistic expectation that desistance should follow punishment—a naïve belief related to the tendency to discount inveterate or unchanging environmental influences on offending behaviour.

The social psychology of causal attributions also plays a critical role. There appears to be a general tendency in our culture for people to be more likely to explain criminal behaviour by reference to personal rather than situational factors. Environmental explanations for offending lack salience and are discounted by members of the public. Moreover, as convictions accumulate, the public make an increasingly character-based approach to punishing the offender. When considering punishing a first offender the seriousness of the crime predominates, but the more times the offender reoffends, the more likely are members of the public to attribute the behaviour to character rather than circumstances; the focus of their punitiveness shifts to the individual.

The public clearly have difficulty in making the distinction—crucial from the perspective of some desert accounts of sentencing—between the act and the actor. Both principal versions of desert theory argue that an offender's characteristics such as his previous convictions should not aggravate the sentence imposed. The public think otherwise, and appear to evaluate the actor as well as the act. As Newman observes, there is a 'real feeling that people have that we cannot clearly separate the particular act of an offender from his prior record' (1983: 55). To a certain degree then, public support for the use of previous convictions reflects 'cognitive errors'. However, at the heart of intuitive reactions to the sentencing of offenders lies a desire to consider factors that lie outside the more circumscribed retributive focus. This tendency explains why the public are moved by offenders who are remorseful.

This volume has now reviewed research pertaining to one of the few universal features of the sentencing process: the recidivist premium. All parties with a stake in the sentencing process—including repeat offenders—appear to agree that previous convictions have some role to play at sentencing. The final chapter explores ways in which the collective response to the use of previous convictions may be accommodated without abandoning important sentencing principles such as proportionality.

10

Reconceptualizing the Recidivist Sentencing Premium

This final chapter reviews the principal findings and conclusions of the volume, provides a discussion of the role that public opinion should play, and then makes some modest proposals with respect to the sentencing of repeat offenders. The principal points emerging from this study include the following:

1. Statutory frameworks around the world all consider an offender's previous convictions at sentencing, although there is considerable variability in the way in which this information influences the severity of sentence imposed. A wealth of historical evidence demonstrates that repetition has featured in legal punishments since records of previous convictions became readily available for the use of sentencers.
2. Analysis of sentencing statistics in a number of different jurisdictions demonstrates that sentencers generally follow a cumulative sentencing model, imposing progressively harsher penalties to reflect the number, nature, and seriousness of the offender's previous convictions. This pattern emerges in jurisdictions that ostensibly pursue a different sentencing model, namely the progressive loss of mitigation.
3. Sentencing theories vary considerably in the way that they justify the imposition of harsher sentences on repeat offenders. From the perspective of incapacitation or individual deterrence, the recidivist sentencing premium is easily justified. Repetition of offending has demonstrated that the previous sentence was insufficient, and that a harsher one must now be imposed. This logic leads to a direct relationship between the severity of the crime and the seriousness of the offender's previous convictions. However, research suggests that a severity premium is unlikely to have much impact on subsequent reoffending rates.

4. Considering previous convictions at sentencing will have some predictive utility, particularly for offenders with long criminal histories. However, it is also necessary to provide a normative justification relating to the offender's conduct rather than simply ascriptions of future risk.
5. Justifying a recidivist premium from the perspective of retributive theories is more difficult. Although early formulations of desert theories argued that offenders with previous convictions are more culpable and therefore more deserving of harsher treatment, until recently, most retributive theorists held the view that previous convictions should play only a limited role in the sentencing process—or no role at all.
6. Repeat offenders interviewed in this study accepted the recidivist sentencing premium as a legitimate and justifiable element of the sentencing process. These individuals evinced little opposition to the recidivist premium, and no support for the view that this practice constitutes double punishment for the same offence. However, they did express resentment about the way that previous convictions were currently considered at sentencing. They perceived the courts to adopt a mechanistic approach to the use of criminal history information.
7. Members of the public strongly support the use of an offender's previous convictions at sentencing. This support is not simply a punitive reaction towards offenders; it reflects a fundamental characteristic of explanations of behaviour. Lay conceptions of culpability and moral blameworthiness incorporate an offender's criminal antecedents, even if these are excluded from some theoretical models of the same concepts.
8. Public support for some kind of recidivist sentencing premium can be explained by reference to public knowledge of offenders, offending, and the sentencing process, as well as lay theories of culpability. At the heart of this analysis is the idea that the intuitive sentencer considers the offender's character in evaluating the appropriate punishment that he or she deserves. Repeat offenders are perceived as being more culpable and hence deserving of harsher punishment. Despite this level of support for consideration of an offender's previous convictions, the public do not lose sight of the importance of proportionality in sentencing.
9. The argument is advanced here that repeat offenders are more culpable as a consequence of their mental state at the time of

the offence, in the same way that offenders who plan their crimes should be considered more blameworthy. According to this analysis, previous convictions should aggravate the severity of sentence imposed to reflect the increased culpability level of repeat offenders. Thus previous convictions are considered relevant to the culpability branch of a proportional sanction.

10. Repeat offenders are more culpable, more worthy of blame, and hence more deserving of punishment. However, recidivists should be allowed to credit efforts to desist against the elevated culpability ascribed to them at sentencing.

Public opinion, sentencing policy, and practice

When a penal dispensation is revolting to the public feeling, that is not of itself a sufficient reason for rejecting it. But it is a reason for subjecting it to a rigorous scrutiny...sentiment excites to reflection, and reflection detects the impropriety of the law. (Bentham 1843: 412)

This volume does not seek to explore the complex relationship between the sentencing process and public opinion (for further discussion of this issue, see Walker and Hough 1988; Roberts 2002; Roberts 2007). Yet it is necessary to return to the question first raised in Chapter 4, namely whether public opinion should play a role in the sentencing process.

A number of retributivist theorists reject any public input into the determination of sentencing policy. For example, Singer (1970) observes that 'in ordinary discourse we do sometimes look to such factors [as previous convictions in] in sentencing...But this innate reaction should be rejected.' (p 72). Bagaric and Edney (2004) also advocate a policy of totally disregarding public views. They argue that 'Seeking public views on sentencing is analogous to doctors basing treatment decisions on what the community thinks is appropriate or engineers building cars, not in accordance with the rules of physics, but on the basis of what lay members of the community "reckon" seems about right' (p 129). But their analogy is hardly appropriate. The rules of physics or of evidence are not improved by community input; the expression of moral reprobation at sentencing is a very different matter.

Why should public views count? The criminal law contains many rules of which the public disapprove. If community values should inform or guide criminal policy with respect to sentencing, why should they not also modify criminal procedures at trial? After all, the public are interested in knowing about a defendant's criminal record long before he is convicted. The strength of the public's desire to ascertain the offender's criminal antecedents can be seen in responses to a British poll which found that almost four out of five respondents wanted juries to learn of the defendant's previous convictions *before* arriving at a verdict (ICM Research 2002). When the same poll asked whether the evidence or the accused's previous convictions would weigh most heavily on their decision if they were a juror, almost half responded that they would assign equal weight to the evidence adduced at trial and the defendant's previous convictions. In a similar way, one of the participants in the qualitative research reported in this volume wryly observed that 'we had had a trial and were found guilty. When they read out the previous convictions the jury was horrified. They wished they had heard them sooner [ie, during the trial].'

Allowing jurors access to the criminal history of the defendant would result in wrongful convictions in cases involving offenders with substantial criminal records, particularly when the priors were similar in nature to the charge for which the defendant is currently on trial. No amount of direction from the judge presiding would eliminate the prejudicial effect of this information. A great deal of previous research has demonstrated that the public infer guilt directly from the existence of prior convictions. If the defendant takes the stand and testifies at trial, the Crown may introduce any previous convictions to raise questions about the defendant's credibility as a witness. However, research involving simulated jurors has clearly demonstrated that jurors infer guilt directly when the offender has prior convictions. Thus Greene and Dodge (1995) found that mock jurors were more likely to convict the defendant when they were aware of a prior criminal conviction, and judges' limiting instructions were ineffective in preventing this inappropriate use of previous convictions (see also Hans and Doob 1976; Steblay et al 2006). If previous convictions are excluded at trial (unless the accused testifies) why should they count after conviction?

Justifying public input into sentencing policy

Two justifications may be offered for considering public views at sentencing. First, sentencing raises very different issues from the trial stage of the criminal process. At trial, the community's representatives are effectively fact-finding, determining whether the State has proved all the elements of the offence beyond a reasonable doubt. Sentencing, however, involves the expression of community censure, and a system which ignored community sentiment would ultimately lose the power to condemn—hence the need to ensure that expressions of censure bear a close connection to public ascriptions of blameworthiness. If legal censure ignores a variable considered by the public to be highly relevant to blameworthiness, the legitimacy of the sentencing process will be undermined.

The second justification for heeding the views of the public concerns the state of public attitudes to the courts. Public opinion surveys routinely reveal widespread disenchantment with sentencing and sentencers. The 1996 administration of the BCS was the first to systematically document these trends which have subsequently been confirmed in later sweeps of the survey (see Hough and Roberts 1998; Mattinson and Mirrlees-Black 2000; Hough and Roberts 2007). The debate over the influence of the public upon sentencers has generally focused on the propriety of allowing community views to influence individual sentencing decisions or the direction of sentencing policy. Few would argue in favour of allowing a sentencing court to hear submissions upon the acceptability of various sanctions prior to the imposition of sentence. On the other hand, if sentencing practices diverged widely and consistently from public opinion the legitimacy of the judicial system would be compromised.

Imagine a sentencing system that ignored proportionality considerations. With proportionality abandoned, theft might be punished more severely than serious assault, manslaughter more harshly than murder, and so forth. Once such penal anomalies were publicized and came to the attention of the public, confidence in criminal justice would surely decline still further. Surveys of the public in Britain and elsewhere have repeatedly revealed that people have less confidence in the courts than other branches of the criminal justice system. For example, while less than one-quarter of the polled public expressed a lack of confidence in the police in Britain, almost half the sample lacked confidence in the courts (see Hough and Roberts 2004, for a review). A sentencing system that ignored an offender's criminal record, and punished (for example) an offender with six previous convictions with no more severity than a first offender convicted of the same offence, would also attract public obloquy. These two concepts—proportionality and the recidivist sentencing premium—appear fundamental to public conceptions of legal punishment.

A previous chapter noted the link between offender perceptions of the legitimacy of the criminal justice system and compliance with the criminal law. A system which fails to be perceived as legitimate will have difficulty ensuring compliance or encouraging desistance. Public perceptions of the legitimacy of the sentencing process are also important. As Robinson and Darley note: 'the compliance power of the criminal law is directly proportional to its moral credibility' (1995: 6). A wide discrepancy between the two with respect to basic principles will lead to public disaffection with the sentencing process and may well undermine compliance.

Generally speaking, the sentencing process is broadly consistent with community opinion. The discrepancy between courts and community would appear to involve overall levels of severity, with the public favouring punishments that are usually, but by no means always, harsher. Although individual sentencing decisions will often spark public ire—particularly when a partial account of the case or the sentencing decision appears in the news media—the essential features of the system are consistent with public expectations. Thus sentencing practices reflect proportionality; the sentencing objectives placed on a statutory footing are mostly ones with which the public are familiar;[1] and rankings of offence seriousness derived from judges and members of the public are highly intercorrelated (eg, Levi and Jones 1985). As long as these features are present the sentencing system will remain within the broad limits of public acceptability or tolerance and will be perceived by most people to be legitimate albeit not necessarily harsh enough (see Walker and Hough 1988; Hough 1996 for discussion). But a departure from community views on an important issue like proportionality or the appropriate use of previous convictions will drain away much of this legitimacy—hence the need to understand community reaction to the use of criminal history information at sentencing.

[1] For example, in England and Wales, section 142(1) of the Criminal Justice Act 2003 directs courts to have regard to: the punishment and rehabilitation of offenders; deterrence; rehabilitation; protection of the public and reparation—these are all sentencing objectives with which the public are familiar.

Prospects for exclusionary models of sentencing

How likely is it that an exclusionary approach to the use of prior convictions will be adopted? The challenge to advocates of this perspective is to convince legislators and the community that it is possible to treat the offence and the offender as separate entities, and to punish the latter for the former, rather than for elements of his or her character or past conduct, particularly actions for which the offender has already been punished. But is it reasonable to ignore a characteristic such as previous offending that the intuitive sentencer will regard as highly relevant to the determination of sentence? It is significant in this context that in research reported by Wilkins (1984) the majority of a diverse population of criminal justice professionals and members of the public agreed with the statement that 'To assess the seriousness of a crime I would need to know something about the offender' (see p 114). This finding underlines the link in the public mind of the act and the actor.

Retributivist sentencing theorists who adhere to a 'flat-rate' exclusionary model may acknowledge that it is impossible to conceive such a system ever being implemented. For example, although he supports a progressive loss of mitigation model rather than the exclusionary alternative, Duff recognizes the practical impediments to some sentencing models: 'One might find my account plausible or attractive as an ideal account, but think it so remote from our existing systems of penality that it lacks application to our actual world' (2001: 167). Indeed, it is hard to conceive any flat rate sentencing schemes which would prove acceptable to the broader community.

Bagaric (2001) proposes a system of fixed penalties—even for offences as serious as murder. Such a sentencing scheme would generate considerable public opposition. More recently still, Bernard Harcourt (2007) advocates a different exclusionary position when he advocates the total elimination of risk considerations from sentencing decisions. He is interested in 'making criminal justice determinations blind to predictions of future dangerousness' (p 5). This seems equally unrealistic, as it would also result in a sentencing system that is likely to encounter considerable community opposition: few members of the public would support a sentencing model which paid no attention to risk factors.

A flat-rate approach to the use of previous convictions lumps together first offenders and multiple recidivists. Criticism of the use of criminal history information sometimes focuses on the stigmatizing effect of such a sentencing policy: the offender with two or three prior convictions is perceived as a persistent offender. Such a judgment is as inaccurate as it is unfair, and it is noteworthy that this is one of the elements of the sentencing process that individuals interviewed for this volume objected to the most. But ignoring prior convictions entirely creates another 'labelling problem': first offenders are classified in the same way as people with long criminal histories. In this way first offenders are denied the opportunity to distinguish themselves from multiple recidivists.

The idea of punishing offenders only for the seriousness of their current offence clearly lacks application to the current penal environment. If the public were less attracted to the proposition that increments in sentence severity would lower the likelihood of reoffending, there may be more room for constraining the use of prior convictions to a greater extent. But shifting the intuitive sentencer away from the belief that culpability for a specific offence is influenced by the offender's past constitutes a far greater challenge. The public would need to reconceptualize their judgments of offender culpability, crime seriousness, and much else before they will accept the flat-rate approach to previous convictions or the principle of the progressive loss of mitigation. The popular approach to the use of previous convictions seems so fundamental—and possibly universal—that transforming it will not be easy.

However, allowing courts free rein to incorporate previous convictions will result in the undermining of proportionality, and a movement towards a system that punishes actors rather than actions. Moreover, a cumulative sentencing model would undermine the principle of proportionality—and therefore public confidence in the sentencing process. Sentencing reformers are confronted with an invidious choice between two equally untenable paths. The solution would appear to involve recognizing the relevance of previous convictions, and then constraining their influence on the determination of sentence.

What might be done to improve the way in which the sentencing process considers an offender's previous convictions at sentencing? A number of steps need to be taken.

Importance of clarity and honesty in sentencing

From a denunciatory-retributive perspective, the system of proportionality should be floating on the waves of public consent, not hidden in the invisible mud of the ocean floor (Davies 1993: 17).

First, the sentencing systems of many common law jurisdictions need to introduce more clarity and transparency. Under the formal sentencing guidelines used in many US jurisdictions the existence and magnitude of the recidivist premium is clear: anyone wishing to know how much additional punishment is imposed on offenders as a result of their previous convictions can simply consult the state or federal sentencing guidelines manual. This is not possible in jurisdictions such as England and Wales, Canada, and other common law jurisdictions. As noted earlier in this volume, under current sentencing arrangements, the magnitude of the recidivist premium is obscured by the total sentence imposed, which reflects a potentially large number of aggravating and mitigating factors. Offenders should be given a much clearer sense of the consequences of reoffending as well as an idea of how they may mitigate these consequences.

Incorporating an offender's previous convictions at sentencing reflects a consensual response to crime and the statutory framework needs to reflect this reality. In addition, while directions to judges regarding this issue will likely remain at a general level, the statute can at least specify the justification for such an approach, as well as the way in which courts should incorporate previous convictions at sentencing.

The role of previous convictions at sentencing should be placed on a statutory footing, as has recently been the case in England and Wales, or clearly articulated in sentencing guidelines. The guidance should include the following:

- articulation of the rationale that justifies the consideration of previous convictions at sentencing, namely enhanced culpability;
- direction that the effect of previous convictions must be constrained by the seriousness of the offence of current conviction;
- direction about the specific dimensions of criminal history that should influence the extent to which priors aggravate the severity of sentence;

- direction to consider any efforts on the part of the offender to change his or her life that may reduce the degree to which the community considers them blameworthy.

Need for education of the public and offenders

> A failure to explain the manner in which [previous convictions are] taken into account does not enlighten the sentencing process...nor does it inform the offender, the Crown and the community of the use which the sentencing judge has made of this factor.[2]

Reconciling the sentencing process with community views involves more than acknowledging the relevance of previous convictions. It is important that the public have a more accurate perception of the nature of the problem and the limitations on the penal response. As Blumstein observes, we need to 'find a means to enhance public education so that the naïve belief that more punishment will lead to less crime...becomes less prevalent' (2004: 75).

Members of the public will not accept a flat-rate model or even the progressive loss of mitigation, but they should understand that a sentencing policy which routinely imposes steeply progressive penalties to reflect an offender's previous convictions would have only a limited effect on the probability of reoffending. Accordingly, agencies responsible for devising sentencing policy and disseminating guidance to sentencers should make a greater effort to improve the level of public knowledge in the area. Despite the increased sensitivity to the views of the public (noted in Chapter 1), efforts to increase the level of public knowledge are rare and modest in nature.

Offenders too need to be provided with more information. A common complaint of defendants in the criminal process is that they are all too often bystanders in the sentencing process. A number of people interviewed for the present volume expressed their confusion at the sentencing process. A typical comment is that made by one individual who stated that: 'The language is all gobbledy-gook and really hard to understand. It's hard to understand what they're saying about you. The language is very outdated.' This perception of being almost incidental to their own sentencing proceedings also emerges from interviews reported by Jacobson and Hough (2007).

[2] *R* v *Walker* [2005] NSWCCA 109 at 32; (New South Wales Court of Criminal Appeal).

Part of the alienation and mystification comes from the speed with which most sentencing hearings are conducted and the language employed by legal professionals. Busy legal professionals concerned with clearing the court's daily docket may have insufficient time or inclination to explain sentencing decisions in any detail. This is regrettable; when the state imposes punishment it also creates an obligation to fully explain the nature, purpose, and consequence of that punishment to the individual on whom it is imposed. This is particularly relevant to the recidivist sentencing premium which may be interpreted by some as additional punishment for previously purged offences, and which is currently perceived by many to be unfairly administered. Judges in a number of common law jurisdictions now conduct brief 'inquiries' in open court to ensure that offenders who plead guilty are aware of the consequences of such a plea. A comparable effort should be made to ensure that an offender understands the logic underlying the sentence he or she receives, as well as the consequences in the event of reconviction.

Limit the impact of previous convictions on sentence severity

Allowing sentence severity to increase dramatically as a function of the offender's criminal record would ultimately swamp proportionality considerations. The consequence would be that pursuit of one sentencing universal (a recidivist premium) would entail loss of the second (proportionality). Offenders convicted of low seriousness crimes but with lengthy criminal records would be punished as harshly as offenders convicted of crimes of intermediate seriousness. And offenders convicted of crimes of intermediate seriousness would attract penal sanctions usually reserved for the most serious offences. Baker and Clarkson (2002) argued that the Home Office sentencing proposals of 2001 (see Chapter 5) would undermine proportionality for this reason, but their point has a general application. There is a clear danger of previous convictions assuming primacy over proportionality in the current penal climate in which so much attention is focused on the repeat offender.

Although I have described proportionality and the recidivist premium as 'universal' sentencing factors, they should not carry equal weight. A sentencing system in which previous convictions trumped crime seriousness would founder in terms of community values, as surely as one in which previous convictions played no role. As noted earlier in this volume, the aggravating power of previous convictions is constrained by other, more important aggravating circumstances, namely those relating to the seriousness of the current offence. The challenge is to incorporate criminal history but not to allow it free rein.

The exception to this general rule involves offenders who accumulate very high numbers of convictions, and whose offending careers appear unaffected by sentencing decisions. The proportionality constraints upon the sentencing of most offenders should be waived in such cases to reflect the highly repetitive nature of such offenders. Sentencers should be given enhanced powers to impose disproportionate sentences for offenders who meet strict criteria of eligibility (based on the number and nature of their convictions). This is the case in some jurisdictions already.

Imposing an incremental quantum of punishment to reflect each additional criminal conviction reflects a simplistic and empirically unsupported assumption about the individual deterrent capacity of the sentencing process. The imposition of a mechanical recidivist premium according to the cumulative sentencing model may well be counter-productive. Moving away from a punitive recidivist premium is likely to engage offenders more in the enterprise of desistance. There is clear resentment against a system which imposes harsher punishments on the basis of an ascribed, aggregate risk score. Mechanistic models that simply assign a more severe sentence for each relevant prior conviction should be abandoned.

How might the influence of an offender's previous convictions be restrained? It will be recalled that under the Swedish sentencing statute the restriction on the use of previous convictions was that courts shall consider priors 'to a reasonable extent'. Similarly, the South African Law Reform Commission proposed a provision which stated that 'The presence or absence of relevant previous convictions may be used to modify the sentence proportionate to the seriousness of the offence to a moderate degree' (South African Law Reform Commission 2000: 42). These formulations are too vague to effectively guide the exercise of discretion in this regard.

Can an offender's previous convictions be incorporated beyond the limit prescribed by the progressive loss of mitigation without dismantling a proportionality-based framework? One way of conceptualizing the question would involve considerations of ordinal proportionality, a requirement of desert-based sentencing (see von Hirsch 1993). Ordinal proportionality carries specific requirements, one being that offenders convicted of crimes of approximately equal seriousness should receive punishments of comparable severity. A second requirement is that the severity of punishments should reflect a rank-ordering of the seriousness of the crimes for which they are imposed: the more serious crimes should be punished with greater severity. Thus rank-orderings of severity should reflect the relative seriousness of offences, not the seriousness of offenders' criminal histories. Ordinal proportionality applies to offenders convicted of the same offence, or between different offences. Creating important distinctions (in terms of the severity of sentence imposed) between two offenders convicted of comparable crimes on the basis that one offender has a longer criminal record thus threatens an essential requirement of ordinal proportionality.

Rankings of ordinal proportionality will not be scrambled by modest increments in sentence severity imposed to reflect the number of previous convictions. For example, if the range of sentence length for a specific offence, X, is 12 to 48 months, with a tariff or entry point of 24 months, an increment, of say, no more than six months to reflect a criminal record, will not irreparably undermine rankings of ordinal proportionality. The reason for this is that the most serious case of crime X should result in a sentence in the 40 to 48 month range, with the longest sentence being imposed on the most serious case committed by the offender with the worst record. But offence seriousness will still account for most of the variance in sentence severity. The enhanced sentence imposed on the multiple recidivist should not take him into the severity range for a much more serious crime.

The proposed model provides for a significant discount for first offenders—more than the modest reduction suggested by the progressive loss of mitigation model. The reason for this is that the difference in culpability between a first offender and one with two or three priors is very important. Another difference between this model and the conventional retributive models is that thereafter sentence severity should rise to reflect the accumulation of additional convictions—but at a more modest rate than suggested by the traditional cumulative model. In this way, the offender's record influences the determination of sentence severity, but not to the extent of swamping proportionality considerations. The third divergence from the traditional models concerns the incorporation of considerations that may qualify or even efface the role of previous convictions.

Counterbalancing the recidivist sentencing premium

In fairness to him, what a man has done that redounds to his credit ought sometimes to be admitted to counterbalance the crime that redounds to his discredit. (Gross 1979: 451).

A recidivist premium that imposes progressively harsher punishments without regard to their efforts to desist constitutes a punitive response to offending; it offers ex-offenders no incentive to change their lives. Greater recognition should be made of any efforts in this direction. The repeat offenders interviewed in this research believed that the courts failed to adequately consider changes that had occurred in their lives. Sentencers in this country may well deny this allegation; the veracity of this perception thus awaits empirical verification.

What kinds of actions should be considered in this way? If previous convictions are regarded as enhancing culpability by placing the current offending in a specific context, countervailing actions should consist of efforts made to desist. These may include efforts to address an addiction, to secure and maintain employment, and the like. If courts allow offenders 'credit' for such actions the sentencing process moves to do more than simply punishing persistence.

Repeat offenders are regarded as more culpable, more blameworthy, to the extent that their life choices embrace offending. The most culpable offender is therefore the one who commits the same offence again in a short interval since having been sentenced and without having made any attempt to address lifestyle issues contributing to his or her offending. Culpability thus declines as the interval between offending increases. This is of course consistent with decay provisions that assign progressively less weight to previous convictions the further in the past they are from the current conviction. However, under current sentencing arrangements, previous convictions count against an offender regardless of any steps he may have taken to resist a relapse into offending (unless the court exercises its discretion to do otherwise). An offender's efforts to desist are generally not formally recognized by the courts, although sentencers may occasionally mitigate the impact of priors when confronted with an offender who has taken such steps.

But this approach to mitigating the impact of previous convictions is essentially passive in nature. Offenders should be given credit for taking steps towards their rehabilitation; recognition should be made of efforts to desist. According to this logic the sentencing system relies on incentives rather than simply the threat of punishment. By allowing the offender's actions to attenuate or efface entirely the impact of previous convictions the system is drawing upon the principle of negative reinforcement—the withdrawal of an aversive stimulus. This is different from punishment which involves the infliction of an aversive stimulus in response to specific forms of behaviour.

The defendant should be able to credit any *relevant* life experiences against the state's ascription of enhanced blameworthiness arising from previous convictions. Some jurisdictions have contemplated incorporating this kind of consideration at sentencing. For example, the current Swedish sentencing statute was preceded by a Commission which issued a report two years earlier by the Swedish Parliament. The Parliamentary Committee's report proposed authorizing a reduction of sentence where 'through the offender's own efforts, a considerable improvement has occurred in his personal and social situation that bears on his criminality'.[3] In the event, the Committee's proposal was not enacted into statutory form (von Hirsch and Jareborg 1989). Courts' alleged failure to reward steps towards rehabilitation or protracted periods of desistance was a clear source of dissatisfaction among the individuals interviewed for this volume. A provision of this nature effectively allows the offender to rebut a presumption of enhanced culpability as a function of his previous convictions.

It is important, however, to make it clear that the credit accorded an offender should be related to the issue of his offending. The credit is extended to recognize his attempts to achieve desistance, not simply any commendable actions on his part. It will be recalled from Chapter 5 that in the state of Victoria, the statutory sentencing considerations include 'any significant contributions made to the community by the offender'. Such a provision is over-broad, can only lead to social accounting sentencing, and is likely to be of particular advantage to defendants with the

[3] Translation cited in von Hirsch and Jareborg (1989: 277).

capacity and resources to make a significant contribution to the community. Thus the sentencing process should not accord mitigation for actions unrelated to the offender's previous offending. For example, an offender convicted of a crime for which custody is warranted should not be spared imprisonment because he, for example, displayed some exceptional act of bravery shortly after committing the crime.

This is not a novel proposal. Courts have long given offenders credit for 'going straight', as manifested in a protracted period of crime-free living. It was noted over a generation ago by Cross and Ashworth (1981). However, the practice is far from widespread, and has received only limited recognition at the appellate level. It is important to increase the visibility of the principle, possibly by placing it on a statutory footing.

It is important, however, that when recognizing (and giving sentence credit for) an offender's efforts to change his life, or overcome criminogenic problems, the court should make this recognition known in open court or in reasons for sentence. In this way, the community and the victim (not to mention the offender) may come to understand why previous convictions, having been considered, are being discounted or ignored.

This proposal would change the graph relating sentence severity to the number of previous convictions. Some offenders with previous convictions will be given significant credit for taking steps to avoid criminal relapse—even though they have ultimately been reconvicted. Their previous offending may carry little or no weight when considered against their life experiences since last conviction. On the other hand an offender with a technically comparable criminal history but who has made no effort to desist will be subject to a recidivist sentencing premium as he will be considered to be more culpable as a consequence of his record. This enhanced culpability justifies a more interventionist state response.

Need to avoid stigmatizing offenders with previous convictions

If thy offences were upon record,
Would it not shame thee, in so fair a troop,
To read a lecture of them?[4]

[4] Shakespeare, *Richard* II, iv. i. 230–2.

Incorporating consideration of the offender's efforts to desist in the determination of the relevance of his or her prior convictions serves another important function. A number of offenders interviewed in the course of this research expressed the view that they had been labelled a 'repeat offender' or a 'rounder'—a label that they resisted and resented. Even individuals who did not use the actual term appeared to feel stigmatized by this sentencing process. If offenders are to be considered more blameworthy as a result of their previous convictions it is important to ensure that they do not become shamed by having their past misconduct automatically considered in the present.

Increased disparity?

Is this counter-balancing model a recipe for greater sentencing disparity or unfairness? There may be fears that such an approach will be of disproportionate benefit to middle class offenders who have the resources to change their lives, and to represent these changes to a sentencing court. Two responses may be made to these objections. First, consistency could be promoted by providing sentencers with guidance as to how to evaluate these aspects of the offender's life. The purpose is not to favour offenders with particular characters any more than the objective of a recidivist premium is to punish an individual for having a bad character. Second, it should be recalled that if previous convictions are relevant to one of the branches of proportional sentencing (offender culpability), the multiple recidivist *deserves* a different sentence from the person with, say, only two prior convictions. The discrepancy between the sanctions imposed upon the two offenders is thus an example of principled disparity.

Encourage ex-offenders to regain their 'first offender' status

In addition to encouraging ex-offenders to mitigate the impact of their criminal histories they should be encouraged to regain their original status as non-offenders. For their own benefit as well as society, offenders need to divest themselves of their criminal records as early as is possible. Reviewing the vast literature upon the effect of a criminal record is beyond the scope of the present volume but many studies have demonstrated that ex-offenders both anticipate and receive differential treatment from the criminal justice system and society in general.[5] Ruddell and Winfree (2006) in one of the rare studies on the use of pardon legislation report that despite the relative ease with which a pardon may be obtained and a criminal conviction expunged, few ex-offenders apply for a pardon. This suggests that simply informing these individuals of the appropriate steps would be of benefit in increasing the proportion of ex-offenders who can shake off their offender status.

Dimensions of criminal history

Finally, the discussion so far has considered previous convictions in a relatively simplistic fashion, assuming that previous convictions enhance culpability in a unidimensional way. But sentencers and sentencing guidelines obviously incorporate many aspects of an offender's criminal record when determining the criminal history score. Sentencers in jurisdictions without formal guidelines also consider a number of aspects of an offender's previous convictions.

The two most obvious dimensions are the recency of the prior convictions, and their relationship to the offence of current convictions (Wasik 1987; Roberts 1997a), but there are many others, including the custody status of the offender at the time of the fresh conviction, whether the priors were committed while the offender was still a juvenile and so forth. Some of these will have a bearing on the degree to which the offender may be considered more blameworthy, others will not. Recency is the most important consideration from a culpability perspective. Imagine two offenders convicted of the same crime of assault. One individual has a prior related conviction five years earlier. The other was convicted of fraud six months ago. The latter would be considered more culpable as the current crime was committed while the previous sentence must have been in the offender's mind. Following this logic, the offender who commits an offence while on probation or parole is most culpable, as he carries the order of the court with him at the time of the fresh offence.

[5] Masden (1978) found that ex-offenders viewed themselves in different ways from other American citizens. For example, they anticipated receiving differential treatment from criminal justice professionals, due solely to the existence of their criminal record.

If the time since the previous conviction is the same, related priors enhance culpability to a greater extent. Consider the case of two offenders convicted of assault, one of whom has a prior assault conviction, the other a prior conviction for car theft. Although the culpability justification applies equally to both offenders, the previous conviction of the first offender provides a different context for judging the current conviction. It is no surprise therefore that most sentencing systems weigh a related previous conviction more heavily than an unrelated prior offence. Unrelated offences are nevertheless still relevant to the determination of the offender's level of culpability.[6] The offender who was last year convicted of extortion and who is now convicted of assault cannot reasonably invoke a first offender discount on the basis that he has not assaulted anyone to this point in time.

From a culpability perspective, it is hard to see the relevance of the seriousness of the previous conviction. Many US guideline schemes assign a higher criminal history score to a more serious prior, and under the federal guidelines, a more serious previous conviction—that resulted in a more severe sentence—is weighed more heavily than a less serious prior conviction. But how does the seriousness of the previous offence make the offender more culpable? Once again consider two offenders, both now convicted of fraud. Individual A has a previous conviction for a relatively minor theft, while Individual B was convicted of a large-scale theft involving thousands of pounds of goods. Both offenders were previously called to account for their prior offending; the harm inflicted by the previous crime should not affect their current level of culpability.

Reconceptualizing the recidivist premium

There are a number of possible ways in which criminal history may be reconceptualised. One alternate way of recognizing the relevance of an offender's previous convictions would be to create a dual sentence structure for sentences of custody. The offender would be assigned two penalties, one to reflect the seriousness of the crime and the other to reflect his previous convictions and

[6] This is another respect in which the model described here differs from another culpability-based justification for a recidivist sentencing premium proposed recently by MacPherson (2002). He proposes a model which assumes that the offender's prior convictions are for the same crime as the offence of conviction.

both would be announced in open court. In order to preserve the proportional requirements of the sentencing process, a formula would be followed in which the magnitude of the recidivist premium would be constrained by the quantum of punishment imposed for the latest offence. How would such a system work? Sentencing tariffs would be determined to reflect factors related to the seriousness of the offence. For a serious crime such as robbery this might result in a range of one to three years, with a significantly higher maximum penalty. Assume that the offender has been convicted of a sentence of middle-range seriousness, and that this results in the imposition of a two-year term. Examination of the offender's previous convictions would permit the court to impose a recidivist premium that would increase the base sentence.

Recidivist sentencing premium as a suspended sentence

The additional punishment imposed for previous offending could be converted into a suspended sentence, to be activated in the event of reconviction. An offender sentenced for, say, burglary might receive a 24 month sentence to reflect the seriousness of the offence and his level of culpability for the crime. To this would be added an additional period of imprisonment which would only be served in the event that the individual reappeared for sentencing. At the subsequent sentencing hearing this component of the sentence would be executed. This scheme has several advantages over present formulations. First, the individual has a clear idea of the additional punishment arising from his or her previous convictions. Second, the ability of the offender to avoid paying 'again' for previous offending is made clear: the recidivist penalty will never be imposed unless and until reconviction occurs. Third, consistent with the concepts promoted in this volume, the ex-offender has a clear incentive to desist from offending. The duration of the recidivist premium would decline over time, and would eventually disappear. The longer the offender goes without reoffending, the less severe would be the punishment imposed for prior offending.

Aggravated forms of offences

There are two ways that the sentencing process recognizes a factor that aggravates the sentence imposed. The presence of the factor may be cited as an aggravating circumstance at sentencing—either because it has been recognized as such by the Court of Appeal or because the factor has been singled out by the legislature by being placed on a statutory footing. Alternatively the factor may result in the offender being sentenced under an aggravated form of the offence. This approach is sometimes adopted with respect to previous convictions and it could be generalized. Many jurisdictions have tiered offence structures for offences such as assault or sexual assault, with the aggravated forms involving greater injury to the victim. An aggravated range of sentence could be created for all offences, but with a precise definition of the aggravated offence.[7] For example, for assault, the aggravated form might involve an offender with a previous conviction for this offence. Aggravated assault could be defined as an assault committed by an individual with a previous conviction for assault.[8] Examples of this approach to punishing persistence exist, but are generally over-broad and stigmatizing.

Coda

Defining the appropriate role for previous convictions in the sentencing process has proved a challenge for all jurisdictions. No theoretical model has attracted the consensus which surrounds proportionality and the consequence is that the manner in which prior convictions are considered at sentencing varies considerably.

This volume has argued that the status quo regarding the punishment of offenders is unacceptable, and contributes to public

[7] I am grateful to Estella Baker for bringing this proposal to my attention. A variation on this proposal may be found in an article by MacPherson (2002) who advocates creation of a number of severity 'plateaus' to reflect different levels of criminal history.

[8] The state would thus have to prove all the elements of the offence as well as the offender's previous conviction. This may encourage plea bargaining, with the Crown offering not to introduce the accused's previous conviction in return for a guilty plea to the lesser and included offence of assault. This exercise of prosecutorial discretion is often observed in the context of tiered offences carrying different penalty levels.

disenchantment with the sentencing process. Considering previous misconduct is an inescapable element of contemporary penality. If we acknowledge this reality and incorporate previous convictions in a limited and reasonable fashion this would remove an important source of public and professional criticism. Otherwise the populist pressures to punish recidivists will result in ever harsher punishments to reflect previous convictions. The rather mechanistic computation of criminal history found in the US sentencing guideline schemes ensure equity of treatment but fail to adequately contextualize an offender's previous misconduct. The linear progression of more severe punishments also fails to reflect risk factors and is more consistent with a punitive model of sentencing. Sentencing schemes that affirm the principle of the progressive loss of mitigation are little better; they create a legal fiction that is at odds with community and professional opinions as well as judicial practice. It is surely time to recognize the inherent relevance of an offender's previous convictions yet limit their impact in order to preserve proportionality in sentencing.

References

Abel, C. and Marsh, F. (1984) *Punishment and Restitution: A Restitutionary Approach to Crime and the Criminal.* Westport, CT: Greenwood Press.

Adler, J. (1991) *The Urgings of Conscience: A Theory of Punishment.* Philadelphia: Temple University Press.

Ahmed, E., Harris, N., Braithwaite, J., and Braithwaite, V. (2001) *Shame Management Through Reintegration.* Cambridge: Cambridge University Press.

Albonetti, C. (1991) 'An Integration of Theories to Explain Judicial Discretion'. *Social Problems*, 38: 247–65.

Alpert, G. and Hicks, D. (1977) 'Prisoners' Attitudes Toward Components of the Legal and Judicial Systems'. *Criminology*, 14: 461–82.

Amelin, K., Willis, M., Blair, C. and Donnelly, D. (2000) *Attitudes to Crime, Crime Reduction and Community Safety in Northern Ireland.* Review of the Criminal Justice System in Northern Ireland. Research Report No. 1. Belfast: Northern Ireland Office.

Andrews, D. and Bonta, J. (1995) *The Level of Service Inventory* (revised edn). Toronto: Multihealth Systems.

—— —— (2003) *The Psychology of Criminal Conduct* (3rd edn). Cincinnati: Anderson Publishing Co.

Applegate, B., Cullen, F., Barton, S., Richards, P., Lanza-Kaduce, L., and Link, B. (1995) 'Public Support for Drunk-Driving Countermeasures: Social Policy for Saving Lives'. *Crime and Delinquency,* 41: 171–90.

—— —— Link, B., Richards, P., and Lanza-Kaduce, L. (1996) 'Determinants of Public Punitiveness toward Drunk Driving: A Factorial Survey Approach'. *Justice Quarterly*, 13: 57–79.

—— —— Turner, M., and Sundt, J. (1996) 'Assessing Public Support for Three-Strikes-and-You're-Out Laws: Global versus Specific Attitudes'. *Crime and Delinquency*, 42: 517–34.

——Davis, R., and Cullen, F. (2007) *Reconsidering Child Saving: The extent and correlates of public support for excluding youths from the juvenile court.* Manuscript under review. Available from: bapplega@ mail.ucf.edu.

Arcuri, A. (1976) 'Lawyers, Judges, and Plea Bargaining: Some New Data on Inmates' Views'. *International Journal of Criminology and Penology*, 4: 177–91.

Aronson, E. (1999) *The Social Animal* (8th edn). New York: Worth Publishers.

Ashworth, A. (1996) 'The Sentencing Guideline System in England and Wales'. *South African Journal of Criminal Justice*, 19: 1–22.

Ashworth, A. (2000) *Sentencing and Criminal Justice* (3rd edn). London: Butterworths.

——(2005) *Sentencing and Criminal Justice* (4th edn). Cambridge: Cambridge University Press.

——and Hough, M. (1996) 'Sentencing and the Climate of Public Opinion'. *Criminal Law Review*, November: 776–87.

Australian Law Reform Commission (1980) *Sentencing of Federal Offenders*. Interim Report No 15. Sydney: Australian Law Reform Commission.

——(2005) *Sentencing of Federal Offenders*. Sydney: Australian Law Reform Commission.

Bagaric, M. (2000a) 'The Errors of Retributivism'. *Melbourne University Law Review*, 24: 1–64.

——(2000b) 'Double Punishment and Punishing Character: the unfairness of prior convictions'. *Criminal Justice Ethics*, 10: 10–28.

——(2001) *Punishment and Sentencing: A Rational Approach*. Sydney: Cavendish Publishing.

——and Amarasekara, K. (2001) 'Feeling Sorry—Tell Someone who Cares: The Irrelevance of Remorse in Sentencing'. *Howard Journal of Criminal Justice*, 40: 364–76.

——and Edney, R. (2004) 'The Sentencing Advisory Commission and the Hope of Smarter Sentencing'. *Current Issues in Criminal Justice*, 16: 125–39.

Baker, E. and Clarkson, C. (2002) 'Making Punishments Work? An Evaluation of the Halliday Report on Sentencing in England and Wales'. *Criminal Law Review*, February: 81–97.

Baker, J. (2003) *The Oxford History of the Laws of England. Volume VI.* Oxford: Oxford University Press.

Baker, T. (1889) 'Systematic Sentencing of Prisoners', in H. Philips and E. Verney (eds.), *'War with Crime'. Being a Selection of Reprinted Papers on Crime, Reformatories etc. by the late T. Barwick Baker.* London: Longmans.

Bakker, L., O'Malley, J., and Riley, D. (1999) *Risk of Reconviction: Statistical Models Predicting Four Types of Re-Offending.* Christchurch: New Zealand Department of Corrections.

Bala, N. (2003) *Youth Criminal Justice Law*. Toronto: Irwin Law.

BBC News (2002) *Attitudes Towards Juries and Sentencing: Survey Results*. Available at <http://www.bbc.co.uk>.

Bean, P. (1981) *Punishment: A Philosophical and Criminological Inquiry.* Oxford: Martin Robertson.

Beattie, J. (1986) *Crime and the Courts in England, 1660–1800.* Princeton: Princeton University Press.

Beccaria, C. (1764; 1963) *On Crimes and Punishments*. London: Collier Macmillan.

Beck, U. (1992) *Risk Society: Towards a New Modernity.* London: Sage.

Beckett, K. and Sasson, T. (2000) *The Politics of Injustice: Crime and Punishment in Contemporary American Politics*. New York: Oxford University Press.

Benaquisto, L. and Freed, P. (1996) 'The Myth of Inmate Lawlessness: The Perceived Contradiction between Self and Other in Inmates' Support for Criminal Justice Sanctioning Norms'. *Law and Society Review*, 30: 481–511.

Bennett, T. and Wright, R. (1984) *Burglars on Burglary: Prevention and the Offender*. Aldershot: Gower.

Bentham, J. (1843) *The Works of Jeremy Bentham*. Volume 1. Edinburgh: W. Tait.

Beresford, S. (2001) 'Unshackling the Paper Tiger—the Sentencing Practices of the ad hoc International Criminal Tribunals for the Former Yugoslavia and Rwanda'. *International Criminal Law Review*, 1: 33–90.

Berman, J. (1976) 'Parolees' Perceptions of the Justice System'. *Criminology*, 13: 507–20.

Birkenmayer, A. and Besserer, S. (1997) *Sentencing in Adult Provincial Courts: A Study of Nine Jurisdictions: 1993 and 1994*. Ottawa: Ministry of Industry.

Blomberg, T., Bales, W., and Reed, K. (1993) 'Intermediate Punishment: Redistributing or Extending Social Control?' *Crime, Law, and Social Change*, 19: 187–201.

Blum-West, S. (1985) 'The Seriousness of Crime: A Study of Public Morality'. *Deviant Behavior*, 6: 83–98.

Blumstein, A. (2004) 'Restoring Rationality in Punishment Policy', in M. Tonry (ed.) *The Future of Imprisonment*. New York: Oxford University Press.

Bottomley, K. and Pease, K. (1986) *Crime and Punishment: Interpreting the Data*. Milton Keynes: Open University Press.

Braithwaite, J. (1999) 'Restorative Justice: Assessing Optimistic and Pessimistic Accounts', in M. Tonry (ed.) *Crime and Justice: A Review of Research*. Volume 25. Chicago: University of Chicago Press.

Brillon, Y., Louis-Guerin, C., and Lamarche, M.C. (1984) *Attitudes of the Canadian Public Toward Crime Policies*. Montreal: Centre for Comparative Criminology, University of Montreal.

Brownfield, D. (2006), 'A Defiance Theory of Sanctions and Gang Membership'. *Journal of Gang Research*, 13: 31–43.

Burbidge, S. (1982) *Public Attitudes Concerning Pardons*. Ottawa: Ministry of the Solicitor General.

Bureau of Justice Statistics (1991) *Statutes Requiring the Use of Criminal History Record Information*. Washington, DC: Government Printing Office.

Bureau of Justice Statistics, U.S. Department of Justice (2000) *Felony Defendants in Large Urban Counties, 2000*. Washington, DC: Bureau of Justice Statistics, U.S. Department of Justice.

Bureau of Justice Statistics, U.S. Department of Justice (2002) *State Court Sentencing of Convicted Felons, 2002. Statistical Tables*. Washington, DC: Bureau of Justice Statistics, U.S. Department of Justice.

Burke, P. and Turk, A. (1975) 'Factors Affecting Post-arrest Dispositions: A Model for Analysis'. *Social Problems*, 22: 313–32.

Calverly, D. (2006) 'Youth Custody and Community Services in Canada, 2003/04'. *Juristat*, 26: 2.

Canadian Committee on Corrections (1969) *Report of the Canadian Committee on Corrections. Toward Unity: Criminal Justice and Corrections*. Ottawa: The Queen's Printer.

Canadian Sentencing Commission (1987) *Sentencing Reform: A Canadian Approach*. Ottawa: Supply and Services Canada.

Carlsmith, K., Darley, J., and Robinson, P. (2002) 'Why do we Punish? Deterrence and Just Deserts as Motives for Punishment'. *Journal of Personality and Social Psychology*, 83: 284–99.

Carroll, J. and Payne, J. (1977) 'Judgements about Crime and the Criminal', in B. Sales (ed.) *Perspectives in Law and Psychology*. Volume 1. New York: Plenum Press.

Casper, J. (1978a) *Criminal Courts: The Defendant's Perspective*. Washington, DC: National Institute of Law Enforcement and Criminal Justice.

——(1978b) 'Having Their Day in Court: Defendant Evaluations of the Fairness of Their Treatment'. *Law and Society Review*, 12: 237–51.

Champion, D. (1994) 'Selective Incapacitation and Recidivism: An Examination of the Issues', in *Measuring Offender Risk: A Criminal Justice Sourcebook*. Westport, CT: Greenwood Press.

Chermak, S. (1998) 'Predicting Crime Story Salience: the effects of crime, victim, and defendant characteristics'. *Journal of Criminal Justice*, 26: 61–70.

Clarke, A., Moran-Ellis, J. and Sleney, J. (2002) *Attitudes to Date Rape and Relationship Rape: A Qualitative Study*. London: Sentencing Advisory Panel.

Commissioners on the Public Records of the Kingdom (1831) *Ancient Laws and Institutes of England*. Volume the First. London: Price & Thorpe.

Conklin, J. (1975) *The Impact of Crime*. New York: Macmillan.

Cox, E. (1877) *The Principles of Punishment as Applied in the Administration of Criminal Law, by Judges and Magistrates*. London: Garland Publishing.

Crime and Justice Institute and Doble Research Associates (2005) *Rethinking Justice in Massachusetts: Public Attitudes Toward Crime and Punishment*. Boston: Crime and Justice Institute.

Cross, R. (1971) *The English Sentencing System* (1st edn). London: Butterworths.

Cross, R. and Ashworth, A. (1981) *The English Sentencing System* (3rd edn). London: Butterworths.

Cullen, F., Clark, G., Cullen, J., and Mathers, R. (1985) 'Attribution, Salience, and Attitudes Toward Criminal Sanctioning'. *Criminal Justice and Behavior*, 12: 305–31.

Cullen, F., Fisher, B. and Applegate, B. (2000) Public Opinion about Punishment and Corrections', in M. Tonry (ed.) *Crime and Justice: A Review of Research*. Chicago: University of Chicago Press.

Cullen, F.T., Link, B.G., and Polanzi, C.W. (1982) 'The Seriousness of Crime Revisited: Have Attitudes Toward White-Collar Crime Changed?' *Criminology*, 20:83–102.

Cumberland, J. and Zamble, E. (1992) 'General and Specific Measures of Attitudes Toward Early Release of Criminal Offenders'. *Canadian Journal of Behavioural Science*, 24: 442–55.

Cunliffe, J. and Shepherd, A. (2007) *Re-offending of Adults: Results from the 2004 Cohort*. Home Office Statistical Bulletin. London: Home Office, Research, Development and Statistics Directorate.

Daily Express (2006) *The Crime Crusader Murdered by Hoodies. Killers Were Freed Just Hours Earlier*. Thursday 13 April, p. 1.

Daily Mail (2006) *Justice Denied. Violent Serial Offenders Walk Free*. 26 June, p. 1.

Daily Record (2005) *Warning. All the Experts Say This Rape Monster Will Strike Again…but the System Has Set Him Free*. Thursday 13 October, p. 1.

Daly, K. (2003) 'Mind the Gap: Restorative Justice in Theory and Practice', in A. von Hirsch, J.V. Roberts, A. Bottoms, K. Roach, and M. Schiff (eds.) *Restorative and Criminal Justice: Competing or Reconcilable Paradigms*. Oxford: Hart Publishing.

Damaska, M. (1968) 'Adverse Legal Consequences of a Conviction and Their Removal'. *Journal of Criminal Law and Criminology*, 59: 542–68.

Darley, J., Carlsmith, K., and Robinson, P. (2000) 'Incapacitation and Just Deserts as Motives for Punishment'. *Law and Human Behavior*, 24: 659–83.

Davies, M. (1993) *Punishing Criminals: Developing Community-Based Intermediate Sanctions*. Westport, CT: Greenwood Press.

Davis, M. (1992) 'Just Deserts for Recidivists', in *To Make the Punishment Fit the Crime: Essays in the Theory of Criminal Justice*. Boulder, CO: Westview Press.

De Keijser, J., Van Koppen, P. and Elffers, H. (2006) *Bridging the gap between judges and the public? An Experimental Study into the Role of Information*. Leiden: Netherlands Institute for the Study of Crime and Law Enforcement.

Departmental Committee on Persistent Offenders (1932) *Report of the Departmental Committee on Persistent Offenders*. London: Her Majesty's Stationery Office.

Diamond, S. (1990) 'Revising Images of Public Punitiveness: Sentencing by Lay and Professional Magistrates'. *Law and Social Inquiry*, 15: 191–219.

Dignan, J. (2005) *Understanding Victims and Restorative Justice*. Maidenhead: Open University Press.

Division of Criminal Justice (1982) *Crime in Colorado: A Survey of Citizens*. Boulder, CO: Division of Criminal Justice.

Doble Research Associates (1994) *Crime and Corrections: The Views of the People of Vermont*. Englewood Cliffs, NJ: Doble Research Associates.

——(1995) *Crime and Corrections: The Views of the People of Oklahoma*. Englewood Cliffs, NJ: Doble Research Associates.

——(1998) *Crime and Corrections: The Views of the People of New Hampshire*. Englewood Cliffs, NJ: Doble Research Associates.

Doble, J. and Klein, J. (1989) *Punishing Criminals: The Public's View: An Alabama Survey*. New York: Edna McConnell Clark Foundation.

Dolan, M. and Doyle, M. (2000) 'Violence Risk Prediction: Clinical and Actuarial Measures and the Role of the Psychopathy Checklist'. *British Journal of Psychiatry*, 177: 303–11.

Doob, A.N. (1995) 'The United States Sentencing Commission Guidelines: If you don't know where you are going, you might not get there', in C. Clarkson and R. Morgan (eds.) *The Politics of Sentencing Reform*. Oxford: Clarendon Press.

——(2001) *Youth Court Judges' Views of the Youth Court System: The Results of a Survey*. Toronto: Centre of Criminology, University of Toronto.

——and Cesaroni, C. (2004) *Responding to Youth Crime in Canada*. Toronto: University of Toronto Press.

——and Roberts, J.V. (1982) *Crime: Some Views of the Canadian Public*. Ottawa: Department of Justice Canada.

————(1983) *An Analysis of the Public's View of Sentencing*. Ottawa: Department of Justice Canada.

————(1988) 'Public Punitiveness and Public Knowledge of the Facts: Some Canadian Surveys', in N. Walker and M. Hough (eds.) *Public Attitudes to Sentencing*. Cambridge Studies in Criminology. Aldershot: Gower.

——and Webster, C. (2003) 'Sentence Severity and Crime: Accepting the Null Hypothesis', in M. Tonry (ed.) *Crime and Justice: A Review of Research*, 30: 143–95. Chicago: University of Chicago Press.

Duff, R.A. (2001) *Punishment, Communication, and Community*. Oxford: Oxford University Press.

Dunbar, I. and Langdon, A. (1998) *Tough Justice: Sentencing and Penal Policies in the 1990s*. London: Blackstone Press Limited.

Durham, A. III (1987a) 'Crime Seriousness and Punitive Severity: An Assessment of Social Attitudes'. *Justice Quarterly*, 5: 131–53.

Durham, A. III (1987b) 'Justice in Sentencing: The Role of Prior Record of Criminal Involvement'. *Journal of Criminal Law and Criminology*, 78: 614–43.

Ekstedt, J. (1988) *Justice in Sentencing: Offender Perceptions*. Research Reports of the Canadian Sentencing Commission. Ottawa: Department of Justice Canada.

English, K., Crouch, J. and Pullen, S. (1988) *Attitudes Towards Crime: A Survey of Colorado Citizens and Criminal Justice Officials*. Boulder, CO: Colorado Department of Public Safety.

Erskine, H. (1974) 'The Polls: Causes of Crime'. *Public Opinion Quarterly*, 50: 288–98.

Ewart, B. and Pennington, D. (1987) 'An Attributional Approach to Explaining Sentence Disparity', in D. Pennington and S. Lloyd-Bostock (eds.) *The Psychology of Sentencing: Approaches to Consistency and Disparity*. Oxford: Centre for Socio-Legal Studies.

Ewing, A. (1929) *The Morality of Punishment*. London: Kegan Paul, Trench, Trubner and Co., Ltd.

Farrell, R. and Swigert, V. (1978) 'Prior Offence Record as a Self-Fulfilling Prophecy'. *Law and Society*, 12: 437–53.

Farrington, D. (1991) 'Childhood Aggression and Adult Violence: Early Precursors and Later Life Outcomes', in D. Pepler and K. Rubin (eds.) *The Development and Treatment of Childhood Aggression*. Hillsdale, NJ: Erlbaum.

Farrington, D., Coid, J., Harnett, L., Jolliffe, D., Soteriou, N., Turner, R., and West, D. (2006) *Criminal Careers up to Age 50 and Life Success up to Age 48: New Findings from the Cambridge Study in Delinquent Development*. Home Office Research Study 299. London: Home Office.

Ferrante, A., Loh, N., Maller, M., Valuri, G., and Fernandez, J. (2005) *Crime and Justice Statistics for Western Australia: 2004*. Crawley, Western Australia: Crime and Justice Research Centre, University of Western Australia.

Finkel, N., Maloney, S., Valbuena, M., and Groscup, J. (1996) 'Recidivism, Proportionalism, and Individualized Punishment'. *American Behavioural Scientist*, 39: 474–87.

Fiske, S. and Taylor, S. (1991) *Social Cognition* (2nd edn). New York: McGraw-Hill.

Fitzmaurice, C. and Pease, K. (1986) *The Psychology of Judicial Sentencing*. Manchester: Manchester University Press.

Flanagan, T. (1987) 'Change and Influence in Popular Criminology: Public Attributions of Crime Causation'. *Journal of Criminal Justice*, 15: 231–43.

——and Longmire, D. (eds.) (1996) *Americans View Crime and Justice: A National Public Opinion Survey*. Beverly Hills, CA: Sage.

Fletcher, G. (1978) *Rethinking Criminal Law.* Boston: Little, Brown and Company.

——(1982) 'The Recidivist Premium'. *Criminal Justice Ethics,* 1: 54–9.

Flood-Page, C. and Mackie, A. (1998) *Sentencing Practice: An Examination of Decisions in Magistrates' Courts and the Crown Court in the Mid-1990s.* Home Office Research Study 180. London: Home Office, Research and Statistics Directorate.

Florida Department of Corrections (1997) *Corrections in Florida: What the Public Thinks: Results of a Survey of Floridians.* Miami: Florida Department of Corrections.

——(2007) *Florida's Punishment Code: A Comparative Assessment.* Florida Department of Corrections. Available at: <http://www.dc.state.fl.us/pub/sg_annual/0506/descoffenses. html>.

Floud, J. and Young, W. (1981) *Dangerousness and Criminal Justice.* London: Heinemann.

Fox, R. (1994) 'The Meaning of Proportionality in Sentencing'. *Melbourne University Law Review*, 19: 489–511.

——(1999) 'When Justice Sheds a Tear: The Place of Mercy in Sentencing'. *Monash University Law Review*, 25: 1–28.

Frase, R. (2005) 'State Sentencing Guidelines: Diversity, Consensus, and Unresolved Policy Issues'. *Columbia Law Review*, 105: 1190–1232.

Freeman, J., Liossis, P., and David, N. (2006) 'Deterrence, Defiance and Deviance: An Investigation into a Group of Recidivist Drink Drivers' Self-Reported Offending Behaviours'. *Australia and New Zealand Journal of Criminology*, 39: 1–19.

Freiberg, A. (2006) *Twenty Years of Changes in the Sentencing Environment and Courts' Responses.* Paper presented at Sentencing Conference, Canberra, 10–12 February.

——and Gelb, K. (eds.) (2008) *Penal Populism, Sentencing Councils and Sentencing Policy.* Cullompton: Willan Publishing/Federation Press.

Furnham, A. and Alison, L. (1994) 'Theories of Crime, Attitudes to Punishment and Juror Bias Amongst Police, Offenders and the General Public'. *Personality and Individual Differences*, 17: 35–48.

Gabor, T. (1986) *The Prediction of Criminal Behaviour: Statistical Approaches.* Toronto: University of Toronto Press.

Galaway, B. (1984) 'A Survey of Public Acceptance of Restitution as an Alternative to Imprisonment for Property Offenders'. *Australian and New Zealand Journal of Criminology*, 17: 108–117.

Galligan, D. (1981) 'The Return to Retribution in Penal Theory', in C. Tapper (ed.) *Crime, Proof and Punishment: Essays in Memory of Sir Rupert Cross.* London: Butterworths.

Gandy, J. and Galaway, B. (1980) 'Restitution as a Sanction for Offenders: A Public's View', in J. Hudson and B. Galaway (eds.) *Victims, Offenders, and Alternative Sanctions*. Toronto: Lexington Books.

Gardiner, L. (1972) *Living it Down: The Problem of Old Convictions*. London: Stevens and Sons.

Gebotys, R. and Dasgupta, B. (1988) 'Attribution of Responsibility and Crime Seriousness'. *The Journal of Psychology*, 121: 607–13.

Gebotys, R. and Roberts, J. (1987) 'Public Views of Sentencing: The Role of Offender Characteristics'. *Canadian Journal of Behavioral Science*, 19: 479–88.

Gelb, K. (2006) *Myths and Misconceptions: Public Opinion versus Public Judgment about Sentencing*. Melbourne: Sentencing Advisory Council.

Gendreau, P., Goggin, C., and Little, T. (1996) *Predicting Adult Offender Recidivism: What Works!* User Report 1996–07. Ottawa: Public Works and Government Services Canada.

Gest, T. (2001) *Crime and Politics: Big Government's Erratic Campaign for Law and Order*. Oxford: Oxford University Press.

Glanz, L. (1994) 'The South African Public's Attitudes towards Imprisonment and the Release of Offenders'. *Acta Criminologica*, 7: 54–80.

Graber, D. (1980) 'Media and Public Images of Criminals and Victims', in *Crime News and the Public*. New York: Praeger Publishers.

Green, D. (2005) 'Public Opinion Versus Public Judgment About Crime: Correcting the "Comedy of Errors"'. *British Journal of Criminology*, 46: 131–54.

Green, E. (1961) *Judicial Attitudes in Sentencing: A Study of the Factors Underlying the Sentencing Practice of the Criminal Court of Philadelphia*. London: Macmillan.

Greenberg, J. and Pyszczynski, T. (1985) 'The Effects of an Overheard Ethnic Slur on Evaluations of the Target: How to Spread a Social Disease'. *Journal of Experimental Social Psychology*, 21: 61–72.

Greene, E. and Dodge, M. (1995) 'The Influence of Prior Record Evidence on Juror Decision Making'. *Law and Human Behaviour*, 19: 67–78.

Gross, H. (1979) *A Theory of Criminal Justice*. New York: Oxford University Press.

Grunhut, M. (1948) *Penal Reform: A Comparative Study*. Oxford: Clarendon Press.

Haas, N., de Keijser, J., and Vanderveen, G. (2007) 'Steun voor eigenrichting. Invloed van Ernst van de aanleiding en mate van planning, een experiment'. *Tijdschrift voor Criminologie*, 49: 45–56.

Hagan, J. and McCarthy, B. (1997) *Mean Streets: Youth Crime and Homelessness*. Cambridge: Cambridge University Press.

Hall, G. (2002) *Sentencing.* Wellington: Butterworths.

Halman, L. (2002) *The European Values Study: A Third Wave.* Tilburg, Netherlands: Tilburg University.

Hamilton, L. and Sanders, J. (1992) *Everyday Justice. Responsibility and the Individual in Japan and the United States.* New Haven, CT: Yale University Press.

Hamilton, V.L. and Rytina, S. (1980) 'Social Consensus on Norms of Justice: Does the Punishment Fit the Crime?' *American Journal of Sociology,* 85: 1117–44.

Hans, V. and Doob, A.N. (1976) 'Section 12 of the Canada Evidence Act and the Deliberation of Simulated Juries'. *Criminal Law Quarterly,* 18: 235–53.

Harcourt, B. (2007) *Against Prediction: Profiling, Policing and Punishing in an Actuarial Age.* Chicago: University of Chicago Press.

Harrel, W. (1981) 'The Effects of Alcohol Use and Offender Remorsefulness on Sentencing Decisions'. *Journal of Applied Social Psychology,* 11: 83–91.

Hawkins, D. (1981) 'Causal attribution and punishment for crime'. *Deviant Behavior: An Interdisciplinary Journal,* 2: 207–30.

Hayes, H. and Daly, K. (2004) 'Conferencing and Re-Offending in Queensland'. *Australian and New Zealand Journal of Criminology,* 37: 167–91.

Hebenton, B. and Thomas, T. (1993) *Criminal Records: State, Citizen and the Politics of Protection.* Aldershot: Avebury.

Heggie, K. (1999) *Review of the NSW Home Detention Scheme.* Research Publication No 41. Sydney: New South Wales Department of Corrective Services.

Heider, F. (1944) 'Social Perception and Phenomenal Causality'. *Psychological Review,* 51: 358–74.

——(1958) *The Psychology of Interpersonal Relations.* New York: Wiley.

Henham, R. (1995) 'Cumulative Sentencing and Penal Policy'. *Journal of Criminal Law,* 59: 420–30.

——(2005) 'Procedural Rules and Trial Practice', in *Punishment and Process in International Criminal Trials.* London: Ashgate Publishing Limited.

Higginbottom, S.F. and Zamble, E. (1988) 'Categorization of Homicide Cases: Agreement, Accuracy and Confidence of Public Assignments'. *Canadian Journal of Criminology,* 30: 351–66.

Hilton, Z. (1993) 'Police Intervention and Public Opinion', in *Legal Responses to Wife Assault.* Newbury Park: Sage Publications.

Hogarth, J. (1971) *Sentencing as a Human Process.* Toronto: University of Toronto Press.

Hollin, C. and Howells, K. (1987) 'Lay Explanations of Delinquency: Global or Offence Specific?' *British Journal of Social Psychology,* 26: 203–10.

Home Office (1969) *The Sentence of the Court: A Handbook for Courts and the Treatment of Offenders*. London: Home Office.

——(1999) Digest 4. *Information on the Criminal Justice System in England and Wales*. London: Home Office, Research, Development and Statistics Directorate.

——(2000) *Prison Statistics: England and Wales 1999*. CM 4805. Norwich: Her Majesty's Stationery Office.

——(2001) *Making Punishments Work: Report of the Sentencing Framework for England and Wales*. London: Home Office.

——(2005) *Sentencing Statistics 2004: England and Wales*. London: Home Office.

——(2006) *Rebalancing the Criminal Justice System in Favour of the Law-abiding Majority. Cutting Crime, Reducing Re-offending and Protecting the Public*. London: Home Office.

——(2007) *Sentencing Statistics 2005: England and Wales*. London: Home Office, Research, Development and Statistics Directorate.

Horan, P., Myers, M., and Farnworth, M. (1982) 'Prior Record and Court Processes: The Role of Latent Theory in Criminology Research'. *Sociology and Social Research*, 67: 40–58.

Hough, M. (1992) *Attitudes to Punishment: Findings from the 1992 British Crime Survey*. London: South Bank University.

——(1996) 'People Talking About Punishment'. *The Howard Journal of Criminal Justice*, 35: 191–214.

——Jacobson, J., and Millie, A. (2003) *The Decision to Imprison: Sentencing and the Prison Population*. London: Prison Reform Trust.

——and Park, A. (2002) 'How Malleable are Attitudes to Crime and Punishment?', in J.V. Roberts and M. Hough (eds.) *Changing Attitudes to Punishment*. Cullompton: Willan Publishing.

——and Roberts, J.V. (1998) *Attitudes to Punishment: Findings from the 1996 British Crime Survey*. Home Office Research Study No 179. London: Home Office.

————(2004) *Confidence in Justice: an international review. Research Findings*. Number 243. London: Home Office.

————Jacobson, J., Bredee, A., and Moon, N. (2007a) *Attitudes to the Sentencing of Offences Involving Death by Driving*. London: Sentencing Advisory Panel.

————(2007b) 'Public Opinion, Crime, and Criminal Justice: The British Crime Survey and Beyond', in M. Hough and M. Maxfield (eds.) *Surveying Crime in the 21st Century*. Crime Prevention Studies. Volume 22. Cullompton: Willan Publishing and New York: Criminal Justice Press.

Hudson, B. (2003) 'Restorative Justice: diversion, compromise or replacement discourse?' in *Understanding Justice* (2nd edn). Maidenhead: Open University Press.

Hutton, N. (2005) 'Beyond populist punitiveness?' *Punishment and Society. The International Journal of Penology*, 7: 243–58.

——(2008) 'Institutional Mechanisms for Incorporating the Public in the Development of Sentencing Policy', in K. Gelb and A. Freiberg (eds.) *Penal Populism: Sentencing Councils and Sentencing Policy*. Cullompton: Willan Publishing.

ICM Research (2002) *BBC Crime Day Poll*. Available at: <http://www.icmresearch.co.uk>.

——(2006a) *BBC Poll*. November 2005. Available at: <http://www.icmresearch.co.uk>.

——(2006b) Crime Survey. Fieldwork: July 12th–16th 2006. Available at: <http://www.icmresearch.co.uk>.

Indermaur, D. (1990) *Crime Seriousness and Sentencing: A Comparison of Court Practice and the Perceptions of a Sample of the Public and Judges*. Mount Lawley: Western Australian College of Advanced Education.

——(1994) 'Offender Perceptions of Sentencing'. *Australian Psychologist*, 29: 140–44.

Ingram, M. (2004) 'Shame and Pain: Themes and Variations in Tudor Punishments', in S. Devereaux and P. Griffiths (eds.) *Penal Practice and Culture, 1500–1900: Punishing the English*. London: Palgrave.

Institute for Social Studies (1999) *Sentencing in South Africa. Public Perception and the Judicial Process*. Capetown: Institute for Social Studies.

Jacobson, J. and Hough, M. (2007) *Mitigation: The Role of Personal Factors in Sentencing*. London: Prison Reform Trust.

Jacoby, J.E. and Cullen, F.T. (1999) 'The Structure of Punishment Norms: Applying the Rossi-Berk Model'. *The Journal of Criminal Law and Criminology*, 89: 245–307.

Jareborg, N. (1995) 'The Swedish Sentencing Reform', in C. Clarkson and R. Morgan (eds.) *The Politics of Sentencing Reform*. Oxford: Clarendon Press.

Jewkes, Y. (2004) *Media and Crime*. London: Sage.

Jones, E. and Davis, K. (1965) 'From Acts to Dispositions: The Attribution Process in Person Perception', in L. Berkowitz (ed.) *Advances in Experimental Social Psychology*. New York: Academic Press.

——and Nisbett, R. (1972) 'The Actor and the Observer: Divergent Perceptions of the Causes of Behavior', in E. Jones, D. Kanouse, H. Kelley, R. Nisbett, S. Valins and B. Weiner (eds.) *Attribution: Perceiving the Causes of Behavior*. New Jersey: General Learning Press.

Justice 1 Committee (2002) *Public Attitudes Towards Sentencing and Alternatives to Imprisonment*. Available at: <http://www.scottish.parliament.uk/business/committees/historic/justice1/reports-02/j1r02-parts-01.htm>.

Klein, R., Newman, I., Weis, D., and Bobner, R. (1983) 'The Continuum of Criminal Offenses Instrument: Further Development and Modification of Sellin and Wolfgang's Original Criminal Index'. *Journal of Offender Counseling, Services & Rehabilitation*, 7: 33–53.

Kleinig, J. (1973) *Punishment and Desert*. The Hague: Martinus Nijhoff.

Kleinke, C., Wallis, R., and Stalder, K. (1992) 'Evaluation of Rapist as a Function of Expressed Intent and Remorse'. *Journal of Social Psychology*, 132: 525–37.

Knight, D. (1965) 'Punishment Selection as a Function of Biographical Information'. *Journal of Criminal Law, Criminology and Police Science*, 56: 325–7.

Kommer, M. (2004) 'The Use of Public Opinion Research in Policy-making: The Dutch Experience', in S. Parmentier et al. (eds.) *Public Opinion and the Administration of Justice: Popular Perceptions and their Implications for Policy Making in Western Countries*. Brussels: Politeia.

Konecni, V. and Ebbesen, E. (1982) *The Criminal Justice System: A Social Psychological Analysis*. San Francisco: W.H. Freeman.

Kowalski, M. and Caputo, T. (1999) 'Recidivism in Youth Court: An Examination of the Impact of Age, Gender, and Prior Record'. *Canadian Journal of Criminology*, 41: 57–85.

Krohn, M. and Stratton, J. (1980) 'A Sense of Injustice? Attitudes toward the Criminal Justice System and Instutional Adaptations'. *Criminology*, 17: 495–504.

Lacey, N. (1988) *State Punishment: Political Principles and Community Values*. London: Routledge.

Landis, J. and Goodstein, L. (1986) 'When is Justice Fair? An Integrated Approach to the Outcome versus Procedure Debate'. *American Bar Foundation Research Journal*, 1986: 675–707.

Landreville, P. (1988) '*Points de vue de détenu-e-s du Québec sur quelques questions soulevées par le mandat de la Commission canadienne sur la détermination de la peine*'. Research Reports of the Canadian Sentencing Commission. Ottawa: Department of Justice Canada.

Law Commission (2005) *A New Homicide Act for England and Wales? A Consultation Paper*. London: Law Commission of England and Wales.

Law Reform Commission of Canada (1976) *Studies on Imprisonment*. Ottawa: Canadian Government Publishing Centre.

Law Reform Commission of Ireland (1993) *Consultation Paper of Sentencing. March 1993*. Dublin: The Law Reform Commission.

Lee Hamilton, V. and Sanders, J. (1992) *Everyday Justice: Responsibility and the Individual in Japan and the United States*. New Haven, CT: Yale University Press.

Madame Le Garde des Sceaux (2007) *Communication au Conseil des Ministres*. Paris: Ministère de la Justice.

Leng, R. and Manchester, C. (1991) *A Guide to the Criminal Justice Act 1991*. London: Fourmat Publishing.

Lerner, M. (1980) *The Belief in a Just World: A Fundamental Delusion*. New York: Plenum.

Levi, M. and Jones, S. (1985) 'Public and Police Perceptions of Crime Seriousness in England and Wales'. *British Journal of Criminology*, 25: 234–50.

Lloyd-Bostock, S. (2006) 'The effects on lay magistrates of hearing that the defendant is of "good character", being left to speculate, or hearing that he has a previous conviction'. *Criminal Law Review*, March: 189–212.

Lyon, J., Dennison, C., and Wilson, A. (2000) *'Tell Them So They Listen': Messages from Young People in Custody*. Home Office Research Study No 201. London: Home Office.

MacPherson, D. (2002) 'The Relevance of Prior Record in the Criminal Law: A Response to the Theory of Professor von Hirsch'. *Queen's Law Journal*, 28: 177–219.

Makkai, T. and Braithwaite, J. (1994) 'Reintegrative Shaming and Compliance with Regulatory Standards'. *Criminology*, 32: 361–85.

Mande, M. and Butler, P. (1982) *Crime in Colorado: A Survey of Citizens*. Denver, CO: Colorado Department of Public Safety, Division of Criminal Justice.

——and English, K. (1989) *The Effect of Public Opinion on Correctional Policy: A Comparison of Opinions and Practices*. Denver, CO: Colorado Department of Public Safety, Division of Criminal Justice.

Manson, A. (2001) *The Law of Sentencing*. Toronto: Irwin Law.

Martinovic, M. (2002) *The Punitiveness of Electronically Monitored Community Based Programs*. Paper presented at the Probation and Community Corrections Conference, Perth, September 2002.

Masden, D. (1978) 'Diversified Opinions Gathered from Sampling of Ex-offenders'. *American Journal of Corrections*, 40: 22–24.

Matravers, M. (2000) *Justice and Punishment: The Rationale of Coercion*. Oxford: Oxford University Press.

Mattinson, J. and Mirrlees-Black, C. (2000) *Attitudes to Crime and Criminal Justice: Findings from the 1998 British Crime Survey*. Home Office Research Study No 200. London: Home Office.

Maxwell, G. and Morris, A. (1996) 'Research on Family Group Conferences with Young Offenders in New Zealand', in J. Hudson, A. Morris, G. Maxwell and B. Galaway (eds.) *Family Group Conferences: Perspectives on Policy and Practice*. Monsey, NY: Willow Tree Press.

—— Kingi, V., Morris, A., Robertson, J., and Anderson, T. (2005) 'Differences in how girls and boys respond to family group conferences: preliminary research results', in L. Walgrave (ed.) *Repositioning Restorative Justice*. Cullompton: Willan.

McAuley, M. and Macdonald, K. (2004) 'Russia and Youth Crime'. *British Journal of Criminology*, 47: 2–22.

McGinnis, J. and Carlson, K. (1982) 'Offenders' Perceptions of their Sentences'. *Journal of Offender Counseling, Services and Rehabilitation*, 5: 27–32.

McTaggert, J. (1896) 'Hegel's Theory of Punishment'. *International Journal of Ethics*, 6: 482–99.

Minnesota Sentencing Guidelines Commission (2006a) *Minnesota Sentencing Guidelines and Commentary*. Available at: <http://www.msgc.state.mn.us>.

——(2006b) *Sentencing Practices: Annual Summary Statistics for Felony Offenders Sentenced in 2005.*

Ministry of Justice (2007) *Penal Policy—a Background Paper.* London: Ministry of Justice, National Offender Management Service.

Missouri Sentencing Advisory Commission (2006) *Recommended Sentencing User Guide, 2006*. St. Louis: Missouri Sentencing Advisory Commission.

Monahan, J. (1982) 'The Case for Prediction in the Modified Desert Model of Criminal Sentencing'. *International Journal of Law and Psychiatry*, 5: 103–13.

——and Ruggiero, M. (1980) 'Psychological and Psychiatric Aspects of Determinate Criminal Sentencing'. *International Journal of Law and Psychiatry*, 3: 143–54.

Montesquieu, Baron de. (1764) *The Spirit of Laws. Volume I.* Cambridge: Collingwood and Sons.

Morris, A. and Maxwell, G. (2003) 'Restorative Justice in New Zealand', in A. von Hirsch, J. Roberts, A. Bottoms, K. Roach and M. Schiff (eds.) *Restorative Justice and Criminal Justice: Competing or Reconcilable Paradigms?* Oxford: Hart Publishing.

Morris, N. and Tonry, M. (1990) *Between Prison and Probation: Intermediate Punishments in a Rational Sentencing System.* New York: Oxford University Press.

Morse, B. and Lock, L. (1988) *Native Offender Perceptions of Sentencing.* Research Reports of the Canadian Sentencing Commission. Ottawa: Department of Justice Canada.

Murphy, J. and Hampton, J. (1988) *Forgiveness and Mercy.* Cambridge: Cambridge University Press.

Murray, C. (2005) 'Simple Justice', in D. Conway (ed.) *Simple Justice. Charles Murray.* London: Civitas.

Myers, M. and Talarico, S. (1987) *The Social Contexts of Criminal Sentencing.* London: Springer-Verlag.

Mylonas, A. and Reckless, W. (1963) 'Prisoners' Attitudes toward Law and Legal Authorities'. *Journal of Criminal Law, Criminology, and Police Science*, 54: 479–84.

National Centre for State Courts (1978) *The Public Image of the Courts.* Virginia: National Centre for State Courts.

New Zealand Department of Justice (1982) *Attitudinal Assessment of New Zealand Judiciary about Sentencing and Penal policy. Part 1. Analytical Summary*. Wellington: New Zealand Department of Justice.

Newman, G. (1983) *Just and Painful: A Case for Corporal Punishment of Criminals*. London: Collier Macmillan.

Nisbett, R. and Ross, L. (1980) *Human Inference: Strategies and Shortcomings of Social Judgment*. Englewood Cliffs, NJ: Prentice-Hall.

Nuttall, C., Eversley, D., Rudder, I. and Ramsay, J. (2003) *Views and Beliefs about Crime and Criminal Justice*. Bridgetown, Barbados: Barbados Statistical Department.

Observer Newspaper (2003) *Crime Uncovered*. April 27, 2003.

O'Connor, M. (1984) 'The Perception of Crime and Criminality: The Violent Criminal and Swindler as Social Types'. *Deviant Behavior*, 5: 255–74.

O'Connell, M. (1999) 'Is Irish Public Opinion toward Crime Distorted by Media Bias?' *European Journal of Criminology*, 14: 191–212.

Office for Criminal Justice Reform (2006) *Public Attitudes to Alternatives to Prosecution*. London: Office for Criminal Justice Reform.

Ohio Criminal Sentencing Commission (2005) *Monitoring Sentencing Reform*. Columbus, OH: Ohio Criminal Sentencing Commission.

O'Neill, M., Maxfield, L., and Harer, M. (2004) 'Past as Prologue: Reconciling Recidivism and Culpability'. *Fordham Law Review*, 73: 245–95.

Oppenheim, A. (1992) *Questionnaire Design, Interviewing and Attitude Measurement*. London: Continuum.

Oppenheimer, H. (1913) *The Rationale of Punishment*. London: University of London Press.

Oregon Criminal Justice Commission (2007) *Statement of Purpose and Principles*. Salem, Oregon: Oregon Criminal Justice Commission.

Orne, M. (1969) 'Demand Characteristics and the Concept of Quasi-controls', in R. Rosenthal and R. Rosnow (eds.) *Artifacts in Behavior Research*. New York: Academic Press.

Pakenham, F. (Lord Longford) (1961) *The Idea of Punishment*. London: Geoffrey Chapman.

Palys, T. (1976) 'An Assessment of Legal and Cultural Stigma Regarding Unskilled Workers'. *Canadian Journal of Criminology and Corrections*, 18: 247–57.

Parker, S. (1998) *Courts and the Public*. Carlton South, Victoria: The Australian Institute of Judicial Administration Incorporated.

Parmentier, S., Vervaeke, G., Doutrelepont, R., and Kellens, G. (2004) *Public Opinion and the Administration of Justice: Popular Perceptions and their Implications for Policy Making in Western Countries*. Brussels: Politeia.

Parton, D.A., Hansel, M., and Stratton, J.R. (1991) 'Measuring Crime Seriousness: Lessons from the National Survey of Crime Severity'. *British Journal of Criminology,* 31: 72–85.

Paulin, J., Searle, W., and Knaggs, T. (2003) *Attitudes to Crime and Punishment: A New Zealand Study.* Wellington: Ministry of Justice.

Petrucci, C. (2002) 'Apology in the Criminal Justice Setting: Evidence for Including Apology as an Additional Component in the Legal System'. *Behavioral Sciences and the Law*, 20: 337–62.

Petersilia, J. and Piper Deschenes, E. (1994) 'Perceptions of Punishment: Inmates and Staff Rank the Severity of Prison Versus Intermediate Sanctions'. *The Prison Journal*, 74: 306–28.

Pillsbury, S. (1998) *Judging Evil: Rethinking the Law of Murder and Manslaughter.* New York: New York University Press.

Piper, S. and Easton, C. (2005) *Sentencing and Punishment: The Quest for Justice.* Oxford: Oxford University Press.

Piquero, A.R., Gomez-Smith, Z., and Langton, L. (2004) 'Discerning Unfairness Where Others May Not: Low Self-Control and Unfair Sanction Perceptions'. *Criminology,* 42: 699–732.

Podgorecki, A., Kaupen, W., Van Houtte, J., Vinke, P., and Kutchinsky, B. (1973) *Knowledge and Opinion about Law.* London: Martin Robertson and Company.

Pratt, J. (2007) *Penal Populism.* London: Routledge.

Prime, J., White, S., Liriano, S., and Patel, K. (2001) *Criminal Careers of Those Born between 1953 and 1978.* London: Home Office, Research, Development and Statistics Directorate.

Princeton Survey Research Associates International (2006) *The National Center for State Courts Sentencing Attitudes Survey: A Report on the Findings.* Available at: <http://www.ncsconline.org>.

Public Safety Canada (2004) *Public Views Toward Effective Corrections and the Correctional System in Canada.* Ottawa: Public Safety Canada.

R v O'Brien & Gloster [1997] 2 VR 714 (VSCA).

Radzinowicz, L. and Hood, R. (1980) 'Incapacitating the Habitual Criminal: The English Experience'. *Michigan Law Review*, 78: 1305–89.

—— ——(1990) *The emergence of penal policy in Victorian and Edwardian England.* Volume 5 of A history of English criminal law and its administration from 1750. Oxford: Clarendon Press.

Raz, J. (1979) *The Authority of Law: Essays on Law and Morality.* Oxford: Oxford University Press.

Redondo, S., Luque, E., and Funes, J. (1996) 'Social Beliefs about Recidivism in Crime', in G. Davies, S. Lloyd-Bostock, M. McMurran, and C. Wilson (eds.) *Psychology, Law, and Criminal Justice: International Developments in Research and Practice.* New York: Walter de Gruyter.

Reed, J. and Nance, D. (1972) 'Society Perpetuates the Stigma of a Conviction'. *Federal Probation*, 2: 27–31.

Reiner, R. (2007) 'Media-made Criminality: The Representation of Crime in the Mass Media', in *Oxford Handbook of Criminology* (4th edn.) Oxford: Oxford University Press.

Reiner, R., Livingstone, S., and Allen, J. (2003) 'From Law and Order to Lynch Mobs: Crime News since the Second World War', in P. Mason (ed.) *Criminal Visions: Media Representations of Crime and Justice.* Cullompton: Willan.

Renaud, G. (2004) *Speaking to Sentence: A Practical Guide.* Toronto: Thomson Carswell.

Report of the Advisory Council on the Penal System (1978) *Sentences of Imprisonment: A Review of Maximum Penalties.* London: Her Majesty's Stationery Office.

Roberts, C., Clawson, E., Doble, J., Selton, C., and Briker, A. (2005) *Rethinking Justice in Massachusetts: Public Attitudes Toward Crime and Punishment.* Available at: <http://crjustice.org/cji/cjipublications.html>.

Roberts, J.V. (1988) *Public Opinion and Sentencing: Surveys by the Canadian Sentencing Commission.* Research Reports of the Canadian Sentencing Commission. Ottawa: Department of Justice Canada.

——(1992) 'Public Opinion, Crime and Criminal Justice', in M. Tonry (ed.) *Crime and Justice: A Review of Research.* Volume 16. Chicago: University of Chicago Press.

——(1994) 'The Role of Criminal Record in the U.S. Sentencing Guidelines'. *Criminal Justice Ethics*, 13: 21–30.

——(1996) 'Public Opinion, Criminal Record and the Sentencing Process'. *American Behavioral Scientist*, 39: 488–99.

——(1997a) 'Paying for the Past: The Role of Criminal Record in the Sentencing Process', in M. Tonry (ed.) *Crime and Justice: A Review of Research.* Volume 22. Chicago: University of Chicago Press.

——(1997b) 'Refining the Role of Criminal Record in the Federal Sentencing Guidelines: A Few Lessons from the States'. *Federal Sentencing Reporter*, 9: 213–15.

——(1999) 'Sentencing Research in Canada: An Overview'. *Canadian Journal of Criminology*, 41: 225–34.

——(2001) *Fear of Crime and Attitudes to Criminal Justice in Canada: A Review of Recent Trends. 2001–2.* Ottawa: Ministry of the Solicitor General.

——(2002a) 'Public Opinion and Sentencing Policy', in S. Rex and M. Tonry (eds.) *Reform and Punishment: The Future of Sentencing.* Cullompton: Willan Publishing.

——(2002b) 'Determining Parole Eligibility Dates for Life Prisoners: Lessons from Jury Hearings in Canada'. *Punishment and Society. The International Journal of Penology*, 4: 103–114.

——(2003a) 'The Pluses and Minuses of Custody: Sentencing Reform in England and Wales'. *Howard Journal of Criminal Justice*, 42: 229–47.

——(2003b) 'An Analysis of the Statutory Statement of the Purposes and Principles of Sentencing in New Zealand'. *Australia and New Zealand Journal of Criminology*, 36: 249–71.

Roberts, J.V. (2003c) 'Public Opinion and Mandatory Sentences of Imprisonment: A Review of International Findings'. *Criminal Justice and Behavior*, 20: 1–26.

——(2004) *The Virtual Prison: Community Custody and the Evolution of Imprisonment*. Cambridge: Cambridge University Press.

——(2005) 'The Fall and Rise of the Recidivist Premium: Recent Developments in England and Wales'. *Federal Sentencing Reporter*, 17: 171–75.

——(2008) 'Theoretical and Historical Perspectives—The Role of the Public and Public Opinion in the Development of Sentencing Policy and Practice', in K. Gelb and A. Freiberg (eds.) *Penal Populism: Sentencing Councils and Sentencing Policy*. Cullompton: Willan Publishing.

——and Baker, E. (2007) 'Sentencing in Common Law Jurisdictions', in S. Shoham, M. Kett and O. Beck (eds.) *International Comparative Handbook of Penology and Criminal Justice*. New York: Taylor and Francis.

——and Birkenmayer, A. (1997) 'Sentencing in Canada: Recent Statistical Trends'. *Canadian Journal of Criminology*, 39: 459–82.

——and Cole, D. (eds.) (1999) *Making Sense of Sentencing*. Toronto: University of Toronto Press.

——Crutcher, N. and Verbrugge, P. (2007) 'Public Attitudes to Sentencing in Canada: Some Recent Findings'. *Canadian Journal of Criminology and Criminal Justice*, 49: 75–107.

——and Hastings, A. (2001) 'Sentencing in Cases of Hate-motivated Crime: An Analysis of the Impact of Sub-paragraph 718.2(a)(i) of the *Criminal Code*'. *Queen's Law Journal*, 27: 93–128.

——and Hastings, R. (2007) 'Public Opinion and Crime Prevention: A Review of International Findings'. *Revue de l'Institut pour la Prevention de la Criminalite*, 1: 193–218.

——and Hough, M. (2005) *Understanding Public Attitudes to Criminal Justice*. Maidenhead: Open University Press.

——and Roach, K. (2003) 'Restorative Justice in Canada: From Sentencing Circles to Sentencing Principles', in A. von Hirsch, J. Roberts, A. Bottoms, K. Roach, and M. Schiff (eds.) *Restorative Justice and Criminal Justice: Competing or Reconcilable Paradigms?* Oxford: Hart Publishing.

—— ——(2005) 'Community Sentencing and the Perspective of Crime Victims: A Socio-legal Analysis'. *Queen's Law* Journal, 30: 560–600.

——and Stalans, L.S. (1997) *Public Opinion, Crime, and Criminal Justice*. Boulder, CO: Westview Press.

————(2004) 'Restorative Justice and the Sentencing Process: Exploring the Views of the Public'. *Social Justice Research*, 17: 315–34.

—— Stalans, L.S., Indermaur, D., and Hough, M. (2003) *Penal Populism and Public Opinion: Lessons from Five Countries*. Oxford: Oxford University Press.

Roberts, J.V., and von Hirsch, A. (1995) 'Statutory Sentencing Reform: The Purpose and Principles of Sentencing'. *Criminal Law Quarterly*, 37: 220–42.

——and White, N. (1986) 'Public Estimates of Recidivism Rates: Consequences of a Criminal Stereotype'. *Canadian Journal of Criminology*, 28: 229–41.

Robinson, P. and Darley, J. (1995) *Justice, Liability, and Blame: Community Views and the Criminal Law*. Boulder, CO: Westview Press.

—— —— (2003) 'The Role of Deterrence in the Formulation of Criminal Law Rules: At Its Worst When Doing Its Best'. *Georgetown Law Journal*, 91: 949–1002.

Robinson, D. T., Smith-Lovin, L., and Tsoudis, O. (1994) 'Heinous crime or unfortunate accident? The effects of remorse on responses to mock criminal confessions'. *Social Forces*, 73: 175–90.

Roche, D. (2003) *Accountability in Restorative Justice*. Oxford: Oxford University Press.

Rose, G. (2000) *The Criminal Histories of Serious Traffic Offenders*. Home Office Research Study No 206. London: Home Office, Research, Development and Statistics Directorate.

Rosenberg, M. (1969) 'The Conditions and Consequences of Evaluation Apprehension', in R. Rosenthal and R. Rosnow (eds.) *Artifacts in Behavior Research*. New York: Academic Press.

Ross, L. (1977) 'The Intuitive Psychologist and His Shortcomings: Distortions in the Attribution Process', in L. Berkowitz (ed.) *Advances in Experimental Social Psychology*. New York: Academic Press.

Rossi, P. and Berk, R. (1997) *Just Punishments: Federal Guidelines and Public Views Compared*. New York: Aldine de Gruyter.

Ruddell, R. and Winfree, L. (2006) 'Setting Aside Criminal Convictions in Canada. A Successful Approach to Offender Reintegration'. *The Prison Journal*, 4: 452–69.

Ruddy, D. (2007) *Reconviction in Northern Ireland: Results from the 2003 Cohort*. Research and Statistics Bulletin 3/2007. Belfast: Statistics and Research Branch of the Northern Ireland Office.

Rugge, T. and Cormier, R. (2005) 'Restorative Justice in Cases of Serious Crime', in E. Elliott and R. Gordon (eds.) *New Directions in Restorative Justice*. Cullompton: Willan Publishing.

Ruscher, J. (1998) 'Prejudice and Stereotyping in Everyday Communication', in M. Zanna (ed.) *Advances in Experimental Social Psychology*. Volume 30. San Diego: Academic Press.

Russell, N. and Morgan, R. (2001) *Sentencing of Domestic Burglary. London: Sentencing Advisory Panel.* Available at: <http://www.sentencing-guidelines.gov.uk/research/index.html>.

Ryberg, J. (2004) *The Ethics of Proportionate Punishment: A Critical Investigation*. London: Kluwer.

Salisbury, H. (2004) *Public Attitudes to the Criminal Justice System: The Impact of Providing Information to British Crime Survey Respondents*. Home Office Online Report 64/04. London: Home Office.

Sanders, J. and Hamilton, V. (1992) 'Legal Cultures and Punishment Repertoires in Japan, Russia, and the United States'. *Law & Society Review*, 26: 117–40.

Scher, S. and Darley, J. (1997) 'How Effective are the Things People Say to Apologize? Effects of the Realization of the Apology Speech Act'. *Journal of Psycholinguistics Research*, 26: 127–40.

Schmideberg, M. (1960) 'The Offender's Attitude Toward Punishment'. *Journal of Criminal Law, Criminology, and Police Science*, 51: 328–34.

Schultz, C. and Allen, H. (1967) 'Inmate and Non-Inmate Attitudes Toward Punitiveness'. *Criminology*, 5: 40–5.

Schwartz, R. and Skolnick, J. (1962) 'Two Studies of Legal Stigma'. *Social Problems*, 10: 133–42.

Sebba, L. (1978) 'Some Explorations in the Scaling of Penalties'. *Journal of Research in Crime and Delinquency*, 15: 247–65.

—— (1980) 'Is Mens Rea a Component of Perceived Offense Seriousness?' *The Journal of Criminal Law and Criminology*, 71: 124–35.

Secretary of State (2002) *Justice for All*. CM 5563. Norwich: The Stationery Office.

Sentencing Guidelines Council (2004) *Overarching Principles: Seriousness*. London: Sentencing Guidelines Council. Available at: <http://www.sentencing-guidelines.gov.uk>.

Sharp, F. and Otto, M. (1909) 'A Study of the Popular Attitude towards Retributive Punishment'. *International Journal of Ethics*, 20: 341–57.

Shaver, K. (1970) 'Defensive Attribution: Effects of Severity and Relevance on the Responsibility Assigned for an Accident'. *Journal of Personality and Social Psychology*, 14: 10–113.

Shepherd, A. and Whiting, E. (2006) *Re-Offending of Adults: Results from the 2003 Cohort*. Home Office Statistical Bulletin 20/06. London: Home Office.

Sherman, L. (1993) 'Defiance, Deterrence, and Irrelevance: A Theory of the Criminal Sanction'. *Journal of Research in Crime and Delinquency*, 30: 445–73.

—— and Strang, H. (2007) *Restorative Justice: the Evidence*. London: The Smith Institute.

Shoemaker, R. (1991) *Prosecution and Punishment: Petty Crime and the Law in London and Middlesex, c. 1660–1725*. Cambridge: Cambridge University Press.

Shute, S. (1998) 'The Place of Public Opinion in the Sentencing Law'. *Criminal Law Review*, July: 465–77.

Shute, S. Hood, R., and Seemungal, F. (2005) *A Fair Hearing? Ethnic Minorities in the Criminal Courts*. Cullompton: Willan Publishing.

Silvey, J. (1961) 'The Criminal Law and Public Opinion'. *Criminal Law Review*, June: 349–58.

Singer, R. (1979) *Just Deserts: Sentencing Based on Equality and Desert*. Cambridge, MA: Ballinger.

Smart, A. (1969) 'Mercy', in H. Acton (ed.) *The Philosophy of Punishment: A Collection of Papers*. London: MacMillan.

Smith, B., Sloan, J., and Ward, R. (1990) 'Public Support for the Victims' Rights Movement: Results of a Statewide Survey'. *Crime and Delinquency*, 36: 488–502.

Snowball, L. and Weatherburn, D. (2006) 'Indigenous Over-representation in Prison: The Role of Offender Characteristics'. *Crime and Justice Bulletin*. Number 99. Sydney: New South Wales Bureau of Crime Statistics and Research.

Sourcebook of Criminal Justice Statistics (2005) *Public Opinion*. Table 2.47. Available at: http://www.albany.edu/sourcebook.

South African Law Commission (2000) *Sentencing (A New Framework)*. Report of Project 82. Available at: <http://www.doj.gov.za/salrc/dpapers.htm>.

South Australia Office of Crime and Statistics Research (2006) *Crime and Justice in South Australia, 2005, Adult Courts and Corrections*. Adelaide, SA: South Australia Office of Crime and Statistics Research.

Spier, P. (2001) *Conviction and Sentencing of Offenders in New Zealand: 1991 to 2000*. Wellington: New Zealand Ministry of Justice.

Spohn, C. (2002) *How do Judges Decide? The Search for Fairness and Justice in Punishment*. Thousand Oaks, CA: Sage.

Stalans, L. and Lurigio, A. (1990) 'Lay and Professionals' Beliefs About Crime and Criminal Sentencing: A Need for Theory, Perhaps Schema Theory'. *Criminal Justice and Behavior*, 17: 333–49.

——and Diamond, S.S. (1990) 'Formation and Change in Lay Evaluations of Criminal Sentencing: Misrepresentation and Discontent'. *Law and Human Behavior*, 14: 199–214.

State of Oregon (2003) *Sentencing Practices: Summary Statistics for Felony Offenders Sentenced in 2001*. Oregon: State of Oregon Criminal Justice Commission.

Steblay, N., Hosch, N., Culhane, S., and A. McWethy (2006) 'The Impact on Juror Verdicts of Judicial Instructions to Disregard Inadmissable Evidence: A Meta-Analysis'. *Law and Human Behavior*, 30: 469–92.

Stephen, K. (1883) *A History of the Criminal Law of England*. New York: Franklin.

Sun, The (2004a) *Laughing Hit-Run Driver With Long Record. Maniac Got Just 6 MONTHS Jail*. Thursday, 15 April, pp. 8–9.

Sun, The (2004b) *Drunk-drivers Face Curbs On Getting Back Licences*. Thursday, 15 April, p. 10.

Sun, The (2006) *200 Murders By Yobs Freed Early*. Saturday, April 22, p. 2.

Sundby, S. (1998) 'The Capital Jury and Absolution: The Intersection of Trial Strategy, Remorse, and the Death Penalty'. *Cornell Law Review*, 83: 1557–98.

Sutton, P. (1978) *Variations in Federal Criminal Sentences: A Statistical Assessment at the National Level*. Washington, DC: U.S. Department of Justice.

Tasioulas, J. (2003) 'Mercy'. *Proceedings of the Aristotelian Society*, CIII: 101–32.

Taylor, C. and Kleinke, C. (1992) 'Effects of Severity of Accident, History of Drunk Driving, Intent, and Remorse on Judgments of a Drunk Driver'. *Journal of Applied Social Psychology*, 22: 1641–55.

Ten, C. (1987) *Crime, Guilt, and Punishment*. Oxford: Clarendon Press.

Thomas, D. (1970) *Principles of Sentencing*. (1st edn). London: Heinemann.

——(1979) *Principles of Sentencing*. (2nd edn). London: Heinemann.

——(2003) 'Judicial Discretion in Sentencing', in L. Gelsthorpe and N. Padfield (eds.) *Exercising Discretion: Decision-Making in the Criminal Justice System and Beyond*. Cullompton: Willan Publishing.

Thomas, M. (2004) 'Adult Criminal Court Statistics, 2003/04'. *Juristat*, Volume 24, Number 12.

Thomas, R. and Diver-Stamnes, A. (1993) *What Wrongdoers Deserve: The Moral Reasoning Behind Responses to Misconduct*. Westport, CT: Greenwood Press.

Tonry, M. (1996) *Sentencing Matters*. New York: Oxford University Press.

——(2004) *Punishment and Politics: Evidence and Emulation in the Making of English Crime Control Policy*. Cullompton: Willan Publishing.

Tornudd, P. (1997) 'Sentencing and Punishment in Finland', in M. Tonry and K. Hatlestad (eds.) *Sentencing Reform in Overcrowded Times*. New York: Oxford University Press.

Tufts, J. (2000) 'Public Attitudes toward the Criminal Justice System'. *Juristat*, Volume 20, Number 12.

——and Roberts, J.V. (2002) 'Sentencing Juvenile Offenders: Comparing Public Preferences and Judicial Practice'. *Criminal Justice Policy Review*, 13: 46–64.

Tyler, T. (2003) 'Procedural Justice, Legitimacy, and the Effective Rule of Law', in M. Tonry (ed.) *Crime and Justice: A Review of Research*. Chicago: University of Chicago Press.

——and Boeckmann, R. (1997) 'Three Strikes and You Are Out, but Why? The Psychology of Public Support for Punishing Rule Breakers'. *Law and Society Review*, 31: 237–65.

U.S. Department of Justice (2002) *Felony Defendants in Large Urban Counties, 2000*. Washington, DC: U.S. Department of Justice.

U.S. Department of Justice (2004) *State Court Sentencing of Convicted Felons, 2002. Statistical Tables*. Washington, DC: U.S. Department of Justice.

U.S. Sentencing Commission (2006) *Guidelines Manual*. Available at: <http://www.ussc.gov>.

Utah Sentencing Commission (2006) *Adult Sentencing and Release Determinations: A Philosophical Approach*. Available at: <http://www.sentencing.utah.gov>.

—— (2007) *2007 Adult Sentencing and Release Guidelines*. Available at: <http://www.sentencing.utah.gov>.

Vallacher, R. and Wegner, D. (1987) 'What Do People Think They're Doing? Action Identification and Human Behaviour'. *Psychological Review*, 94: 3–15.

Vanfraechem, I. (2005) 'Evaluating Conferencing for Serious Juvenile Offenders', in E. Elliott and R. Gordon (eds.) *New Directions in Restorative Justice: Issues, Practice, Evaluation*. Cullompton: Willan Publishing.

Van Ness, D. and Strong, K. (2002) *Restoring Justice* (2nd edn). Cincinnati, OH: Anderson Publishing.

Versele, D., Goffin, R., Tsamadou, C., Legros, P., and van Haecht, A. (1972) *Justice Penale et Opinion Publique*. Bruxelles: Editions de l'Universite de Bruxelles.

Victoria Department of Justice (2006) *Victoria Sentencing Manual*. Available at: <http://www.justice.vic.gov.au/emanuals/VSM/Previous Convictions.htm>.

Victorian Sentencing Committee Report (1988) *Sentencing: The Report of the Victorian Sentencing Committee*. Melbourne: Victorian Attorney-General's Department.

Vidmar, N. (2002) 'Retributive Justice', in M. Ross and D. Miller (eds.) *The Justice Motive in Everyday Life*. Cambridge: Cambridge University Press.

——and Miller, D. (1980) 'Socialpsychological Processes Underlying Attitudes Toward Legal Punishment'. *Law and Society Review*, 14: 565–602.

von Hirsch, A. (1976) *Doing Justice: The Choice of Punishments*. Boston: Northeastern University Press.

——(1981) 'Desert and Previous Convictions in Sentencing'. *Minnesota Law Review*, 65: 591–634.

——(1985) *Past or Future Crimes: Deservedness and Dangerousness in the Sentencing of Criminals*. New Brunswick, NJ: Rutgers University Press.

——(1991) 'Criminal Record Rides Again'. *Criminal Justice Ethics*, 10: 55–57.

—— (1993) *Censure and Sanctions.* Oxford: Clarendon Press.

von Hirsch, A. (2002) 'Record-enhanced Sentencing in England and Wales: Reflections on the Halliday Reports Proposed Treatment of Prior Convictions', in S. Rex and M. Tonry (eds.) *Reform and Punishment: The Future of Sentencing.* Cullompton: Willan Publishing.

——and Ashworth, A. (2005) *Proportionate Sentencing: Exploring the Principles.* Oxford: Oxford University Press.

———— and Shearing, C. (2003) 'Specifying Aims and Limits for Restorative Justice: A "Making Amends" Model?', in A. von Hirsch, J. Roberts, A. Bottoms, K. Roach, and M. Schiff (eds.) *Restorative Justice and Criminal Justice: Competing or Reconcilable Paradigms?* Oxford: Hart Publishing.

—— Bottoms, A., Burney, E., and Wikstrom, P.-.O. (1999) *Criminal Deterrence and Sentence Severity: An Analysis of Recent Research.* Oxford: Hart Publishing.

—— and Jareborg, N. (1989) 'Sweden's Sentencing Statute Enacted'. *Criminal Law Review,* April: 275–80.

—— and Roberts, J.V. (2004) 'Legislating Sentencing Principles: The Provisions of the Criminal Justice Act 2003 Relating to Sentencing Purposes and the Role of Previous Convictions'. *Criminal Law Review,* August: 639–52.

Wake, R., Homes, A., and Wright, O. (2006) *Attitudes to Alternatives to Prosecution—Discussion Groups with Victims and Witnesses.* London: Home Office, Office for Criminal Justice Reform.

Walker, M. (1978) 'Measuring the Seriousness of Crimes'. *British Journal of Criminology,* 18: 348–64.

Walker, N. (1965) 'Recidivists', in *Crime and Punishment in Britain.* Edinburgh: University Press.

——(1980) *Punishment, Danger and Stigma: The Morality of Criminal Justice.* Oxford: Blackwell.

——(1985) *Sentencing: Theory, Law and Practice.* London: Butterworths.

——(1999) *Aggravation, Mitigation and Mercy in English Criminal Justice.* London: Blackstone Press.

——and Argyle, M. (1964) 'Does the Law Affect Moral Judgments?' *British Journal of Criminology,* 4: 570–81.

——and Hough, M. (eds.) (1988) *Public Attitudes to Sentencing: Surveys from Five Countries.* Aldershot: Gower.

——and Padfield, N. (1996) *Sentencing: Theory, Law and Practice* (2nd edn.) London: Butterworths.

Warner, S. (1992) *Making Amends: Justice for Victims and Offenders.* Avebury: Aldershot.

Washington State Sentencing Guidelines Commission (1992) *A Statistical Summary ofAdult Felony Sentencing.* Olympia, WA: Washington State Sentencing Guidelines Commission.

Washington State Sentencing Guidelines Commission (2005) *Recidivism of Adult Felons, 2004*. Olympia, WA: Washington State Sentencing Guidelines Commission.

——(2006) *Adult Sentencing Manual 2006*. Available at: <http://www.sgc.wa.gov/pubs/Adult_Manual/Adult_sentencing_manual_2006.htm>.

Wasik, M. (1987) 'Guidance, Guidelines and Criminal Record', in M. Wasik and K. Pease (eds.) *Sentencing Reform: Guidance or Guidelines?* Manchester: Manchester University Press.

——and Taylor, R. (1991) *Blackstone's Guide to the Criminal Justice Act 1991*. London: Blackstone Press Limited.

——and von Hirsch, A. (1994) 'Section 29 Revised: Previous Convictions in Sentencing'. *Criminal Law Review*, June: 409–18.

Weatherburn, D. and Indermaur, D. (2004) 'Public Perceptions of Crime Trends in New South Wales and Western Australia'. *Crime and Justice Bulletin*. Sydney: NSW Bureau of Crime Statistics and Research.

Weiner, B. (1980) *Human Motivation*. New York: Holt, Rinehart, & Winston.

Wilkins, L. (1984) *Consumerist Criminology*. London: Heinemann.

Wolfgang, M., Figlio, R., Tracy, P., and Singer, S. (1985) *The National Survey of Crime Severity*. Washington, DC: U.S. Department of Justice, Bureau of Justice Statistics.

Wood, J. and Viki, G. (2004) 'Public perceptions of crime and punishment', in J. Adler (ed.) *Forensic Psychology: Concepts, Debates and Practice*. Cullompton: Willan Publishing.

Wright, M. (2005) 'Is it Time to Question the Concept of Punishment?', in E. Elliott and R. Gordon (eds.) *New Directions in Restorative Justice: Issues, Practice, Evaluation*. Cullompton: Willan Publishing.

Zamble, E. and Kalm, K. (1990) 'General and Specific Measures of Public Attitudes toward Sentencing'. *Canadian Journal of Behavioural Science*, 22: 327–37.

Zimmerman, S., Van Alstyne, D., and Dunn, C. (1988) 'The National Punishment Survey and Public Policy Consequences'. *Journal of Research in Crime and Delinquency*, 25: 120–49.

Index